FAST BASIC: Beyond TRS-80™ BASIC

GEORGE A. GRATZER
University of Manitoba
Winnipeg, Manitoba
Fort Richmond Software Co.

assisted by **THOMAS G. GRATZER**
Fort Richmond Software Co.

John Wiley & Sons, Inc.

New York • Chichester • Brisbane • Toronto • Singapore

. . . it takes all the running *you* can do,
to keep in the same place. If you want
to get somewhere else, you must run at
least twice as fast as that!

—L. Carroll in *Through the Looking Glass*

Dedicated to the people
who did all the running:

to the mathematicians
who worked out the algorithms
utilized in the TRS-80 ROM;

to the programmers
who put it all together;

to the many experts
who, through their writings and correspondence,
taught us the secrets of TRS-80 BASIC.

Publisher: Judy V. Wilson
Editor: Dianne Littwin
Composition and Make-up: Cobb/Dunlop, Inc.

Library of Congress Cataloging in Publication Data
Gratzer, George A.
FAST BASIC
Includes index.
1. Basic (Computer program language) 2. TRS-80 (Computer)—Programming. I. Gratzer, Thomas G. II. Title.
QA76.73.B3G7 001.64'24 81-16207
ISBN 0-471-09849-3 AACR2

Printed in the United States of America

82 83 10 9 8 7 6 5 4 3 2

Contents

Preface

Promise, large promise,
is the heart of any advertisement.

—S. Johnson in *The Idler*

The TRS-80* computer is equipped with an excellent programming language: TRS-80 BASIC (called Level II BASIC in the Model I and Model III BASIC in the Model III). The design of TRS-80 BASIC emphasizes ease of operation, and so it is not surprising that in some business and game programs the computer is too slow to respond. This book suggests a solution. Write your programs in FAST BASIC.

FAST BASIC is introduced in two stages. The first stage is called CONTROLLED BASIC: the systematic use of PEEK and POKE to gain control over TRS-80 BASIC. To program in CONTROLLED BASIC we must have a good understanding of the structure of TRS-80 BASIC. Many of your wishes for an improved TRS-80 BASIC can come true with a few PEEKs and POKEs *if you know where.* In CONTROLLED BASIC you can send to the printer what is displayed on the screen, merge BASIC programs in a cassette system, and check the status of the printer or the disk.

The presentation of CONTROLLED BASIC is self-contained. Some readers may find CONTROLLED BASIC adequate for the improvements they seek; they should read Parts I and II of this book.

The second stage is FAST BASIC itself: We use TRS-80 BASIC to accomplish what TRS-80 BASIC can do well, but enhance it with machine language routines to overcome some of its shortcomings.

Almost any task FAST BASIC has to do in machine language can be built up from the routines that can be found in the TRS-80 ROM (read-only memory; the ROM is a part of the TRS-80 computer). By learning how to use *fewer than 20 machine language instructions* and the names of about 60 ROM routines, we can write our enhancements.

Examples in this book demonstrate that we can easily make our programs run faster by a factor of 3 to 4 for arithmetic calculations, and by a factor of 1000 for string sorts.

Machine language programming has two main drawbacks: the hundreds of instructions one has to learn and the difficulty of debugging long pro-

*TRS-80 is a trademark of Tandy Corporation.

grams. These problems do not arise in FAST BASIC. In a few minutes any user of TRS-80 BASIC can learn the few machine language instructions needed in FAST BASIC. All tasks, for example, addition, are performed by ROM routines. Debugging is done in BASIC.

In FAST BASIC we select the time-consuming lines, especially FOR NEXT loops, from a BASIC program and replace each by a small group of machine language program lines, mostly subroutine calls to the ROM. These small groups of machine language instructions are presented in this book; almost no machine language debugging is needed.

Finally, we consider enhancing FAST BASIC with machine language routines that are not translations of BASIC program lines. We do this when even FAST BASIC is not fast enough or when we want to implement something that cannot be done in TRS-80 BASIC.

To understand what is happening in the computer's memory, we have to speak the language of the computer; this language is written in binary and hex. In Part I we teach you binary numbers, the shorthand representation of binary numbers—hex—and ways of representing negative numbers. We also discuss the various codes, including ASCII and the codes for the BASIC keywords. If you are familiar with these topics, you can safely skip Part I.

CONTROLLED BASIC and FAST BASIC rely heavily on how the memory is organized. In Part II we learn the organization of the memory and the significance of many memory locations. Dozens of applications are interspersed throughout the discussion.

In Part III we acquire a rudimentary knowledge of the Z-80 microprocessor, along with some machine language instructions.

FAST BASIC is developed in Part IV. We start with the most important ROM routines that carry out arithmetic operations and move variables around. Then we learn how to do FOR NEXT loops. We achieve a great increase in speed (a loop that takes 48 to 99 seconds in BASIC is executed in less than 0.5 second in FAST BASIC).

We then learn how to handle string variables. This means extra work on our part but the reward—a 984 times increase in the speed of our benchmark program—makes the effort worthwhile.

A step-by-step guide is given for turning a BASIC program into FAST BASIC.

To illustrate how FAST BASIC can be enhanced, several new Z-80 instructions are introduced and their utilities demonstrated. We conclude the discussion with a case study. This provides a rather dramatic example of the speedup from BASIC to enhanced FAST BASIC: In TRS-80 BASIC the FIND command of the example program takes about 5 hours and 20 minutes to search the complete (64K) memory; in enhanced FAST BASIC this is accomplished in 1 second. The machine language enhancement that makes this speedup possible is only 83 bytes (about the length of an average BASIC line).

We assume that the reader has some familiarity with TRS-80 BASIC and, preferably, has access to a Model I or Model III TRS-80. To understand Parts

III and IV, the reader should also have an assembler such as the Radio Shack Editor Assembler.

We often refer to the TRS-80 BASIC Manual. For Model I users this is the *Level II BASIC Reference Manual;* for Model III users this is the "BASIC Language Section" of the *TRS-80 Model III Operation and BASIC Language Reference Manual.*

Most of the material covered in this book applies to both the TRS-80 Model I and Model III computers, although the examples are oriented a bit more toward the Model I. The differences between Model I and Model III, as they relate to this book, are discussed in Appendix 9. When reading a chapter, the Model III user should refer to the corresponding section in Appendix 9.

With small modifications FAST BASIC can be used for any computer that uses Microsoft BASIC (TRS-80 Model II, Heath, Sorcerer, Apple II with the Z-80 card, and so on). The ideas of FAST BASIC can be adopted for any microcomputer where enough information is available about the interpreter.

We would like to express our appreciation to H. McCracken and his son, Iain; to the members of the TRS-80 Users Group, in particular to D. Rigg, D. Toews, and D. Wood, who made many helpful suggestions; to Prof. H. Lakser, who was always there to help us out with an explanation when we needed it the most; and to C. Dillon, our developmental editor, for a most professional job.

George A. Gratzer
Thomas G. Grätzer

PART I
Background for Controlled BASIC

CHAPTER ONE

Representing the Contents of Memory Locations

Practice yourself, for heaven's sake, in little things;
and thence proceed to greater.
—Epictetus in *Discourses*

CONTROLLED BASIC uses the BASIC functions PEEK and POKE to gain control over TRS-80 BASIC. These two BASIC functions can read information in the computer's memory and change it.

In Part I you learn in what form information is stored in the computer's memory. We use this in Part II to make TRS-80 BASIC send to the printer what is displayed on the screen, merge BASIC programs in a cassette system, and so on.

In this chapter we discuss a representation of memory contents: binary numbers. Because binary numbers tend to be long and cumbersome, we also introduce a shorthand: hex.

BINARY NUMBERS

Memory Locations

A memory location in the TRS-80 computer has an "address": the address can be any integer from 0 to 65535.

Turn the computer on and make sure it shows the BASIC READY prompt. To find the contents of a memory location of a given address we use the BASIC PEEK function. For instance,

```
PRINT PEEK(2423)
```

will return the number 205. If the address, X, is greater than 32767, we should replace X by −1 * (65536 − X). (See the TRS-80 BASIC Manual.) Thus to find the contents of the memory location with address 65535, type PRINT PEEK (-1) since –1* (65536–65535) = –1.

The BASIC PEEK function represents the contents as an integer from 0 to 255. Another way of representing the contents of a memory location is provided by the program TUTOR.

TUTOR

We shall often refer to the program TUTOR. We assume that you either purchased the program on cassette or disk, or copied it in from Appendix 8 for your own use.

RUN the program TUTOR and respond to the question:

```
TYPE THE NUMBER OF THE DESIRED OPTION?_
```

by typing 1 (and press the ENTER key). Answer the prompt

```
TYPE IN ADDRESS (0 - 65535)?_
```

with any address from 0 to 65535; we get a response such as

```
(2423) = 1100 1101
```

indicating that the contents of memory location 2423 are 1100 1101. (To make it easier to read TUTOR puts a space between the first 4 and last 4 digits.) To get the contents of memory location 65535 type 65535; there is no need to do any subtraction when you work with TUTOR.

Even if we have a system with 16K memory (that is, the computer has memory at locations 0 to 32767), we can still request numbers over 32767. The computer does not know how much memory it has. Observe, however, that the contents of such nonexistent high memory are always 1111 1111.

There is no memory at addresses 12288 to 15359. At these locations TUTOR will give us mostly 1111 1111; however, a few locations will yield varying results. This will be explained in Part II.

Examine the contents of memory locations 0 to 12287; these contain Microsoft's BASIC Interpreter, the program that makes the TRS-80 computer run. At locations 15360 to 16385 we are looking at the memory locations containing what is displayed on the screen. Since, as a rule, most of the screen is blank, we usually get 0010 0000, the code for a blank (see Chapter 2).

As the program TUTOR suggests, the contents of a memory location can be represented by a sequence of zeros and ones, an 8-digit "binary number." Thus our understanding of memory locations has to start with binary numbers.

What is really at a memory location? Imagine that a memory location contains eight light bulbs; each bulb can be on or off. We can describe the contents by naming which bulbs are on and which are off, for instance: on on off off off on on off. By writing 1 for on and 0 for off, we can represent the contents by 11000110.

In reality the contents of a memory location are magnetic rather than electric. However, the little magnets also have *two* states that can be represented by a 0 and 1, so again we can represent the magnetic contents by 11000110.

Remember: PEEK represents the contents of a memory location with a number from 0 to 255 whereas TUTOR represents it with an 8-digit binary number!

Binary Numbers

What is a binary number? We know that the number 592 stands for

$$5 \times 100 + 9 \times 10 + 2$$

If we agree to write 10^2 (10 squared or 10 to the power 2) for 100, 10^1 (10 to the power 1) for 10, and 10^0 (10 to the power 0) for 1, then our number becomes

$$5 \times 10^2 + 9 \times 10^1 + 2 \times 10^0$$

This is called the "expanded form" of 592. Numbers expressed in powers of 10 are called "base 10" or "decimal" numbers; 5, 9, and 2 are the "digits."

If we replace base 10 by base 2 and permit only 0 and 1 as digits, then we get "binary numbers." Examples:

$$101 = 1 \times 2^2 + 0 \times 2^1 + 1 \times 2^0 = 4 + 0 + 1 = 5$$
(the decimal number 5)

$$1000 = 1 \times 2^3 + 0 \times 2^2 + 0 \times 2^1 + 0 \times 2^0 = 8 + 0 + 0 + 0 = 8$$
(the decimal number 8)

0110 1001 =

$$0 \times 2^7 + 1 \times 2^6 + 1 \times 2^5 + 0 \times 2^4 + 1 \times 2^3 + 0 \times 2^2 + 0 \times 2^1 + 1 \times 2^0 =$$
$$0 + 64 + 32 + 0 + 8 + 0 + 0 + 1 =$$
105
(the decimal number 105)

In a binary number 0 and 1 are called "binary digits," or "bits" for short. To make the binary numbers easier to read we put a space after every fourth digit (starting from the right).

We saw above that we can represent the contents of a memory location by an eight-character string of zeroes and ones, for example, 0110 1110. We shall regard this as an 8-bit binary number.

An 8-bit binary number is called a "byte," and its bits are numbered from 0 to 7, from right to left. We illustrate this with the byte 0110 1001:

```
bits:   7 6 5 4    3 2 1 0
        ↓ ↓ ↓ ↓    ↓ ↓ ↓ ↓
        0 1 1 0    1 0 0 1
```

Bit 7 often is called the "high-order bit" and bit 0 the "low-order bit." Note that the bit number corresponds to the exponent of 2 when 0110 1001 is written in the expanded form.

Set and Reset

In the early days of electronics binary numbers were used to denote whether an electric switch was set or reset. We still use this terminology. If the bit in a binary number is 1, we say the bit is "set"; if it is 0, we say the bit is "reset." For instance, in the binary number 0110 1001 bit 6 is set and bit 1 is reset.

Converting Binary to Decimal

What is 1100 1101 in decimal? Writing the binary number in expanded form:

$$1 \times 2^7 + 1 \times 2^6 + 0 \times 2^5 + 0 \times 2^4 + 1 \times 2^3 + 1 \times 2^2 + 0 \times 2^1 + 1 \times 2^0 =$$
$$128 + 64 + 0 + 0 + 8 + 4 + 0 + 1$$
$$= 205$$

So 1100 1101 is 205 in decimal. Surprise! Compare this with PEEK(2423) and the contents of 2423 as given by TUTOR. We conclude that the *PEEK* function *gives the decimal conversion of the binary representation of the contents of a memory location.*

Practice binary to decimal conversion with option 2 of TUTOR.

Table 1.1 lists the first 16 powers of 2. This table is useful in converting from binary to decimal.

TABLE 1.1. Powers of 2

2^0 =	1	2^8 =	256
2^1 =	2	2^9 =	512
2^2 =	4	2^{10} =	1024
2^3 =	8	2^{11} =	2048
2^4 =	16	2^{12} =	4096
2^5 =	32	2^{13} =	8192
2^6 =	64	2^{14} =	16384
2^7 =	128	2^{15} =	32768

Binary Arithmetic

Binary addition and multiplication are very easy to learn. There are only 2 digits, so there are only four pairs of numbers to learn to add and multiply.

$$0 + 0 = 0 \qquad 0 + 1 = 1$$
$$1 + 0 = 1 \qquad 1 + 1 = 10$$

$$0 \times 0 = 0 \qquad 0 \times 1 = 0$$
$$1 \times 0 = 0 \qquad 1 \times 1 = 1$$

It is convenient to represent addition and multiplication in tabular form:

+	0	1
0	0	1
1	1	10

×	0	1
0	0	0
1	0	1

As you see, the only rule to learn is $1 + 1 = 10$, which in multidigit addition will take the form: $1 + 1 = 0$ and carry 1. Now let us do a multidigit addition:

```
      1 0 1 1              1 1 1 1 0      Carry line
 +  1 1 1 1 0                1 0 1 1
 ------------        +     1 1 1 1 0
                     ---------------
                         1 0 1 0 0 1      Result line
```

We start the addition from the right, that is, in the last column: $1 + 0 = 1$ (write 1 in the result line) with no carry (carry 0 is written on the carry line one column to the left); moving one column to the left, $0 + 1 + 1 = 0$ (write 0 in the result line), carry 1 (write this in the carry line); next, $1 + 0 + 1 = 0$, carry 1, and so on.

We can subtract binary numbers in much the same way as decimal numbers. For a closer look at binary arithmetic turn to Appendix 4. Option 3 of TUTOR will help you practice.

Keep in mind, however, that our primary goal is to recognize and understand the contents of a memory location. We shall always have help (from BASIC or from machine language instructions) in carrying out arithmetic operations.

Logical Operations

In addition, there are also logical operations (also called "Boolean operations") that can be performed on the binary digits: AND, OR, exclusive OR (XOR), and negation (NOT). TRS-80 BASIC users do not have much difficulty learning the logical operations. After all, if we start a BASIC line with

```
IF X = 0 AND Y = 9
```

we use AND exactly as we do in everyday English.

OR and XOR are quite different. XOR (exclusive OR) means one or the other, but not both. A OR B is TRUE if A is TRUE and B is FALSE, or if A is FALSE and B is TRUE, or if both A and B are TRUE. A XOR B is TRUE if A is TRUE and B is FALSE, or if A is FALSE and B is TRUE. If A and B are both TRUE, then A OR B is TRUE while A XOR B is FALSE.

Examples: The lawn is wet if it rains or if it has been watered. Tonight we go to the movies; we go to the Odeon Theater or to the Venus Theater. In the first sentence "or" means OR; in the second, "or" means XOR (we cannot go to both theaters at the same time).

In conditional statements in BASIC (IF condition THEN . . .) we very seldom need XOR. TRS-80 BASIC does not provide XOR; if you find it convenient to use it, substitute

> (condition1 OR condition2) AND NOT (condition1 AND condition2)
> for XOR.

The logical operations are applied to TRUE and FALSE; the result is again TRUE or FALSE. Table 1.2 describes the logical operations.

If you think of 0 as FALSE and 1 as TRUE, Table 1.3 repeats the information of Table 1.2.

To perform AND on 0 and 1: First find the AND table; at the intersection of the 0 line and 1 column is 0; so 0 AND 1 is 0. Similarly, 1 XOR 1 is 0. NOT has only one argument; the NOT of 0 is 1 and the NOT of 1 is 0.

The logical operations can be applied to bytes as well, carrying them out bit by bit:

```
     0100 1110            1100 1010              1110 0001
AND  1000 0010       OR   0001 1110       XOR    1010 1010
--------------       --------------       ----------------
     0000 0010            1101 1110              0100 1011

NOT  0010 1100
--------------
     1101 0011
```

We carry out the AND in eight steps: first, for bit 7 (0 AND 1 is 0), then for bit 6 (1 AND 0 is 0), and so on.

This may help explain how the logical operations work in BASIC. We have seen in the foregoing example that 0100 1110 AND 1000 0010 = 0000 0010. Now 0100 1110 is 78 decimal; 1000 0010 is 130 decimal; 0000 0010 is 2 decimal. Thus in BASIC the logical expression

```
78 AND 130
```

TABLE 1.2. Logical Operations

TRUE AND TRUE = TRUE
TRUE AND FALSE = FALSE
FALSE AND TRUE = FALSE
FALSE AND FALSE= FALSE

TRUE OR TRUE = TRUE
TRUE OR FALSE = TRUE
FALSE OR TRUE = TRUE
FALSE OR FALSE= FALSE

TRUE XOR TRUE = FALSE
TRUE XOR FALSE = TRUE
FALSE XOR TRUE = TRUE
FALSE XOR FALSE = FALSE

NOT TRUE = FALSE
NOT FALSE= TRUE

TABLE 1.3. Logical Operations on Bits

AND	0	1
0	0	0
1	0	1

OR	0	1
0	0	1
1	1	1

XOR	0	1
0	0	1
1	1	0

NOT	0	1
	1	0

is evaluated as 2. Try this out by typing in the line:

```
IF (78 AND 130) = 2 THEN PRINT "TRUE" ELSE PRINT "TOUGH LUCK"
```

The computer will display TRUE, verifying that

```
78 AND 130 = 2
```

As you can see, we are not only learning what is in a memory location, but we are also getting a better understanding of BASIC by seeing how logical expressions are evaluated.

It is not very difficult to understand that, by substituting 0 and 1 for FALSE and TRUE, the logical operations can also be used for binary and decimal numbers. However, it is somewhat tricky to keep in mind that TRS-80 BASIC stores TRUE and FALSE as –1 and 0. Thus the value of the logical expression

```
X = 2
```

is –1 (that is, TRUE) if X is indeed 2, otherwise it is 0 (that is, FALSE).

Applications

Logical operations have many uses. Here are a few examples.

1. Let A be an 8-bit binary number; we want to test whether bit 6 of A is 0. Form A AND 0100 0000. The result is all 0's, except possibly bit 6, which equals bit 6 of A. This procedure is called "masking": We masked all the bits except bit 6. Similarly, ANDing with 0000 1111 masks the 4 "high-order bits" (bits 7 to 4), and so on.
2. For any byte A, A XOR A = 0000 0000. We often use this in machine language programming to give A the value 0.
3. Let A and B be 8-bit binary numbers; to check whether *both* equal zero form A OR B; if the result is zero, then both A and B are zero. This is often used in machine language programming, but we can also use it in BASIC. Instead of

```
IF A = 0 AND B = 0 THEN ...
```

we write

```
IF (A OR B) = 0 THEN ...
```

to shorten the line.

Packing

Binary numbers may look awkward to us, but they are immensely useful. Here is an example. We are filing away the responses of our employees to a questionaire: they were requested to respond to eight yes or no questions. We file the answers in the form YYNYYYNN as an eight-character string. We shall see in Chapter 4 that this requires 14 bytes of memory. But why not store it in 1 byte as 1101 1100? This reduces our storage requirement 14 to 1! Consider the following program.

Program 1.1. Packing

```
10 X% = 0 : A% = 1
20 FOR I=1 TO 8
30 PRINT "RESPOND TO QUESTION #"; I; " (Y/N)"
40 INPUT R$
50 IF R$="Y" THEN X% = X% OR A%
60 A% = 2*A%
70 NEXT
```

If X% = 10011000_B, the responses were (packed from right to left) no, no, no, yes, yes, no, no, and yes. "Unpacking" the byte to yes and no answers is just as easy.

Converting from Decimal to Binary

It is often necessary to convert from decimal to binary. We do this by repeated division by 2, keeping track of the remainders. Let us convert 250 into binary; in each step we write the result of the division below the number and the remainder to the right:

```
250      remainder 0    ← Low-order bit of result
125                1
 62                0
 31                1
 15                1
  7                1
  3                1
  1      ←————————        High-order bit of result
```

We carry on with the divisions until we get 0 or 1. The binary number is the final result and the remainders read from bottom to top; or 1111 1010 in the example. Practice this with the conversion exercises (option 3) in the program TUTOR!

For more details about binary arithmetic see Appendix 4.

HEX AND BASE 256

Hex

As much as binary numbers are indispensable to understanding the workings of a computer, they are cumbersome to write and impossible to remember. For instance, 0011100000001000 is the address of the memory location that can tell us if X, Y, or Z is pressed on the keyboard. Could you possibly remember this number?

Hex can be viewed as a device to help us work with long binary numbers. An 8-bit or a 16-bit binary number can be written in groups of 4 digits:

01010001 = 0101 0001
0011100000001000 = 0011 1000 0000 1000

There are 16 4-bit groups, and we can label each possible value of a group as shown in Table 1.4.

TABLE 1.4. Coding with Hex Digits

0000	0	1000	8
0001	1	1001	9
0010	2	1010	A
0011	3	1011	B
0100	4	1100	C
0101	5	1101	D
0110	6	1110	E
0111	7	1111	F

The resulting numbers are base 16, hex, numbers. Our two binary examples become 51 and 3808 in hex.

For hex (hexadecimal) numbers we need digits 0 to 15; it is customary to use A, B, C, D, E, and F for the digits representing 10 to 15 respectively. Thus the digits used for hex numbers are 0, 1, 2, 3, 4, 5, 6, 7, 8, 9, A, B, C, D, E, F. The hex number 2A45 stands for

$$2 \times 16^3 + 10 \times 16^2 + 4 \times 16^1 + 5 \times 16^0$$

Examples:
Binary numbers: 10, 101, 1001 (no single digit larger than 1)
Decimal numbers: 10, 157, 7010 (no single digit larger than 9)
Hexadecimal numbers: 10, 157, FFA7 (no single digit larger than F)

Here are some numbers expressed in each of the three bases.

Binary	Decimal	Hex
10	2	2
1000	8	8
1010	10	A
0001 0000	16	10
101	5	5
0010 1110	46	2E
0001 0011	19	13
1010 0000	160	A0

In hex our memory addresses are from 0 to FFFF. Isn't FFFF easier to remember than the decimal number 65535?

Observe that the number 10 can represent a binary number, but it can also represent a decimal number and a hex number. Likewise, 157 represents a decimal number, but it can also be hex. How can we tell which one we mean? Let us agree to write 10_B, 10_D, 10_H to avoid confusion. (Note: Throughout the book, if the base of a number is not clear from the context, it is assumed to be in base 10.) The computer's video display (and many books on computers) does not have the capability to write subscripts. So be prepared to read and write FFABH for the hex number $FFAB_H$. (In assembly language programming a hex number starting with A–F is prefixed with 0; instead of FFABH one writes 0FFABH.)

Hex Conversion

We convert from binary to hex by writing the binary number in groups of 4 digits (pad the number on the left with 0's if the number of digits is not divisible by 4) and then substitute the 4-bit groups as shown in Table 1.4. Hex to binary conversion is also easy: replace each hex digit by the corresponding 4-bit binary in Table 1.4; thus $9A0F_H$ is $1001\ 1010\ 0000\ 1111_B$.

We convert from decimal to hex by repeated division by 16. As an example, let us convert 65000_D:

65000	remainder 8	← Low-order hex digit
4062	remainder 14 = E	
253	remainder 13 = D	
15 = F ←		High-order hex digit

Thus, reading from bottom to top, we get the hex number FDE8. This is a time-consuming procedure. If you want to see whether you have mastered it, use the option: BASE CONVERSION in the program TUTOR in the EXERCISE mode. The UTILITY mode of the same program and the hex conversion table in Appendix 5 will help you to convert.

Hex Arithmetic

In CONTROLLED BASIC it is often useful, although not indispensable, to add hex numbers. We add hex numbers as we add decimal numbers, except that we use the hex addition table of Appendix 5 to help us add digits. Here is an example:

```
                         1 0 1 0      Carry line
       F 0 A 9             F 0 A 9
+      1 A B 3       +     1 A B 3
  -------------      -------------
                         1 0 B 5 C    Result line
```

Starting in the last column, 9 + 3 = C (from the hex addition table) with carry 0, so we write C in the result line and 0 in the carry line one column to the left. Next, 0 + A + B = 5 with carry 1, so we write 5 in the result line and 1 in the carry line one column to the left, and so on.

Here is a simple example of hex addition and multiplication: The video display shows the contents of the memory locations $3C00_H$ to $3FFF_H$. Each line occupies $64_D = 40_H$ locations. What is the address of line 6, character 15_D? The answer is (the computation is shown in hex):

$$3C00 + 40 \times 5 + F = 3C00 + 140 + F = 3C00 + 14F = 3D4F_H$$

Practice hex addition with option 3 of TUTOR.

Base 256

Since memory addresses are stored by TRS-80 BASIC in base 256, we discuss base 256 for an encore. To convert a decimal number to base 256 we carry on dividing by 256. In base 256 we need 256 digits. We shall use (decimal) 0 to 255 in pointed brackets as base 256 digits. As an example, let us convert 11121934_D to base 256:

11121934	remainder 14	←	Low-order base 256 digit
43445	remainder 181		
169	←———————		High-order base 256 digit

Thus $11121934_D = <169><181><14>_{256}$.

Since a memory location can store a number between 0_D and 255_D (a base 256 digit), we can store the number 11121934_D in three memory locations! This method of storing a number yields, on the average, a 70 percent saving. Can you see the application of this for storing many large numbers (large numeric data bases)?

The conversion from decimal to base 256 is completed in one step for numbers from 0 to 65535. As an example, let us convert 35643:

35643	remainder 59	←	Low-order base 256 digit
139	←———————		High-order base 256 digit

So $35643 = <139><59>_{256}$.

Numbers from 0 to 65535 are very important: They are the addresses of memory locations. Addresses are stored as base 256 numbers, first the low-order base 256 digit and then the high-order base 256 digit.

Let X be an address and let H be the high-order base 256 digit and L the low-order base 256 digit of L. The formulas for H and L are

```
H = INT(X/256)

L = X - 256*H
```

Now we store this at address Y:

```
POKE Y, L: POKE Y + 1, H
```

Be careful, however, to replace Y by $-1*(65536-Y)$ if $Y > 32767$; similarly for Y + 1.

Example: Let X = 35643 and Y = 29131. Then

$$H = \text{INT}\ (35643/256) = 139$$

and

$$L = 35643 - 139*256 = 59$$

Indeed, 35643 = 139*256 + 59. So we POKE:

```
POKE 29131, 59 : POKE 28132, 139
```

Question 26 in the Review and Programming Practice shows the tight connection between base 16 and base 256.

Review and Programming Practice

1. Define binary, PEEK, and POKE.
2. What are the contents of memory location 2423? What is the difference between the answer provided by PEEK and the answer given by the program TUTOR?
3. What is the PEEK of 3192 and 33121? (Consult the TRS-80 BASIC Manual on PEEKing at 33121.)
4. What is meant in this book by (2423)?
5. What do we get when we PEEK at nonexistent high memory?
6. Define bit and byte.
7. What does 101 stand for as a decimal number? What does 101 stand for as a binary number?
8. Which is bit 7 of the byte 0011 1111? Which is bit 0?
9. Fill in the following table for binary additions:

+	0	1
0		
1		

10. Do the previous exercise for × (times), AND, OR.
11. What is 0010 1000 AND 1010 1010 in binary?
12. What is NOT 1001 1010 in binary?
13. Convert the binary number 1010 0011 to a decimal number.
14. Convert the following decimal numbers to binary: 35, 17, 101, 5.
15. In Program 1.1 assume that the responses are no, no, no, yes, yes, no, no, and yes (as in the text). What is X% after each response?
16. Let the BASIC variable X% contain an integer from 0 to 255. Write a BASIC program that checks whether bit 5 is set (that is, whether it is 1).
17. Write a BASIC program using OR that checks if the integer variables X and Y are both 0.
18. The TRS-80 computer's lineprinter sets bit 7 of (14312) (that

is, the contents of the memory location 14312) when it is busy; otherwise the bit is reset. (The printer is "busy" when it is printing a character and it is not yet ready to receive a new character for printing.) Write a BASIC program line that checks whether the printer is busy.

19. Redo Program 1.1 for the following situation. There are four questions and each question can be answered in four ways: 0 to 3. Pack the four answers in a byte.
20. Convert to hex the following binary numbers: 01, 101, 1100 0100, 1 0001 1111.
21. Convert to binary the following hex numbers: 2, A0, F0F0.
22. Convert to hex the following decimal numbers: 29, 129, 2001, 62548. (Use TUTOR and Appendix 5 to check your answers.)
23. A machine language program starts at 7010_H and is 3012_D bytes long. What is the address of the last byte?
24. Write 25432_D in base 256.
25. Write a BASIC program to convert a decimal number (0 to 65535) to base 256.
26. How do we convert a hex number to base 256?

Answers

There are many correct answers to the programming questions. The answers provided here are only guidelines by which to judge your own answers.

1. Binary: a sequence of zeroes and ones.

   PEEK: a BASIC function; PEEK (X) gives in decimal the contents of the memory location X.

   POKE: a BASIC function; POKE X, Y places Y in memory location X.
2. PRINT PEEK (2423) will display 205; this is the contents of memory location 2423 in decimal. TUTOR displays

```
(2423) = 1100 1101
```

   giving the memory contents in binary.
3. PEEK(3192) = 46. The value of PEEK (–1*(65536–33121)) will depend on what happens to be currently in your computer's memory. (Recall: We have to type PEEK (–1*(66536–X)) if X exceeds 32767.)
4. The contents of the memory location 2423.
5. 255 (decimal) or 1111 1111 (binary).

6. A bit is a binary digit, that is, 0 or 1. A byte is an 8-bit binary number, e.g., 10010001.
7. In decimal: $101 = 1 \times 10^2 + 0 \times 10^1 + 1 \times 10^0$

   In binary: $101 = 1 \times 2^2 + 0 \times 2^1 + 1 \times 2^0 = 5$ decimal.
8. Bit 7 is the first bit on the left: 0; bit 0 is the first bit on the right: 1.
9.

+	0	1
0	0	1
1	1	10

10.

×	0	1
0	0	0
1	0	1

AND	0	1
0	0	0
1	0	1

OR	0	1
0	0	1
1	1	1

11. 0010 1000.
12. 0110 0101.
13. 163.
14. 10 0011, 1 0001, 110 0101, 101.
15. 0, 0, 0, 8, 24, 24, 24, 152, or in binary 0000 0000, 0000 0000, 0000 0000, 0000 1000, 0001 1000, 0001 1000, 0001 1000, 1001 1000.
16.

```
10 IF X% AND 32 = 0 THEN PRINT "BIT 5 NOT SET" ELSE PRINT "BIT  5
   IS SET"
```

17.

```
10 IF X OR Y = 0 THEN PRINT "BOTH ZERO" ELSE PRINT "AT LEAST  ONE
   NOT ZERO"
```

18. PR is the memory location where bit 7 signifies whether the printer is busy. In decimal, AND 128 masks all bits but bit 7:

```
10 PR = 14312 : IF PEEK(PR) AND 128 = 0 THEN PRINT "PRINTER
   AVAILABLE" ELSE PRINT "PRINTER BUSY"
```

19

```
10 DEFINT A - Z
20 X = 0 : A = 1
30 FOR I = 1 TO 4
40 PRINT "RESPOND TO QUESTION #"; I; "(0 - 3)";
50 INPUT R
60 X = X OR (A*R)
70 A = A*4
80 NEXT
```

20. 1_H, 5_H, $C4_H$, $11F_H$.

21. 0010, 1010 0000, 1111 0000 1111 0000.

22. $1D_H$, 81_H, $7D1_H$, $F454_H$.

23. $7BD3_H$ or 31699_D ($7010_H + 3012_D - 1$).

24. $25432 = 99*256 + 88 = <99><98>_{256}$.

25.

```
10 INPUT X : PRINT "HIGH ORDER BASE 256 DIGIT IS"; INT(X/256);
   PRINT "NEXT DIGIT IS"; X - 256*INT(X/256)
```

26. Write the hex digits in groups of two from the right. The groups of hex digits are the base 256 digits. For instance, take $F013_H$. Write it as F0 13; the base 256 digits are F0 and 13 in hex or 240 and 19 in decimal. Thus $F013_H = <240><19>_{256}$.

CHAPTER TWO

Binary Codes

and eas'd the putting off
These troublesome disguises which we wear,

—J. Milton in *Paradise Lost*

In Chapter 1 we learned to represent the contents of memory locations by binary numbers. This suggests that we can store a positive integer by converting it into binary and storing the result.

But there is a lot more to store in the memory of the TRS-80 computer than positive numbers. At the very least we have to be able to store negative numbers, fractions, and characters. We have to agree on rules on how to represent these as binary numbers. This procedure is called "binary coding." By using the codes we can store and manipulate negative numbers, characters, and BASIC keywords in the memory.

In this chapter we emphasize recognition and conversion rather than manipulation.

NEGATIVE NUMBERS

In Chapter 1 we discussed 8-bit integers and 16-bit integers. To distinguish them from the types of integers we introduce in this chapter, we refer to them as "unsigned integers."

Signed Integers

We shall agree that in a "signed 8-bit integer" bit 7 (the high-order bit) is the sign bit. If bit 7 is set (that is, equals 1), then the number is negative; if bit 7 is 0, then the number is either 0 or positive. Examples:

0010 0110 = 38 1010 0110 = –38

The largest decimal number we can represent as a signed 8-bit integer is 0111 1111 = 127 and the smallest is 1111 1111 = –127.

Signed 8-bit integers cannot be added in the usual way. For instance,

```
    0010 0110    (38)
+   1000 0110    (–6)
    ---------
    1010 1100
```

and the result is –44; it should be 32.

Two's Complement

This problem is partly overcome by the 8-bit "two's complement representation." The 8-bit two's complement representation of a positive 8-bit binary number (or 0) whose bit 7 is 0 is the binary number itself. We obtain the representation of a negative binary number –X (where X is an 8-bit binary number whose bit 7 is 0) in two steps:

1. NOT ("complement") the 8-bit number X.
2. Add 1.

For example, what is the 8-bit two's complement representation of –38? In this case X = 38, or in 8-bit binary, X = 0010 0110.

1. Complement X: NOT X = 1101 1001.
2. Add 1: 1101 1001 + 1 = 1101 1010.

So the 8-bit two's complement representation of –38 is 1101 1010.

Let us now try an addition: 40 + (–38). As 40 in binary is 0010 1000, the 8-bit two's complement representation of 40 is 0010 1000. The 8-bit two's complement representation of –38 is 1101 1010:

```
0010 1000
1101 1010
---------
0000 0011
```

with a carry 1 from bit 7. Ignoring the carry from bit 7, the result is 0000 0010 in binary or 2 in decimal. Indeed, 40 + (–38) = 2, and we got the correct result.

For a second example we find the 8-bit two's complement representation of –44. Then X = 44; in 8-bit binary form X = 0010 1100.

1. Complement X: NOT X = 1101 0011.
2. Add 1: 1101 0011 + 1 = 1101 0100.

So the 8-bit two's complement representaton of –44 is 1101 0100.

If we are given an 8-bit binary number and are told that it is the 8-bit two's complement representation of a number, how do we find out which number? First, look at bit 7 (the high-order bit). Just as with signed integers, if bit 7 is 0, then the number is positive, and so it represents itself. However, if bit 7 is 1, we have to reverse the two rules given above:

1. Reset bit 7 (that is, make it 0).
2. Take away 1.
3. Complement.

Examples: The 8-bit two's complement of a number is (a) 0110 1010, (b) 1001 0101, (c) 1001 0110. What is the number?

In (a) the high-order bit is 0, and thus the number is 0110 1010, that is, 106 in decimal.

In (b), bit 7 is 1:

1. Reset bit 7: we get 0001 0101.
2. 0001 0101 –1 = 0001 0100.
3. NOT 0001 0100 = 1110 1011 or 235 decimal.

Thus the number is –235.

In example (c):

1. Reset bit 7: 0001 0110.
2. 0001 0110 – 1 = 0001 0101.
3. NOT 0001 0101 = 1110 1010 or 236 decimal.

In (c) the number is –236.

In step 2 taking away 1 is easy if bit 0 is 1: We replace the 1 by 0. If bit 0 is 0 as in (c), we have to know how to take away 1. The rule is simple:

$$10 - 1 = 01,\ 100 - 1 = 011,\ 1000 - 1 = 0111$$

and so on.

What is the range of the numbers that have an 8-bit two's complement representation? Obviously the largest positive number is 127, represented by 0111 1111. The smallest number is 1000 0000, which represents –128. Thus the range is –128 to +127, an asymmetry that we have to keep in mind. (This will come up in the explanation of Z–80 instructions, for example, the JR, or jump relative, in Chapter 10.)

Two's complement has a big advantage over signed integers: It is easy to tell when adding two's complement numbers yields the correct result. (See Appendix 4 for a detailed discussion.) Remember, however, our priority is to learn how to convert to and from two's complement representation. BASIC or machine language instructions will do the arithmetic for us.

Everything we said in this section applies to 16-bit integers as well. The range for unsigned 16-bit integers is 0 to 65535 (= $2^{16} - 1$) and –32768 to 32767 is the range for the numbers that have 16-bit two's complement representation.

Two's complement representation is very important for us. As we shall see, most integers in BASIC are stored in this form.

INTEGERS

Integers in BASIC

In TRS-80 BASIC there are three kinds of numeric variables: integer, single precision, and double precision (see the TRS-80 BASIC Manual). All integer variables are stored as 16-bit two's complement integers. (We shall see in Chapter 4 how single- and double-precision variables are stored.) This explains some of the odd numbers we had to learn in TRS-80 BASIC. We get an overflow error if an integer variable exceeds 32767 or goes below –32768. (This is the range for the 16-bit two's complement.)

Integers in Machine Language

If you turn on your computer and you respond to the MEMORY SIZE? question with 65000, you obviously are not typing in a BASIC integer (it could not exceed 32767). Indeed, the MEMORY SIZE? question comes from a machine language routine. Integers can be of arbitrary size in machine language. In fact, the Interpreter uses 16-bit unsigned integers very often, for memory addresses and BASIC line numbers.

Since our main goal in this chapter is to recognize what is stored in the memory, it is very important to remember the following rule. The storage of 16-bit integers (of all forms) is inverted: first comes the "less significant (second) byte" (LSB), and then the "more significant (first) byte" (MSB).

Let us take an example from the end of Chapter 1: How is the address 35643_D stored in the memory location 30000_D and 30001_D? We know that 35643 = 138*256 + 59. Hence 138_D is the MSB and 59_D is the LSB. When *writing* or *displaying* a number we always start with the most significant digit. When *storing* 16-bit integers we start with the less significant (base 256) digit; so we first store 59_D in 30000_D and then 138_D in 30001_D.

The "address at location X" is, in fact, at X and X + 1: (X) = LSB and (X+ 1) = MSB. Use DISPLAYING AN ADDRESS in the program TUTOR to experiment with this.

There are also unsigned 8-bit integers in TRS-80 BASIC: For example, the X in CHR$ (X) is an unsigned 8-bit integer, hence its range is 0 to 255.

The PEEK and POKE Rule

In Chapter 1 we had to learn a strange rule with PEEK and POKE. If the address X at which we PEEK or POKE is over 32767, then we have to replace X by –1* (65536 –X). Let us try to understand why.

Memory addresses are unsigned 16-bit integers, hence in decimal they range from 0 to 65535. Table 2.1 shows some decimal values X from 32768 to 65535 in decimal and hex in the first two columns. The last two columns show the number –1* (65536 –X) in two forms: decimal and 16-bit two's complement representation.

For instance, let X = 65534_D. In hex X = $FFFE_H$. Then –1*(65536 – X) = –2; in 16-bit binary 2 is 0000 0000 0000 0010. To get the 16-bit two's complement representation, we complement this and add 1:

```
1111 1111 1111 1101
                  1
-------------------
1111 1111 1111 1110
```

(there is a carry from bit 15, which we ignore). Converting this binary number into hex, we obtain FFFE, as shown in Table 2.1.

The conclusion is clear: For a decimal number X from 32768 to 65535 the unsigned binary representation is the same as the 16-bit two's complement representation of –1*(65536 – X). This explains the PEEK and POKE rule.

CHARACTERS AND KEYWORDS

ASCII

It has often been said that without the ability to handle text the computer is just a supercalculator. We have to use codes to store text and graphics characters in the computer memory. Although at one time there were as many codes as there were computer manufacturers, very few coding systems survived: ASCII (American Standard Code for Information Interchange) and the IBM EBCDIC (Extended Binary Coded Decimal Interchange Code) are the standard ones. TRS-80 BASIC uses (mostly) ASCII and all computers (including those of IBM) can communicate in ASCII.

Most coding systems agree that a character is coded in a byte, although the character set contains only 128 characters. Thus the character set can be, and in fact is, coded in 7 bits: bit 6 through bit 0. The handling of bit 7 changes from system to system. TRS-80 BASIC simply resets it.

TABLE 2.1. Illustrating the PEEK and POKE Rule

X Decimal	X Hex	–1*(65536 – X) Decimal	–1*(65536 – X) 16-bit Two's Complement Representation (written in hex)
32768	8000	–32768	8000
32769	8001	–32767	8001
. . . . .			
65534	FFFE	–2	FFFE
65535	FFFF	–1	FFFF

The complete code is presented in Appendix C in the TRS-80 BASIC Manual. Read the table with great attention. Study the various control codes and how numbers are assigned to the characters. This knowledge can help you to program better.

Applying ASCII

TRS-80 BASIC contains a number of functions that allow us to utilize our knowledge of ASCII. CHR$ (X) is a character whose ASCII is X (X can range from 0 to 255). ASC(X$) is the ASCII of the first character of X$. Less often used, but nevertheless very useful, is STRING$ (X,Y), which produces a string repeating X times the character whose ASCII is Y. (Both X and Y range from 0 to 255; Y can be substituted by the actual character in quotation marks.)

An important part of every program is "input verification." For instance, we may ask for an INPUT A$ to input an integer. The following will test the input as to whether all characters are digits from 0 to 9.

```
100 FOR J% = 1 TO LEN(A$) : I% = ASC(MID$(A$,J%)) : IF 47 < I%
    AND I% < 58 THEN NEXT : ELSE PRINT "INPUT ERROR"
```

This program line takes the characters one at a time and puts in I% the ASCII of the character. The ASCII's of the digits (see Appendix C of the TRS-80 BASIC Manual) are 48, 49, 50, 51, 52, 53, 54, 55, 56, and 57. Thus if 47 < I% and I% < 58, then I% is the ASCII of a digit. A similar test checks for letters, and so on.

CHR$(X) is often used in BASIC programs to produce letters and digits. It can also be very useful with control characters. Example: The ASCII for line feed (start a new line) is 10. Did you ever need in your own text editor a "skip N lines" command? Here it is:

```
LPRINT STRING$(N,10)
```

(However, the Radio Shack lineprinter uses 138 for line feed, so do LPRINT STRING$ (N, 138).)

It is often useful to know the actual decimal number representing a character. For instance, suppose that X$ contains a hex digit and we want to convert it to decimal (Y is to contain the converted value). This can be done in 16 lines:

```
100 IF X$ = "0" THEN Y = 0
101 IF X$ = "1" THEN Y = 1
...

109 IF X$ = "9" THEN Y = 9
110 IF X$ = "A" THEN Y = 10
...

115 IF X$ = "F" THEN Y = 16
```

Knowing the actual ASCII values we can use the formula:

```
100 Y = ASC(X$) : IF Y < 65 THEN Y = Y - 48 ELSE Y = Y - 55
```

BASIC Keyword Codes

Another set of 8-bit codes is the BASIC keyword codes (also called "tokens"). There are 122 BASIC keywords, that is, special words used in BASIC statements: FOR, RUN, CLOAD, NEXT, GOTO, and so on. The BASIC program stores each in 1 byte: FOR is 81_H (129_D), DEFINT is 99_H (153_D), and INT is $D8_H$ (216_D). Note that bit 7 is set for all keyword codes. A listing is given as an appendix in the TRS-80 BASIC Manual (Appendix E for Level II and Appendix D for Model III).

EPILOGUE

Having reached this far in the book you understand the descriptions of the various codes and practiced with the program TUTOR. Now nothing stands in your way to becoming a CONTROLLED BASIC programmer.

We start to use CONTROLLED BASIC in the next chapter. But before we conclude this part, let us pause to consider the following problem, which will illustrate much of what we have learned so far.

The contents of a memory location are represented by an 8-bit binary number; this 8-bit number could be any one of the following.

1. An unsigned 8-bit integer
2. A signed 8-bit integer
3. The first byte of an unsigned 16-bit integer
4. The second byte of an unsigned 16-bit integer
5. The first byte of a signed 16-bit integer
6. The second byte of a signed 16-bit integer
7. An 8-bit two's complement representation of an integer
8. The first byte of a 16-bit two's complement representation of an integer

9. The second byte of a 16-bit two's complement representation of an integer
10. The ASCII of a character
11. The code of a BASIC keyword

For instance, let us consider the byte 1001 0101:

- As an unsigned 8-bit integer it is 149.
- As a signed 8-bit integer it is –21.
- As an 8-bit two's complement it is –107.
- As a graphics character it represents a vertical line.
- As a BASIC keyword it represents ELSE.

It can also stand for one-half of a 2-byte integer of various formats. As if this were not enough, it can represent a byte of a binary fraction, of a machine language instruction, of a single-precision variable (see Chapters 4 and 7, and Appendix 4), and many other things. The question is: How does the computer know what the byte represents?

If we work in BASIC, the BASIC Interpreter tells the computer how to regard the byte. In CONTROLLED BASIC *we* have to know what we are doing. We have to know how to interpret the byte we are PEEKing at and the byte we POKE. Finally, if we work in machine language or in FAST BASIC (a mixture of BASIC and machine language), again *we* have to remember the meaning of each byte in memory. We learn what many of the bytes mean as we progress through the following chapters.

The following story illustrates this point. A program segment was published in a computer magazine. We are supposed to attach this segment to our BASIC program, run the merged program, and then delete the segment. It is claimed that now all the PRINT statements in our BASIC program have become LPRINT statements.

The idea is simple enough: The program segment, through PEEKs and POKEs, changes 178 (the code for PRINT) to 175 (the code for LPRINT) throughout our BASIC program (skipping only the first 4 bytes of each line). This works if the graphics character 178 is not present in our BASIC program (which is normally the case)! But if it is present, all occurrences of it are replaced by the graphics character 175, thus creating havoc!

How does your BASIC Interpreter know whether 178 is LPRINT or a graphics character? As the Interpreter reads a BASIC statement, it sets a flag when it enters a PRINT statement. Within the PRINT statement any byte with bit 7 set is interpreted as a graphics character or a space compression character. Otherwise, any such byte is interpreted as a BASIC keyword. However, if we do PEEKs and POKEs, we have to keep track of where we are, and find out whether 178 is LPRINT or a graphics character.

The moral of the story is simple. We have two choices:

1. We should let Microsoft's BASIC Interpreter do all our work and stay away from PEEKs and POKEs.

2. We do PEEKs and POKEs and we accept the responsibility of knowing the role of the bytes with which we are tampering.

Review and Programming Practice

1. Which is the sign bit of a signed 8-bit integer?
2. Convert the following signed binary numbers into decimal numbers: 0001 0000, 1001 0001, 1111 0101.
3. Recall the two steps of finding the 8-bit two's complement representation of a negative binary number.
4. Let X = 0100 0101 (decimal 69). Carry out the two steps to find the two's complement representation of –69.
5. Find the 16-bit two's complement representation of –400 and –12123.
6. What are the MSB and LSB of 0011 0101 1100 1100 (MSB and LSB are defined in Chapter 1)?
7. The 16-bit binary number 0011 0101 1100 1100 is stored at location 12125. Which byte is stored at 12125 and which is stored at 12126?
8. Is there any way to tell whether a byte is an unsigned or a signed binary number?
9. Use Appendix C of the TRS-80 BASIC Manual to find the code of A, a, 9, compress 15 spaces.
10. What is the CHR$ of 32, 78, 96, 101, and 168?
11. What is the BASIC keyword code in decimal for RUN, RND, and ASC? (Use the appropriate appendix of the TRS-80 BASIC Manual.)
12. Use the BASIC ASC function to write a BASIC line to check whether the input (a string) is all lowercase letters.
13. Use the BASIC ASC function to write a BASIC subroutine that checks whether an input is all lowercase and uppercase letters and substitutes all lowercase letters by their uppercase forms.
14. Use the BASIC ASC function to write a BASIC line that checks whether the input is a hex number.
15. Using STRING$, write a BASIC program that (a) fills the screen with the letter A, and (b) whites out the screen.
16. Simplify the BASIC lines:

```
100 IF H$ = "A" THEN GOTO 200
110 IF H$ = "B" THEN GOTO 250
120 IF H$ = "C" THEN GOTO 300
```

17. By PEEKing we find that the first byte of the text of the first line of a BASIC program is 148. What happens when we RUN this program?
18. Locations 6EFF$_H$, 6F00$_H$, and 6F01$_H$ contain the bytes 0101 0010, 1100 0001, and 0000 0010 respectively. What does 1100 0001 stand for in the 11 cases listed in the Epilogue?

Answers

There are many correct answers to the programming questions. The answers provided here are only guidelines by which to judge your own answers.

1. Bit 7.
2. 16, −17, −117.
3. (1) Complement. (2) Add 1.
4. 1011 1011.
5. 1111 1110 0111 0000 and 1101 0000 1010 0101.
6. MSB: 0011 0101. LSB: 1100 1100.
7. (12125) = 1100 1100, (12126) = 0011 0101. Remember we always store the LSB first.
8. No, there is not.
9. 65, 97, 57, 207 (in decimal).
10. Space, N, @ (lowercase, that is, shifted), e, a graphics character (a rectangle).
11. 142, 222, 246 (in decimal).
12.

```
100 FOR I = 1 TO LEN(A$) : IF ASC(MID$(A$,I)) < 97 OR
    ASC(MID$(A$,I)) > 127 THEN PRINT "NOT ALL LOWER CASE" : STOP
    : ELSE NEXT : PRINT "ALL LOWER CASE"
```

13. The input is in A$; S$ in the converted string. The subroutine is lines 1000 to 1060; lines 10 to 30 are given so the program can be RUN in this form.

```
10 INPUT A$
20 GOSUB 1000
30 PRINT S$ : STOP
1000 IF LEN(A$) = 0 THEN RETURN
1010 S$ = ""
1020 FOR I = 1 TO LEN(A$)
1030 AS = ASC(MID$(A$,I))
1040 IF (90 < AS AND AS < 97) OR (AS < 65) OR (121 < AS)
     THEN PRINT "NOT UPPER OR LOWER CASE LETTERS" : STOP
1050 IF AS > 96 THEN S$ = S$ + CHR$(AS - 32) ELSE S$ = S$ +
     CHR$(AS)
1060 NEXT
1070 RETURN
```

14.

```
10 INPUT A$
20 GOSUB 1000
30 PRINT "HEX NUMBER" : STOP
1000 Y = LEN(A$) : IF Y = 0 THEN RETURN
1010 FOR X% = 1 TO Y
1020 AS = ASC(MID$(A$,X%))
1030 IF AS < 48 OR (AS > 57 AND AS < 65) OR AS > 70 THEN
     PRINT "NOT HEX NUMBER" : STOP
1040 NEXT
1050 RETURN
```

15. (a)

```
100 CLEAR 600
110 CLS
120 FOR I = 1 TO 4
130 PRINT STRING$(255, "A");
140 PRINT "A";
150 NEXT
```

(b)

```
100 CLEAR 600
110 CLS
120 FOR I = 1 TO 4
130 PRINT STRING$(255, 191);
140 PRINT CHR$(191);
150 NEXT
```

16.

```
100 ON ASC(H$) - 64 GOTO 200, 250, 300
```

17. 148 is the BASIC keyword code for STOP. Thus STOP is the first instruction in the BASIC program. It STOPs.

18. Remember, in 3, 4, 5, 6, 8, and 9 a 16-bit integer is always stored with LSB first!
   (1) The unsigned 8-bit integer, 193_D.
   (2) The signed 8-bit integer, -65_D.
   (3) At memory location $6F00_H$ 1100 0001 is the first byte of a 16-bit integer. Hence the second byte (at $6F01_H$) is 0000 0010. The LSB is 1100 0001 and the MSB is 0000 0010. Thus the binary number is 0000 0010 1100 0001; in decimal, 705_D.
   (4) The MSB of the unsigned 16-bit integer, 49490_D.
   (5) The first byte of the signed 16-bit integer, 705_D.
   (6) The second byte of the signed 16-bit integer, -16722_D.
   (7) The 8-bit two's complement representation of the integer -63_D.
   (8) The first byte of the 16-bit two's complement representation of the integer -16126_D.
   (9) The second byte of the 16-bit two's complement representation of the integer -16046_D.
   (10) Compress one space.
   (11) USR.

PART II
Controlled BASIC

CHAPTER THREE

PEEKing and POKEing

In case of doubt, don't.
—St. Augustine

CONTROLLED BASIC is TRS-80 BASIC enhanced by the systematic use of PEEK and POKE. These two BASIC instructions enable us to examine any memory location and to change any memory location in RAM—we can change PRINTs to LPRINTs, merge programs, write an improved trace function, speed up graphics, control the cursor, check for printer availability and for write protection of a disk, and so on.

In this chapter we learn how to PEEK and POKE. We lay the foundation for PEEKing and POKEing (and also for CONTROLLED BASIC and FAST BASIC) by learning the memory organization of TRS-80 BASIC, in particular, the role of certain memory locations. This information is presented in three tables. Many applications are given following the tables. Others follow in Chapters 4 and 5.

GENERAL MEMORY ORGANIZATION

ROM and RAM

To formulate the fundamental rule of POKEing we have to familiarize ourselves with the expressions ROM and RAM. "Read-only memory," or ROM, is a part of the memory that can only be read. Memory that can be overwritten as well as read is called "random access memory," or RAM. ("Random" simply means that we can access directly any memory location as opposed to "sequential," which means that we have to access location 0 first, then 1, and so on—the cassette is sequential.)

Let us display memory contents using the program TUTOR. Observe that it is impossible to distinguish whether an address is in ROM or in RAM just by PEEKing. In other words, we can PEEK at any address. However, POKEing has no effect in ROM. Hence the fundamental rule of POKEing: Never POKE in ROM.

Memory Organization

Table 3.1 gives some general information about memory organization. This table also shows which addresses are in ROM and RAM and which are in neither.

(Model III users: See the slightly modified Table 3.1 in Appendix 9.)

Note the use of hex and decimal in Table 3.1. We would like to discourage the use of decimal numbers for addresses; nevertheless, since TRS-80 BASIC requires the use of decimal numbers for PEEKing and POKEing, we shall continue to give both.

The bottom of Table 3.1 is the top of the memory. In the explanations, referring to the memory "on top" means having a higher address. The higher the address, the further down it is in the tables.

Keep in mind that a higher-order address is below a lower-order address in this table and on all representations of the memory. For example, a 16-bit integer $0FA1_H$ is stored in memory with A1 coming first and 0F on top of ("below") it. Here is a 16-bit integer at address X:

Address X	LSB of integer
Address X + 1	MSB of integer

To avoid this confusion we could reverse the top and bottom in our tables. Unfortunately, assembly language programs have to be written with the lowest address at the top and the highest address at the bottom. So we follow the convention of starting the tables with the low memory.

Disk Systems

For a disk system there are memory areas not shown in Table 3.1. At power-up a check is made as to whether the computer is connected with an expansion interface. If it is, the BREAK key is checked. If the BREAK key is not pressed, it is assumed that a disk operating system is available in drive 0. The Interpreter reads in 256 bytes of program from the disk. This, then, loads in the "resident program" of the "disk operating system" (DOS) starting at 4200_H (16896_D). When BASIC is called, it loads into the area 5200_H to $6A24_H$ (20992_D to 27172_D). Disk BASIC refers to our TRS-80 BASIC with its disk extensions.

Between the resident DOS and the Disk BASIC area is the DOS "overlay area." DOS commands will bring in programs from the disk, placing them in the overlay area. Some of these programs (e.g., DIR, displaying the disk directory), in fact, go up to $6FFF_H$ (28671_D). (These will overwrite Disk BASIC.) This explains why protected memory in a disk system must not be below 7000_H (28672_D).

Storing and Passing Data

POKE writes into the memory. Therefore, POKE can be used to store data, for instance, data generated by the packing program (Program 2.1) of Chap-

TABLE 3.1. General Memory Organization

Address	Description
0_H–$2FFF_H$ 0_D–12287_D	Low memory ROM Level II BASIC Interpreter
3000_H–$3BFF_H$ 12288_D–15359_D	No memory Input/output area See Table 3.2
$3C00_H$–$3FFF_H$ 15360_D–16383_D	Video display RAM
4000_H–$42E8_H$ 16384_D–17128_D	RAM BASIC work area See Table 3.2
$42E9_H$– 17129_D– $6A24_H$– 27172_D–	RAM Level II BASIC program (in a cassette system) TRS-DOS Version 2.3 BASIC program
	RAM Simple variable table (built during execution of program)
	RAM Array variable table (built during execution of program)
. . . .	RAM
	RAM BASIC stack area
	RAM String space (set aside by CLEAR)
	RAM Protected area
top of the memory $7FFF_H = 32767_D$ $BFFF_H = 49151_D$ $FFFF_H = 65535_D$	 For 16K systems For 32K systems For 48K systems High memory

ter 2. We can also use POKE to pass variables to a program to which we are chaining.

We pass variables by using the protected area. For instance, in a 16K system, if we answer the MEMORY SIZE? question with 32100, then to pass the integer variable X from PROG1 to PROG2:

```
500 X1 = INT(X/256) : POKE 32100, X - X1*256: POKE 32101, X1
510 RUN "PROG2"
```

(or CLOAD "P" and RUN in a cassette system, where "P" is the name of PROG2 on the tape) and in PROG2:

```
10 X = PEEK(32101)*256 + PEEK(32100)
```

We pass characters by POKEing their ASCII and recover them by PEEKing and taking CHR$.

If we chain in a cassette system in TRS-80 BASIC and there is not enough room at the top of the memory to pass data, we can use the BASIC keyword jump area (4152_H to $41A5_H$; 16722_D to 16805_D) see Table 11.1, but one should be careful. If we are pressed for room, we can store data in a part of the BASIC program text that is not needed any more (for instance, data statements used to initialize variables); of course, after BREAKing the program, we shall not be able to RUN it again.

THE BASIC WORK AREA

The BASIC Interpreter and the Work Area

In looking at Table 3.1 we see that 0 to 12K (where K = 1024), that is, 0 to $2FFF_H$, is ROM containing the BASIC Interpreter; from 15360_D ($3C00_H$) on the computer's memory is RAM. The Interpreter is a fixed program that cannot be changed; for instance, it contains the routine that sends characters to the line printer. What do we do if we have a printer that requires different control signals? How can one make a fixed program flexible?

This problem was solved by augmenting the ROM with a "work area" in RAM. The connections are set up by unchangeable addresses (pointers, really—also called "vectors") in ROM. Since the work area is in RAM, we can make subtle changes in it.

To illustrate this, let us examine what the Interpreter does when it comes across a PRINT "A" statement. The program that displays A on the screen starts at $58D_H$ (1421_D) in the ROM. But the Interpreter does not go to $58D_H$! Rather, it goes to the work area, to 4026_H (16422_D), which contains the address $58D_H$. Here 4026_H is the pointer; it is recorded in the ROM and cannot be changed. The memory location 4026_H is in the work area, and so, if necessary, the address recorded there can easily be changed.

When the computer is powered up, it goes through an intricate procedure in setting up the work area. Then it activates the keyboard scanning routine to await instructions. The instruction typed in will activate one of the many components of the Interpreter:

1. The BASIC editor (in response to AUTO or the typing of a BASIC program)
2. The machine language monitor (in response to SYSTEM)
3. A system utility program (for instance, CLOAD activates the program that reads in a cassette tape)
4. The Interpreter proper (by typing a BASIC line without a line number, which calls in the Interpreter to execute the line, or by typing RUN, which calls in the Interpreter to run a program)

The Interpreter proper is the program that actually reads a BASIC line, analyzes it, and executes it.

BASIC Tables

To store and run a BASIC program the Interpreter has to set up a number of tables—some of fixed size and some of variable size.

An example of a fixed-size table is the "variable type table." This table contains 26 bytes, with each byte corresponding to a letter from A to Z. TRS-80 BASIC initializes this table by placing 4_H in each byte. If the program declares DEFINT S, a marker (namely, 2_H) will be placed in the byte corresponding to S. Any time a variable is used without a type qualifier ($, %, #, !) and the name of the variable starts with S, then the entry under S is checked; since the entry is 2_H all such variables will be integer variables. The marker for string variables is 3_H, for double precision it is 8_H, and for single precision it is 4_H, the default.

A variable-size table changes its size either when the program is written or when the program is RUN. The most important variable-size tables are the following.

1. The BASIC program
2. The simple variable table (contains the nondimensioned—that is, simple—numeric variables and the addresses of the nondimensioned string variables)
3. The array variable table (contains the dimensioned numeric variables and the addresses of the dimensioned string variables)
4. The string space (contains the strings that are not defined in the BASIC program)
5. The BASIC stack (used for temporary storage, including the return addresses from subroutine calls and the FOR NEXT table)

In addition, there is the protected area (set aside—for instance, for machine language programs or for storage—when answering the MEMORY SIZE? question at power-up or when BASIC is called in a disk system).

The BASIC work area contains pointers to keep track of the locations and extent of these tables. Some of these are discussed in greater detail in Chapter 4.

Address Table

The highlights of the input/output area and the BASIC work area are given in Table 3.2. This table also shows some examples of the housekeeping done by the Interpreter (e.g., $403D_H$, 4099_H, and $409A_H$).

Table 3.2 contains a very great deal of information. Some of it (for instance, the software accumulator) will be used only in Part IV. The examples in this chapter should give you plenty of experience in the use of this table.

BASIC Program Size

How do we find the size of a BASIC program? Let us look at the following two lines from Table 3.2.

40A4 – 40A5	16548 – 16549	BASIC program start address
40F9 – 40FA	16633 – 16634	Starting address of simple variable table

The address at $40A4_H$ (16548_D) is the starting address of the BASIC text. The address at $40F9_H$ (16633_D) is the start of the simple variable table. Table 3.1 shows that the simple variable table is on top of the BASIC program. The start of the simple variable table thus marks the end of the BASIC program. Hence the size of the program is displayed by:

```
PRINT PEEK(16634)*256 + PEEK(16633) - PEEK(16549)*256 -
PEEK(16548)
```

Try this out with the following one-line program.

```
10 REM THIS IS A BASIC PROGRAM
```

You should get 32. Why? If you do not know the answer, consult Chapter 4.

This is nice, but is it of any use? Suppose we want to calculate the memory requirement of a program in order to see whether the program would run on a 16K computer or whether it could coexist with another BASIC program or a machine language utility. Table 3.2 contains the entry:

40FD – 40FE	16637 – 16638	Address of last byte in array variable table

We accomplish our task by changing 16633 and 16634 in the above formula

TABLE 3.2. Address Table

Hex Address	Decimal Address	Description
		Low memory
37E0	14304	Interrupt address port: Bit 7 is set for clock, bit 6 is set for disk
37E1	14305	Disk drive select
37E4	14308	Cassette 1 or 2 select (0 or 1)
37E8	14312	Lineprinter address port
37EC	14316	Disk command/status
37ED	14317	Disk track select
37EE	14318	Disk sector select
37EF	14319	Disk data
3800 – 3840	14336 – 14400	Keyboard address ports
3C00 – 3FFF	15360 – 16383	Video display memory
4003 – 4005	16387 – 16389	RST 10H transfer address
4012 – 4015	16402 – 16405	RST 38H transfer address
4015 – 401C	16405 – 16412	Keyboard control block
401D – 4024	16413 – 16420	Video control block
4025 – 402C	16421 – 16428	Printer control block
403D	16445	Cassette port and print-size flag (bit 3) copy
4041 – 4046	16449 – 16454	Time area (seconds, minutes, hours, year, day, month)
4049 – 404A	16457 – 16458	DOS memory size
408E – 408F	16526 – 16527	USR starting address
4099	16537	INKEY$ storage
409A	16538	Error code
409C	16540	Output flag (–1, 0, or 1)
40A0 – 40A1	16544 – 16545	String space start address
40A2 – 40A3	16546 – 16547	Current line number in BASIC program
40A4 – 40A5	16548 – 16549	BASIC program start address
40AA – 40AC	16554 – 16556	Seed for RND
40AB	16555	This byte is changed by RANDOM
40AF	16559	Variable-type flag for the software accumulator
40B1 – 40B2	16561 – 16562	Last byte of memory available for BASIC
40D6 – 40D7	16598 – 16599	Next usable byte in string space
40DF – 40E0	16607 – 16608	Entry point of system tape
40E6 – 40E7	16614 – 16615	Points at terminator of the last executed BASIC statement
40EA – 40EB	16618 – 16619	Line number with error
40F9 – 40FA	16633 – 16634	Starting address of simple variable table
40FB – 40FC	16635 – 16636	Starting address of array variable table
40FD – 40FE	16637 – 16638	Address of last byte in array variable table
4101 – 411A	16641 – 16666	Variable-type table
411D – 4124	16669 – 16676	Software accumulator (SA)
4127 – 412E	16679 – 16686	Alternate software accumulator (SA_1)
4152 – 41AF	16722 – 16815	DOS interface area
41A6 – 41A8	16806 – 16808	Used by BASIC for error messages
		High memory

to 16637 and 16638, respectively, since the address at $40FD_H$ (16637_D) points to the end of the variable tables:

```
PRINT PEEK(16638)*256 + PEEK(166_7) - PEEK(16549)*256 -
PEEK(16548)
```

Of course, we have to add to this N if the string area was set by CLEAR N (N = 50 is the default). Finally, we have to estimate our stack requirement (which depends on the number of FOR NEXT loops that run concurrently, the levels of nesting of GOSUBs), and add this to the number we obtained before.

For instance, if a program takes 2012 bytes, with the variable table's 2309 bytes, we leave 200 bytes for the stack and CLEAR 250 saves 250 bytes for the strings, and then the program requires all told 4771 memory locations.

Merge

A more practical application is the implementation of MERGE in TRS-80 BASIC. Merging is very important. For instance, we have a complex subroutine debugged and tested. Whenever we need it, we just merge it with the new program.

We have the BASIC programs PROG1 and PROG2 on cassette and we would wish to merge them. We assume that the line numbers of PROG1 are smaller than the line numbers of PROG2. First, CLOAD PROG1. When we are CLOADing the address at $40A4_H$ (16548_D) is checked and it is used as the starting address of the loaded program. After the loading is complete, the address is $40F9_H$ (16633_D) points to the first location after the program. So we copy this address minus 2 to $40A4_H$ (we subtract 2 to take care of the end-of-file marker, see Chapter 4). Now if we CLOAD PROG2, it will load from the new address. Finally, the original address is reset at $40A4_H$. The program in memory is now the merged program, ready to run. To recap:

Step 1.

```
X = PEEK(16548) : Y = PEEK(16549) : PRINT X : PRINT Y
```

write down X and Y.

Step 2.

```
CLOAD "P"
```

where "P" is PROG1.

Step 3.

```
V = PEEK(16633) : U = PEEK(16634)
```

Subtract 2 from U*256 + V and write it as U1*256 + V1. Use the formulas we discussed in Chapter 1 to convert from decimal to base 256: U1 = INT((U*256 + V)/256) and V1 = U*256 + V – U1*256.

Step 4.

```
POKE 16548, V1 : POKE 16549, U1
```

Step 5.

```
CLOAD "Q"
```

where "Q" is PROG2.
Step 6.

```
POKE 16548, X : POKE 16549, Y
```

If we have more than two programs to merge, we repeat steps 3 and 4.

USR

In TRS-80 BASIC the starting address of a machine language subroutine has to be POKEd at $408E_H$ (16526_D). It should be mentioned that if there are many machine language subroutines, each starting address has to be POKEd in as needed. So there is no real restriction in TRS-80 BASIC on the number of machine language subroutines one can utilize.

Top of Memory

Changing entries listed in Table 3.2 does not always bring the desired result. An interesting example is top of memory.
In Table 3.2 we find the entry:

40B1 – 40B2	16561 – 16562	Last byte of memory available for BASIC

Thus the address at $40B1_H$ (16561_D) is the last byte available for BASIC, which is one less than the answer to the MEMORY SIZE? question. Would it not be nice to change the size of the protected area by POKEing the new size at the beginning of a BASIC program? Try it and it may not work.

To understand what is happening take a look at Table 3.1. If the size of the protected area is increased, it will overlap with the string space; hence the string space, and also the stack area, will have to be moved. These moves will be accomplished by CLEAR N. To recap: To protect X bytes of memory (T# is the Top of the Memory, both X and T# are decimal):

```
Z% = INT((T# - X)/256) : POKE 16561, T# - X - 256*Z% : POKE
16562, Z% : CLEAR N
```

Status Checking

The TRS-80 hangs up (that is, appears to have stopped) if it LPRINTs to a printer that is not turned on. To make sure that this does not happen, we may insert before the first LPRINT statement in our program the following lines.

```
90 ST = PEEK(14312) AND 128 : IF ST <> 0 THEN PRINT "TURN PRINTER
   ON : HIT C TO CONTINUE" ELSE 100
92 ST$ = INKEY$ : IF ST$ <> "C" THEN GOTO 92
100 REM START OF PROGRAM
```

In line 90 we PEEK at 14312, which is the lineprinter address port (Table 3.2). AND 128 masks all bits but bit 7. Thus ST = 0 if bit 7 is reset and ST <> 0 if bit 7 is set, and so ST signifies whether the printer is busy. A simple machine language variant of this program can also be written and be made permanently resident in protected memory.

We do not want to write data on a write-protected disk ("write protected" means that we can only read from the disk, we cannot write on it). For disks,

```
POKE 14305, 1 : POKE 14316, 208
```

requests a status report from disk 0 (POKE 2, 4, and 8 for drives 1, 2, and 3). Then the status report is given in 14316:

```
PRINT PEEK (14316) AND 64
```

is 0 if the drive is not write protected, and it is 64 if the drive is write protected. We use this in Chapter 5 to write a subroutine that checks whether or not a disk is write protected.

THE CONTROL BLOCKS

Control Block Table

The details of the control blocks are given in Table 3.3. Note that "P" stands for the ASCII of P (an assembly language convention). In this table the most important information is the address of the driver. The zeros designate unused locations.

(Model III users: See the slightly modified Table 3.3 in Appendix 9.)

Changing Drivers

Table 3.3 may give you the most fun with POKEing. The second and third locations of each control block contain the driver address. Whenever a character is to be received from or sent to a device (keyboard, video, or printer), a subroutine call is made to this address. Hence by POKEing in a new address you can (1) swap existing drivers or (2) replace drivers by new ones. The video driver is used by the PRINT and LIST statements and the printer driver is utilized by LPRINT and LLIST.

A software company sells a program that rewrites, in a BASIC program, all PRINTs to LPRINTs so that what is normally displayed on the screen will be sent to the printer. Knowing about drivers, we can do this ourselves:

```
X = PEEK(16414): Y = PEEK(16415)

POKE 16414, PEEK(16422) : POKE 16415, PEEK(16423)
```

TABLE 3.3. Control Blocks

Keyboard	Video	Printer
$4015_H = 16405_D$ Device type = 1	$401D_H = 16413_D$ Device type = 7	$4025_H = 16421_D$ Device type = 6
$4016_H = 16406_D$ LSB of driver address $= E3_H = 227_D$	$401E_H = 16414_D$ LSB of driver address $= 58_H = 88_D$	$4026_H = 16422_D$ LSB of driver address $= 8D_H = 141_D$
$4017_H = 16407_D$ MSB of driver address $= 03_H = 3_D$	$401F_H = 16415_D$ MSB of driver address $= 04_H = 4_D$	$4027_H = 16423_D$ MSB of driver address $= 05_H = 5_D$
$4018_H = 16408_D$ 00_H	$4020_H = 16416_D$ LSB of cursor position	$4028_H = 16424_D$ Number of lines on a page = 67
$4019_H = 16409_D$ 00_H	$4021_H = 16417_D$ MSB of cursor position	$4029_H = 16425_D$ Line counter
$401A_H = 16410_D$ 00_H	$4022_H = 16418_D$ ASCII of character replaced by cursor	$402A_H = 16426_D$ 00_H
$401B_H = 16411_D$ "K"	$4023_H = 16419_D$ "D"	$402B_H = 16427_D$ "P"
$401C_H = 16412_D$ "I"	$4024_H = 16420_D$ "O"	$402C_H = 16428_D$ "R"

This saves the printer driver address and also copies it into the video control block. Hence everything that was to be displayed on the screen will be sent to the printer. To restore the video driver:

```
POKE 16414, X : POKE 16415, Y
```

Notice that we can do this even if what we type is invisible!

Reversing this procedure, we can RUN a program with LPRINTs even if we do not have a printer. We can also interchange the effects of PRINT and LPRINT—but why would anyone want to do this?

Such magic can be applied not only in BASIC programs but in all programs that use (some or all of) the same control blocks. For instance, in a disk system,

```
CLS : POKE 16414, PEEK(16422) : POKE 16415, PEEK(16423) : CMD"S"
```

exits to DOS; now DIR will send the directory listing to the printer. (Notice that DIR will not appear on the screen but it will be printed.)

It is enough to know two or three machine language instructions to write a short machine language program that will neutralize PRINT or LPRINT (e.g., cause PRINT to be ignored—the video display will stay blank), slow down LIST (with speed control, see Program 7.2), and so on.

Using a Diablo Printer

The control blocks are important to users who have unusual devices. For instance, we have a DEC word processor (a computer used for text handling) with an expensive Diablo printer. Instead of buying a printer for the TRS-80, we bought an RS-232-C interface board. Now the two computers can communicate. To make the system complete, however, we had to change BASIC so that BASIC will send LPRINTed characters to the communication interface. Nothing to it: We copied the communication program (from page 27 of the Interface Manual mentioned in Appendix 7) to high memory, starting at $FFE0_H$, and we POKEd $E0_H = 224_D$ into 16422_D and FF_H into 16423_D. Now everything LPRINTed or LLISTed goes through the DEC word processor (for editing and printing).

Trace

TRON turns the trace on in TRS-80 BASIC. The trace displays the current line number at the current cursor position. Thus for programs that use the video display the TRS-80 BASIC trace is of limited value. Let us write a trace that displays the current line number at locations of our own choosing.

Let C1, C2, L, LC be variables not used in the BASIC program for which we are writing the trace. We use the following entry from Table 3.2.

40A2 – 40A3	16546 – 16547	Current line number in BASIC program

Thus the current BASIC line number being processed is

```
PEEK(16547)*256 + PEEK(16546)
```

and the current cursor position from Table 3.3 is

```
PEEK(16417)*256 + PEEK(16416)
```

This is utilized in the following BASIC subroutine.

```
301 L = PEEK(16547)*256 + PEEK(16546) - 1: GOSUB 10000

10000 C1 = PEEK(16416) : C2 = PEEK(16417)
10010 LC = LC + 1 : IF LC > 16 THEN LC = 0
10020 PRINT @58 + LC*64, "<"; L; ">";
10030 POKE 16416, C1 : POKE 16417, C2
10040 RETURN
```

Line 301 is inserted after line 300 in the text; it stores the current line number (namely, 300). Line 10000 stores the current cursor position (in C1 and C2). LC is the line on which we print the trace; it is updated in line 10010. At the end of line LC we print the current line number of the BASIC program. Finally, we restore the cursor position.

This gives us a trace function that may not interfere with the video display. If the right margin is needed for the display, change the PRINT in line 10020 to direct the trace to an unused part of the video screen.

It is easy to implement the improved trace with a disk system. With AUTO 11, 10 (this is an editor command; it generates line numbers 11, 21, 31, . . .) we create a file where each line is just ' (the shorthand for REM). We save it with the A (ASCII) option. We write a program that opens this file for input, and until EOF (end of file) inputs A$ (a line), cuts off the last character of A$ (') and concatenates A$ with

```
L = PEEK(16547)*256 + PEEK(16546) - 1 : GOSUB 10000
```

Let us call this file TRON. We MERGE our program with TRON, delete the TRON lines where we do not want a trace, and RUN it.

POKEing into Machine Language Programs

POKE may be used to alter machine language programs, whether user-written programs or system programs. Here is an often-used example.

It may be desirable in a BASIC program to disable the BREAK key. This may prevent an accidental abortion of the program. In a cassette-based TRS-80 BASIC system this can be accomplished by

```
POKE 16396,175
```

and in TRS-DOS by

```
POKE &H4312, &HAF : POKE &H4313, &HC9
```

Unfortunately, these POKEs no longer set flags; they rewrite a part of the operating system. Although one can disable the BREAK key by this procedure, we would strongly recommend against using it. Such POKEs assume that we know what is in a particular location. If the system has been changed in any way, these POKEs may have disastrous consequences.

The safe way to disable the BREAK key is by intercepting the video driver with a machine language program that tests whether or not the BREAK key is depressed. If it is, the program waits for the release of the BREAK key and then continues normal execution. Chapter 12 contains an illustration of how to POKE a change into a machine language program and avoid this pitfall.

A Project

We hope this chapter has convinced you of how important it is to know the role of some memory locations. You have learned a few here, but there literally are thousands more. We suggest that you make yourself a memory map.

Print all hex addresses of the memory locations. At each address of interest, enter the significance of the address and the source where the information was found (title of book, issue of magazine, etc.). Of special interest is the BASIC work area. As a start, put in your memory map the information from this chapter.

Review and Programming Practice

1. What do ROM and RAM stand for?
2. (2423) = 205. After POKE 2423, 60 we do PRINT PEEK(2423). What is displayed?
3. What are the bottom and top of your computer's memory?
4. Which is higher in memory, the BASIC Interpreter or a BASIC program?
5. Use Table 3.1 to answer the following questions.
   (a) Where is the BASIC Interpreter?
   (b) Is 15892_D in the video display RAM?
   (c) Could 26025_D be in a BASIC program in a cassette system? Is it necessarily there? How about a disk system?
   (d) Is 42329_D available in a 16K system?
6. Use Table 3.2 to answer the following questions.
   (a) What are the locations of the three control blocks?
   (b) Let the current line number in a running BASIC program be 28310. It is stored as an unsigned 16-bit integer. Where is it stored? Give the contents of these locations.
7. Use PEEK to find the keyboard driver address. Is this address in ROM or in RAM?
8. RUN a BASIC program and BREAK it. Use PEEK to find
   (a) The start of the program
   (b) The current line number
   (c) The start of the simple variable table
   (d) The last byte of memory available for BASIC
9. RUN the program VIEW/MOD (see Appendix 8) and use it to examine the program itself. How many bytes per line are unreadable?
10. Write a BASIC program that stores in the protected area a line of text typed in.

11. Write a BASIC program that reads and displays the text stored by the program of the previous exercise.
12. Write a BASIC program line that causes all output sent to the video display to be sent to the lineprinter.
13. Write a BASIC program that will LOAD a program 2000 bytes higher than normal.
14. MERGE is given in six steps in this chapter. What happens if we omit step 4 and after step 6 we LIST?
15. After you disable the BREAK key with POKE 16396, 175, how do you enable it again?
16. LLIST sends the BASIC program listing to the lineprinter. You want the program printed out 60 printed lines per page. How do you accomplish that?

Answers

There are many correct answers to the programming questions. The answers provided here are only guidelines by which to judge your own answers.

1. ROM: read-only memory. RAM: random access memory.
2. 205. POKEing into ROM does not change the memory location.
3. The bottom of the memory is 0; the top is $7FFF_H$ (32767_D) for a 16K system, $BFFF_H$ (49151_D) for a 32K system, and $FFFF_H$ (65535_D) for a 48K system.
4. The BASIC program is higher up.
5. (a) $0 - 2FFF_H$ ($0 - 12287_D$).
   (b) Yes.
   (c) Yes. No, not necessarily. It could not be in a BASIC program in a disk system.
   (d) No.
6. (a) $4015_H - 402C_H$ ($16405_D - 16428_D$).
   (b) (16546_D) = 150_D, (16457_D) = 110_D.
7. $3E3_H$ (995_D) is in ROM. [In Model III 0625_H (1573_D).]
8. Do PRINT PEEK(X) + 256*PEEK(X + 1) for the following values.
   (a) X = 16548
   (b) X = 16546
   (c) X = 16663
   (d) X = 16561
9. 5 bytes a line are, as a rule, unreadable.
10. We terminate the text with a 00_H byte:

```
10 INPUT A$
20 IF LEN(A$) = 0 THEN GOTO 10
30 FOR I = 1 TO LEN(A$)
40 POKE 32255 + I, ASC(MID$(A$,I))
50 NEXT I
60 POKE 32255 + LEN(A$) + 1, 0
```

You can easily write a variant that stores many lines of text. Use the following scheme: The first byte is the length of the string; a 00_H byte indicates the end of the text.

11. According to the program in the previous exercise we search for the 00_H byte that terminates the text.

```
10 I = 1
20 X = PEEK(32255 + I)
30 IF X = 0 THEN STOP
40 PRINT CHR$(X);
50 I = I + 1
60 GOTO 20
```

12.

```
POKE 16414, PEEK(16422) : POKE 16415, PEEK(16423)
```

13.

```
10 W = PEEK(16548) + PEEK(16549)*256 + 2000
20 POKE 16548, W - 256*INT(W/256) : POKE 16549, INT(W/256)
30 LOAD "PROG"
```

In line 30 use CLOAD "P" in a cassette system.

14. PROG2 is listed.

15. Before disabling the BREAK key, PRINT PEEK(19396). To enable the BREAK key, POKE 19396, the number you found (196).

16.

```
POKE 16424,60 : LLIST
```

CHAPTER FOUR

Five BASIC Tables

For Art and Science cannot exist but in minutely organized Particulars.

—W. Blake in *Jerusalem*

In this chapter we discuss the structure of the five most important BASIC tables: the BASIC program, the simple and the array variable tables, the string space, and the BASIC stack. By knowing the organization of these tables we can make TRS-80 BASIC perform more efficiently.

THE BASIC PROGRAM

Organization

We already know (see Table 3.2) that the address at $40A4_H$ (16548_D) is the starting address and the address at $40F9_H$ (16633_D) is 1 byte past the end of the BASIC program.

The organization of the program is very simple. The first 2 bytes contain the starting address of the next line; this is a 16-bit unsigned integer called the "next line pointer." The next 2 bytes contain the line number (regardless of whether it is 1 or 65512) as a 16-bit unsigned integer. This is followed by the text of the first line terminated by the byte 00_H. Every character is stored by its ASCII (bit 7 is 0) and the BASIC keywords are stored by their code (bit 7 is 1).

The next line follows the same structure, with a pointer to the following line, etc. The end-of-file marker is 2 bytes: 00_H, 00_H.

Let us return to the example of Chapter 3, the BASIC program:

```
10 REM THIS IS A BASIC PROGRAM
```

We claimed in Chapter 3 that this program occupies 32 memory locations. Indeed, 4 bytes are taken up by the line pointer and the line number (10). The blank before REM automatically is put in after the line number; it is not part of the program. REM is a BASIC keyword that takes 1 byte. The text of the line starts with the blank; it contains 24 characters. The end-of-the-line marker is 1 byte, and the end-of-file marker takes 2 bytes:

$$4 + 1 + 24 + 1 + 2 = 32$$

When a new line is added to a BASIC program or when an existing line is edited, all the pointers must be recalculated. This explains the delay of several seconds before the appearance of the READY prompt after editing a line in a long program.

The BASIC program has no other tables for line numbers. When the program is being RUN, apart from the program text, only the start, the end of the BASIC text, and the current line number are available.

GOTO

How does the Interpreter find a line? Suppose that we are at line 295 of a BASIC program and it contains the instruction GOTO (or GOSUB) NN. If NN < 295, then the Interpreter returns to the first line. If the first line number is NN, then it is executed; if not, then, using the pointer to the next line, the Interpreter checks whether the next line is NN. This continues until NN (or the end of file) is found. Of course, if NN ≥ 295, then the search starts at line 295.

Simple, isn't it? Still, many useful conclusions can be drawn from it.

Program 4.1. Line Number Scanning

```
1 REM

...

297 REM
298 REM
299 IF X% = 1000 THEN STOP
300 X% = X% + 1 : GOTO 299
```

(Lines 2 to 296 are all REM.) Program 4.1 takes 41 seconds to run. However, if we delete lines 2 to 298, it takes only 11 seconds to RUN. Thus the Interpreter scans 9900 line numbers per second.

We can speed up the execution of a program by:

1. Placing an often-used subroutine close to and following the GOSUB lines or near to the beginning of the program
2. Avoiding jumping back a few lines in a loop
3. Replacing GOTOs by FOR NEXT loops wherever possible

Lost Programs

The computer may be reset accidentally (by unintentionally pressing the reset button or by a power surge) or intentionally (by pressing the reset button when the computer "hangs up," that is, appears to go dead). This does not erase the BASIC program, nor does it change the BASIC pointers. However, calling BASIC (or typing NEW) does change some of the pointers: (1) The pointer to the second line (the first 2 bytes of the program) is changed to 00_H, 00_H. (2) The starting address of the simple variable table at $40F9_H$ (16633_D) is changed.

After a reset, restore the BASIC program as follows:

1. Set the starting address of the simple variable table (remember, this address is one larger than the end of the BASIC program) well out of harm's way (say, beginning of BASIC program + 10000; this will ensure that the variables used in steps 2 and 3 will not overwrite the program).
2. Type

```
B = PEEK(16549)*256 + PEEK(16548)
```

B is the beginning of the BASIC program. Now search for the first 00_H byte. (Be careful! Do not type line numbers in the next two steps.)

```
FOR I = 4 TO 255: IF PEEK(B + I) = 0 THEN N = B + I + 1 : PRINT N
ELSE NEXT
```

The number displayed, N, is the address of the first byte of the next line. We have to POKE this into the beginning of the first line:

```
POKE B, N - INT(N/256)*256 : POKE B + 1, INT(N/256)
```

3. Now we look for the end of the program:

```
FOR I = 4 TO 10000 : IF (PEEK(B + I) AND PEEK(B + I + 1) AND
PEEK(B + I + 2) = 0) THEN E = B + I + 3 : PRINT E ELSE NEXT
```

We record the address E at $40F9_H$ and $40FB_H$:

```
POKE 16633, E - INT(E/256)*256 : POKE 16634, INT(E/256)
POKE 16635, E - INT(E/256)*256 : POKE 16636, INT(E/256)
```

Now we can LIST the program again.

THE SIMPLE VARIABLE TABLE

Organization

To examine the simple variable table, RUN the program VARPTR listed in Appendix 8. Table 4.1 shows how this program displays some entries from the simple variable table. (The memory locations in the table show that we ran VARPTR on a 16K system.) The program gives you the choice of hex or decimal for the addresses; in Tables 4.1 and 4.2 we have the hex format.

In Tables 4.1 and 4.2

```
<---- VARPTR
```

shows the byte whose address is given by the BASIC function VARPTR. For instance, in entry 2, VARPTR(SP) = $54FA_H$. (Of course, VARPTR gives the decimal conversion of $54FA_H$, that is, 21754_D.)

To find a (simple) variable X, type PRINT VARPTR(X); the address displayed points inside the simple variable table. As you can see, the 3 bytes preceding this are also interesting.

1. The first byte is the variable-type flag: 02_H for integers, 03_H for strings, 04_H for single-precision numbers, and 08_H for double-precision numbers. The flag also indicates the number of locations (including where VARPTR is pointing) used up by the variable entry.
2. The next 2 bytes contain the ASCII of the two characters in the variable name, reversed. However, if the variable name is only one character long, the code for the second character is 00_H.

The storage of integer variables is in the form of a 16-bit signed integer, LSB followed by MSB.

The storage of single- and double-precision variables is a bit more complicated. Suppose the number we want to store is 298. First we look for the "exponent." The exponent is the largest integer n such that 2^n does not exceed 298. In looking at Table 1.1 we see that the exponent for 298 is 8. This exponent is stored as the last byte of the entry in the following form: bit 7 is set (= 1) if the exponent is positive, otherwise it is reset; bits 6 to 0 contain the (unsigned) exponent as a 7-bit binary number.

We do not concern ourselves any further with the storage of single- and double-precision numbers. It is enough for us to understand the exponent and to know how many bytes of storage the numbers take. For a full discussion see Appendix 4.

Observations

Run the program VARPTR a couple of times; add a REM line and see the changes in the addresses. Introduce a new variable and look for it. Experimentation will tell you:

1. The location of a variable changes if the BASIC program

TABLE 4.1. The Simple Variable Table

```
ENTRY # 1 IN THE SIMPLE VARIABLE TABLE (HEX FORMAT)

(54F2) = 2      TYPE FLAG FOR INTEGER VARIABLE
(54F3) = 4E     CODE FOR SECOND LETTER IN VARIABLE NAME: N
(54F4) = 49     ASCII OF FIRST LETTER IN VARIABLE NAME: I
(54F5) = 2      LSB OF VALUE   <---- VARPTR
(54F6) = 0      MSB OF VALUE


ENTRY # 2 IN THE SIMPLE VARIABLE TABLE (HEX FORMAT)

(54F7) = 4      TYPE FLAG FOR SINGLE PRECISION VARIABLE
(54F8) = 50     CODE FOR SECOND LETTER IN VARIABLE NAME: P
(54F9) = 53     ASCII OF FIRST LETTER IN VARIABLE NAME: S
(54FA) = 0      LSB OF VALUE   <---- VARPTR
(54FB) = 20     BYTE 2 OF VALUE
(54FC) = 71     MSB OF VALUE
(54FD) = 91     EXPONENT IS 11


ENTRY # 3 IN THE SIMPLE VARIABLE TABLE (HEX FORMAT)

(54FE) = 8      TYPE FLAG FOR DOUBLE PRECISION VARIABLE
(54FF) = 42     CODE FOR SECOND LETTER IN VARIABLE NAME: B
(5500) = 44     ASCII OF FIRST LETTER IN VARIABLE NAME: D
(5501) = 0      LSB OF VALUE   <---- VARPTR
(5502) = 80     BYTE 2 OF VALUE
(5503) = 1E     BYTE 3 OF VALUE   (5504) = 9F   BYTE 4 OF VALUE
(5505) = F5     BYTE 5 OF VALUE   (5506) = D7   BYTE 6 OF VALUE
(5507) = 68     MSB OF VALUE
(5508) = A9     EXPONENT IS 29
ENTRY # 4 IN THE SIMPLE VARIABLE TABLE (HEX FORMAT)

(5509) = 3      TYPE FLAG FOR STRING VARIABLE
(550A) = 31     CODE FOR SECOND LETTER IN VARIABLE NAME: 1
(550B) = 53     ASCII OF FIRST LETTER IN VARIABLE NAME: S
(550C) = 2      LENGTH OF THE STRING    <---- VARPTR
(550D) = 4D     LSB OF STARTING ADDRESS
(550E) = 44     MSB OF STARTING ADDRESS

44D2  ---->   HI
```

```
ENTRY # 5 IN THE SIMPLE VARIABLE TABLE (HEX FORMAT)

(550F) = 3      TYPE FLAG FOR STRING VARIABLE
(5510) = 32     CODE FOR SECOND LETTER IN VARIABLE NAME: 2
(5511) = 53     ASCII OF FIRST LETTER IN VARIABLE NAME: S
(5512) = 9      LENGTH OF THE STRING     <---- VARPTR
(5513) = F7     LSB OF STARTING ADDRESS
(5514) = 7F     MSB OF STARTING ADDRESS

 7FF7  ---->    HI GEORGE
```

TABLE 4.1 continued

changes—this should be clear from Table 3.1. The start of the table is the end of the BASIC text.

2. The variables in the table are "in order of their appearance" in the BASIC program. When a variable is needed the table is searched from the beginning. If the table is large, it takes time to find a variable near the end of the table. Therefore, at the beginning of a program we should initialize the often-used variables. As a rule the loop counters should be at the very beginning!
3. Remember, the array variable table sits on top of the simple variable table. When a simple variable is introduced into the program the whole array variable table is moved! If the table is large, this rearrangement may take a few seconds. To avoid this initialize all the variables at the beginning of the program.

To experiment with the rearrangement of the variable tables, RUN the program:

```
1 DIM X(40,200)
2 PRINT "WATCH NOW"
3 W = 0
4 PRINT "TABLE MOVED UP"
```

This takes about 2 seconds.

An obvious, but important, observation is that integer, single-precision, and double-precision variables require 5, 7, and 11 bytes of storage respectively. Use the type of variable that requires the least amount of storage but still has the required precision.

Packing

Knowing how variables are stored will prove to be crucial for FAST BASIC. Let us present a simple application in BASIC.

We can ask how many bits we need for the most economic storage of the integer N. One bit can pack 0 and 1; two bits can pack 0 to 3; three bits can pack 0 to 7; . . .; K bits can pack 0 to ($2^K - 1$). So we are looking for the smallest integer K such that N does not exceed $2^K - 1$. If N is provided in double-precision format, we find this K in the "exponent byte" as explained above. Program 4.2 calculates this number K.

Program 4.2. Packing

```
10 INPUT A#
20 IF A# = 0 THEN K = 1 : GOTO 50
30 X = VARPTR(A#)
40 K = PEEK(X + 7) - 128
50 PRINT "# OF BITS NEEDED FOR"; A#; "IS"; K : GOTO 10
```

Powers of 2

It may be useful to know more about the storage of single- and double-precision variables. For instance, if a double-precision variable A# is a power of 2, then the number is represented by the exponent; the 7 bytes, starting with VARPTR(A#), are all 00_H. Program 4.3 utilizes this information.

Program 4.3. Powers of 2

```
10 INPUT A#
20 X = VARPTR(A#)
30 FOR I = 0 TO 6
40 IF PEEK(X + I) <> 0 GOTO 70
50 NEXT I
60 PRINT "POWER OF 2" : GOTO 10
70 PRINT "NOT POWER OF 2" : GOTO 10
```

String Variables

Entries 4 and 5 in Table 4.1 show string variables. As you can see, the table entry takes 6 bytes, of which the last 2 point to where the string is actually stored (the "pointer" to the string).

If the string is defined in the program (in the form A$ = " . . .") and not changed during program execution (a "string constant"), then the string is stored in the BASIC program. The value of the string pointer of entry 4 shows that S1$ is a string constant.

If the string is defined during program execution, then it is stored in the string space on a first come, first entered basis. In entry 5 the string variable S2 goes to the start (the top) of the string space. The speed-up rule about numeric variables also applies to string variables: the most-often-used string variables should be initialized first.

As we have just seen, VARPTR can be used to find the location of a string variable. This is useful in many ways. Here are two examples:

1. Pack a machine language program into a string constant. Use VARPTR to find where the string is, so that the user subroutine (USR) can be given a starting address. (We demonstrate this in Chapter 10.)
2. Put a variable, say, A$ = "", into the BASIC program so that the start of the string can be used to locate a part of the text.

   This trick is always useful when we have to change something that cannot be represented by a string variable.

   To illustrate this, imagine that we have a program plotting curves SIN(X), COS(X), TAN(X), etc. We have a line

```
PRINT "1. LOG  2. EXP  3. COS  4. SIN  5. TAN  6. ATN" :
INPUT "CHOOSE FUNCTION YOU WISH PLOTTED"; F%
```

   and we have a line with the formula:

```
A$ = "" : Y = SIN(X)
```

   In this line SIN should be replaced by LOG, EXP, COS, SIN, TAN, or ATN, according to the input. This is accomplished as follows:

```
AD = PEEK(VARPTR(A$) + 1) + PEEK(VARPTR(A$) + 2)*256 :
POKE AD + 4, 222 + F%
```

   To understand 222 + F% at the end of the last line, observe that the BASIC keyword codes for LOG, EXP, COS, SIN, TAN, and ATN are 223_D to 228_D. Program 4.4 gives a simple illustration.

Program 4.4. Replacing a Trig Function

```
10 I = 0
20 A$ = "" : Z = SIN(1) : IF I = 0 THEN 30 ELSE PRINT Z
30 PRINT "1. LOG  2. EXP  3. COS  4. SIN  5. TAN  6. ATN"
40 I = I + 1
50 INPUT "CHOOSE FUNCTION"; F%
60 IF F% < 1 OR F% > 6 THEN GOTO 50
70 A# = VARPTR(A$) : AD# = PEEK(A# + 1) + PEEK(A# + 2)*256 : POKE
   AD# + 4, 222 + F%
80 GOTO 20
```

Among the many other applications the following are a few examples.

1. Change the + in X + Y to –, thus transforming an addition routine to a subtraction routine.

2. Change a line number in a GOTO statement (remember, these numbers are represented by the ASCII of the digits).
3. Change the line number pointer in the first line to the last line and RUN the program by GOTO 20 (this will stop the uninitiated from LISTing the program).
4. For Disk BASIC or Level III BASIC users: Change UU in FNUU to the desired user-defined function.

THE ARRAY VARIABLE TABLE

Organization

We now turn our attention to the storage of array variables.

Table 4.2 shows examples of entries in the array variable table. As you can see, it takes 8 bytes to record the array type of a variable of dimension 1 [DIM A(5) dimensions a one-dimensional array]; for a variable of dimension 2 [e.g., DIM B(120,2)] it takes 10 bytes. The table gives the typeflag, the variable name, the number of bytes in the array starting from the byte "NUMBER OF DIMENSIONS" (so in fact the whole entry uses up 5 more bytes), the number of dimensions, and then 2 bytes each for the size of each dimension.

The elements of an array are stored in the same way as simple variables (without the typeflag and the variable name). They are in the natural order: DB#(0), DB#(1),. . . . If the dimension is higher than one, for example, DIM A(2,1), then the listing is A(0,0), A(1,0), A(2,0), A(0,1), A(1,1), A(2,1). In other words, the first "index" increases to its limit, then the second is increased by one and the first is again increased to its limit, and so on.

Note that the program VARPTR does not distinguish between DIM A(5) and DIM A(2,1). In both cases we have six entries listed for the array.

THE STRING SPACE

Organization

The next important area to investigate is the string space. We already know that it stores all string variables but the string constants. To experiment with the string space, RUN the following program.

TABLE 4.2. The Array Variable Table

```
ARRAY # 1 OF ARRAY VARIABLE TABLE (HEX FORMAT)
(55DD) = 8      TYPE FLAG FOR DOUBLE PRECISION VARIABLE ARRAY
(55DE) = 42     CODE FOR SECOND LETTER IN VARIABLE NAME: B
(55DF) = 44     ASCII OF FIRST LETTER IN VARIABLE NAME: D
(55E0) = 2B     LSB OF THE ARRAY STORAGE SIZE
(55E1) = 0      MSB OF THE ARRAY STORAGE SIZE
(55E2) = 1      NUMBER OF DIMENSIONS
(55E3) = 5      LSB OF DIMENSION #1
(55E4) = 0      MSB OF DIMENSION #1
ELEMENT # 2 OF THE ARRAY
(55ED) = 0      LSB OF VALUE   <---- VARPTR
(55EE) = 0      BYTE 2 OF VALUE
(55EF) = 58     BYTE 3 OF VALUE   (55F0) = BC   BYTE 4 OF VALUE
(55F1) = 48     BYTE 5 OF VALUE   (55F2) = C1   BYTE 6 OF VALUE
(55F3) = 35     MSB OF VALUE
(55F4) = A5     EXPONENT IS 25


ARRAY # 2 OF ARRAY VARIABLE TABLE (HEX FORMAT)
(560D) = 3      TYPE FLAG FOR STRING VARIABLE ARRAY
(560E) = 31     CODE FOR SECOND LETTER IN VARIABLE NAME: 1
(560F) = 53     ASCII OF FIRST LETTER IN VARIABLE NAME: S
(5610) = 12     LSB OF THE ARRAY STORAGE SIZE
(5611) = 0      MSB OF THE ARRAY STORAGE SIZE
(5612) = 1      NUMBER OF DIMENSIONS
(5613) = 5      LSB OF DIMENSION #1
(5614) = 0      MSB OF DIMENSION #1
ELEMENT # 2 OF THE ARRAY
(5618) = 4      LENGTH OF THE STRING    <---- VARPTR
(5619) = E0     LSB OF STARTING ADDRESS
(561A) = 7F     MSB OF STARTING ADDRESS

 7FE0  ---->   HIHI


ARRAY # 5 OF ARRAY VARIABLE TABLE (HEX FORMAT)
(5657) = 2      TYPE FLAG FOR INTEGER VARIABLE ARRAY
(5658) = 4E     CODE FOR SECOND LETTER IN VARIABLE NAME: N
(5659) = 49     ASCII OF FIRST LETTER IN VARIABLE NAME: I
(565A) = 19     LSB OF THE ARRAY STORAGE SIZE
(565B) = 0      MSB OF THE ARRAY STORAGE SIZE
```

```
(565C) = 1       NUMBER OF DIMENSIONS
(565D) = B       LSB OF DIMENSION #1
(565E) = 0       MSB OF DIMENSION #1
ELEMENT # 2 OF THE ARRAY
(5661) = DC      LSB OF VALUE   <---- VARPTR
(5662) = 5       MSB OF VALUE
```

Program 4.5.

```
10 CLEAR 55
20 A$ = "  123  "
30 A$ =A$ + A$
40 B$ = LEFT$(A$,4) + RIGHT$(A$,4)
44 DIM D$(1)
50 D$(0) = "  567  "+"  "
60 E$ = B$ + "  "
70 D$(1) = "  999  "+"  "
72 STOP
75 A$ = "123456"+"  "
80 STOP
```

Now let us display the string space (. stands for blank):

Bottom of string space   Top of string space

↓ ..999 . . . . . 1223 . . . . . 567 . . . . . 1223 . . 23 . . . . 12 . . 123 . . . . 123 . . ↓

This shows the following arrangement.

D$(1), E$, D$(0), B$, "23 . . . . 12", A$

A$ = " . . 123 . . . . 123 . . " as the first string variable "in order of appearance" is placed at the top; then below it (on the left) we find B$ = " . . 1223 . . ", D$(0) = " . . 567 . . . ", E$ = " . .123 . . .", and finally D$(1) = " . . 99 . . . " as we would expect it. What may not have been expected is the string below A$: "23 . . . . 12". This was left over from the computation in line 40: Some temporary variables were created by the Interpreter and placed in the string space. Unfortunately, at the end of the computation this string was not cleared out.

Now RUN Program 4.5 with line 40 modified as follows:

```
40 B$ = LEFT$(A$,4)
```

Then the string space is as follows:

Bottom of string space　　　　　　Top of string space

↓　　　　　　　　　　　　　　　　　　　　　　　　↓
. . 999 . . . . . 12 . . . 567 . . . . . 12 . . 123 . . . . 123 . .

This shows the following arrangement.

D$(1), E$, D$(0), B$, A$

(When comparing this with the previous display, keep in mind that B$ and E$ have been redefined.) As you can see, the one extra string needed in handling the new line 40 was cleared out by the Interpreter.

Junk is also created by the redefinition of a string. Type CONT to CONTinue running the program; A$ is redefined as "123456.". We shall find "123456 ." at the bottom of the used area of the string space and the old A$ (. . 123 . . . . 123 . .) becomes junk.

When the string space gets filled up, a special subroutine is called in to delete all the junk. This is easy to illustrate: Restore line 40 of Program 4.1 and RUN it; we are left with 5 bytes in the string space when the program STOPs at line 72. CONTinue the program. When line 75 is executed there is no room at the bottom of the string space for the 7 bytes of the redefined A$, hence the string space is rearranged:

Bottom of string space　　　　　　　　　　　　Top of string space

↓　　　　　　　　　　　　　　　　　　　　　　　　　　　　↓
123456 . . . 999 . . . . . 1223 . . . . . 567 . . . . . 1223 . . . .123 . . . . 123 . .

Enough junk (but not all) was eliminated to make room for the new A$. With many string variables, such rearrangements may "hang up" the program for a considerable time. (In a checkbook program all the data were put into string variables and sorted; the program occasionally hung up in excess of two hours!) Take care to avoid the creation of junk if possible.

Swapping

We can utilize our understanding of the string space to write a CONTROLLED BASIC "swap" for string variables. In BASIC we swap A$ and B$ as follows:

```
C$ = A$ : A$ = B$ : B$ = C$
```

Program 4.6 shows how to accomplish the same in CONTROLLED BASIC.

Program 4.6.

```
10 A% = VARPTR(A$) : X1% = PEEK(A% + 1) : X2% = PEEK(A% + 2) :
X3% = PEEK(A%)
20 B% = VARPTR(B$)
30 POKE A% + 1, PEEK(B% + 1) : POKE A% + 2, PEEK(B% + 2) : POKE
A%, PEEK(B%)
40 POKE B%, X3% : POKE B% + 1, X1% : POKE B% + 2, X2%
```

This does not involve the string space. Thus we can save considerable time in string sorts.

THE BASIC STACK

Two More BASIC Tables

Finally we come to the BASIC stack. (We learn more about stacks in Chapter 7.) A stack is the work area of a machine language program. However, the BASIC stack is used for some BASIC tables: the subroutine call table and the FOR NEXT table.

Any time a subroutine is called a 7-byte entry is made in the subroutine call table; nesting subroutines may result in extensive use of the stack area. We make no use of this table in CONTROLLED BASIC or FAST BASIC.

A FOR instruction results in an 18-byte entry in the BASIC stack. The first and last bytes repeat the BASIC keyword code of FOR. In between, all the information about the FOR NEXT loop is recorded. When a NEXT instruction is encountered the entries are searched from last entry to first. If we jump out of a FOR NEXT loop without terminating it, the entry in the table is not erased. This may create trouble later in the program.

Review and Programming Practice

1. Name five BASIC variable-size tables.
2. Which tables vary in size during execution?
3. Are all strings stored in the string space?
4. What are the end-of-line marker and end-of-file marker for a BASIC program?
5. What do the first 2 bytes of a BASIC program contain? What do the following 2 bytes contain?
6. Name three ways of speeding up a BASIC program.
7. How much is Program 4.1 speeded up if we replace lines 299 and 300 by a FOR NEXT loop?
8. What does the BASIC stack contain?

9. We PEEKed at locations 16458, 16459, and 16633 to 16638 and obtained the numbers: 217, 104, 246, 104, 250, 104, 251, 104, 251, 104. What conclusions can you draw?
10. Where does the VARPTR of X% point?
11. The following BASIC line was RUN.

```
X% = 3 : E% = PEEK(VARPTR(X%) - 2)
```

What does E% contain?

12. Swap two integer variables using the VARPTR function.
13. Do the same as in Review Question 12, but for single-precision variables.
14. Do the same as in Review Question 12, but for double-precision variables.
15. Do the same as in Review Question 12, but for string variables.
16. The following program was RUN.

```
10 A = 0 : DIM X(20)
20 DB = PEEK(16637) + PEEK(16638)*256
30 PRINT DB
40 W = 0 : Y = 2
50 DE = PEEK(16637) + PEEK(16638)*256
60 PRINT DE
```

Explain the difference between the values of DB and DE.

17. Run the following program.

```
10  A$ = "GEORGE"
20  B$ = "TOM"
30  B$ = B$ + B$
```

Find out where A$ and B$ are stored. Is either A$ or B$ in the string space?

18. Type in and RUN the following BASIC program.

```
10 FOR I = 1 TO 10
20 IF I = 5 THEN 40
30 NEXT I
40 FOR J = 1 TO 10
50 FOR I = 1 TO 5
60 NEXT I
70 NEXT J
```

Although for every FOR there is a NEXT, we get an error message: NEXT WITHOUT FOR IN 70. Can you explain why? (*Hint:* The FOR NEXT table is scanned from the bottom up when a FOR statement is encountered.)

19. Explain why Program 4.2 works.
20. Write the alternative for Program 4.3. Compare A# with powers of 2. Which is faster?
21. How large can N be in DIM D#(N, 23) in a 48K computer?
22. Explain how Program 4.6 works.
23. Write a program that changes the positive sign to a negative sign in the line:

```
10 S$ = "" : X = X + Y
```

Answers

There are many correct answers to the programming questions. The answers provided here are only guidelines by which to judge your own answers.

1. The five BASIC variable-size tables are (1) the BASIC program, (2) the simple variable table, (3) the array variable table, (4) the string space, and (5) the BASIC stack.
2. All of them vary in size during program execution except the BASIC program.
3. No. String constants are stored in the BASIC program.
4. A 00_H byte terminates a BASIC line; two 00_H bytes terminate a BASIC program.
5. The first 2 bytes of a BASIC program contain the address of the second line as a 16-bit unsigned integer. The next 2 bytes contain the line number of the first line as a 16-bit unsigned integer.
6. Here are three ways of speeding up your BASIC program.
   (a) Place often-used subroutines close to and following the GOSUBs or at the beginning of the program.
   (b) Avoid jumping back a few lines in a loop.
   (c) Replace GOTO's by FOR NEXT loops wherever possible.
7. The new program is:

```
299 FOR X% = 0 TO 1000
300 NEXT
```

   This executes in 1.6 seconds—a speed-up by a factor of 25.
8. The BASIC stack contains some BASIC tables, for example, the FOR NEXT table and the subroutine call table; it is also used as a work area for machine language programs.
9. The program starts at 26841 = 217 + 256*104 and ends at 26869 = 246 + 256*104 – 1. The simple variable table goes

from 26870 to 26876 (one single-precision variable). The array variable table goes from 26877 to 26877. (It is empty.)

10. The VARPTR of X% points to the LSB of the 16-bit two's complement representation of the integer.
11. E% equals 2, the typeflag for an integer variable.
12.

```
10  DEFINT A - Z
20  INPUT X : INPUT Y
30  VX = VARPTR(X)
40  VY = VARPTR(Y)
50  E = PEEK(VX - 3)
60  FOR I = 0 TO E - 1
70  S = PEEK(VX + I)
80  POKE VX + I, PEEK(VY + I)
90  POKE VY + I, S
100 NEXT
110 PRINT X : PRINT Y
```

13. Change line 10 in the solution to Review Question 12 to:

```
10 DEFSP A - Z
```

14. Change line 10 in the solution to Review Question 12 to:

```
10 DEFDBL A - Z
```

15. Change line 10 in the solution to Review Question 12 to:

```
10 DEFSTR A - Z
```

16. DB and DE both point at the beginning of the array variable table. However, in between the two PRINTs the array variable table was moved up by 21 bytes. The introduction of the three single-precision variables (two in line 40 and one in line 50) caused the simple variable table to expand, pushing the array variable table up.
17. The address where A$ is stored is displayed by:

```
PRINT PEEK(VARPTR(A$) + 1) + PEEK(VARPTR(A$) + 2)*256
```

Similarly, the address where B$ is stored is:

```
PRINT PEEK(VARPTR(B$) + 1) + PEEK(VARPTR(B$) + 2)*256
```

B$ is in the string space.

18. At line 10 an entry is made in the FOR NEXT table for I. The I loop is aborted in line 20. The entry stays in the table because the NEXT was not reached.

Execution continues with line 40: An entry is made for J in the FOR NEXT table. This table now contains two entries—I on top and J below it. At line 50 an I loop is encountered. The FOR NEXT table is searched and an entry for an I loop is found; this entry is rewritten for the new I loop and the pointer to the bottom of the FOR NEXT table points at the new I entry. (This pointer always points at the last entry.) Hence the J loop entry is lost. Encountering NEXT J in line 70, a search is made for a J entry and none is found. The computer displays an error message.

19. In line 40 PEEK(X + 7) returns the value of the byte containing the exponent. Since bit 7 is set, we have to subtract 128 to get the value of the exponent.

20.

```
10 INPUT A#
20 J% = 1
30 FOR I = 1 TO A#
40 J% = 2*J%
50 IF J% = A# THEN PRINT "POWER OF 2" : I = A#
60 IF J% > A# THEN PRINT "NOT POWER OF 2" : I = A#
70 NEXT
```

21. On a 48K computer there are about 48,000 bytes for a TRS-80 BASIC program. Thus N has to be smaller than 48,000/8, that is, 6000. In Disk BASIC, N has to be smaller than 39,000/8, that is, 4,875.

22. In line 10 Program 4.6 copies the length and address of A$ into X1%, X2%, and X3%. In line 30 the length and address of B$ is copied into the length and address of A$. Finally, the stored length and address of A$ overwrite the length and address of B$.

23. The following lines change the + to a – in the statement X = X + Y:

```
20 DB = PEEK(VARPTR(S$) + 1) + PEEK(VARPTR(S$) + 2)*256
30 POKE DB + 10, 206
```

CHAPTER FIVE

Devices

And imagined such a device as they are not able to perform.
—Psalm xxi,11 in *The Book of Common Prayer*

In this chapter we discuss the most important devices used by the TRS-80: the video display, the keyboard, the cassette recorder, and the disk.

BUSES AND PORTS

We have carefully avoided discussing the hardware of the TRS-80; it does not seem necessary for understanding the aspects of CONTROLLED BASIC covered in the previous chapters. However, to program input/output in CONTROLLED BASIC, we should know something about "buses" and "ports."

CPU

The heart of the computer is the "central processing unit" (CPU). The CPU of the TRS-80 is a Z-80 microprocessor. This is really the computer; it carries out the instructions of the machine language program. We discuss the Z-80 microprocessor in Part III.

Buses

In this section we discuss how the Z-80 microprocessor is connected with the rest of the computer. The connections are made through a 16-line "address bus," an 8-line "data bus," and a 4-line "control group." There are a few more wires but we need not concern ourselves with them in this discussion.

Each line (wire) can carry a bit. Thus the address bus can carry a 16-bit number and the data bus can carry a byte. By way of example, let us assume that the CPU wishes to store byte $A2_H$ in memory location $9F21_H$. The CPU puts $9F21_H$ on the address bus and the number $A2_H$ on the data bus. The CPU then sends signals through the control group that will cause $A2_H$ to be sent to location $9F21_H$.

The address bus is unidirectional; it carries 16-bit numbers from the CPU. The data bus is bidirectional; it can carry a byte of data to or from the CPU. In fact this is the only way data can be passed between the CPU and the outside world.

Address Decoder

The 16-bit number placed on the address bus carries vital information. This 16-bit number may be the address of a ROM memory location, the address of a RAM memory location, or the address in the special RAM used by the video display. Finally, it may signify an "address port," which may not be a memory location. An address port connects the CPU with a peripheral device such as the keyboard or the printer.

It is the task of the "address decoder" to analyze the 16-bit number on the address bus and to decide on the appropriate category. For instance, $9F21_H$ is a RAM memory location, so in the foregoing example $A2_H$ is sent to memory. If the CPU places $37E8_H$ on the address bus, then the address decoder connects the data bus directly with the printer. The address port of the printer is $37E8_H$ (14312_D).

Memory Mapping

Peripheral devices that have address ports are called "memory mapped." This is very misleading; with the exception of the video display, *there is no memory* at the addresses of the address ports. It would seem to be more appropriate to call these devices "address mapped"; however, the name "memory mapped" is too well entrenched to be changed.

The lineprinter, the keyboard, the video display, and the disks are memory mapped. The video display uses 1024_D address ports that are in a special memory chip.

Ports

There is another way in which the Z-80 can be connected to devices. The Z-80 has 256 "ports." For instance, the cassette uses port 255_D (FF_H). The CPU communicates with the ports by using the first eight lines of the address bus and the data bus. The control group signifies that the data bus should be connected with a port.

From the point of view of the BASIC programmer, there is not much difference between ports and address ports. We send a byte of data, 23_D, to the address port $37E8_H$ (14312_H) by POKE 14312, 23; we send it to port 255_D by OUT 255, 23. We receive a byte of data from the address port $37E8_H$ (14312_D) by PEEK(14312) and from the port 255_D by INP(255).

THE VIDEO DISPLAY

The video display is the simplest memory-mapped device. The screen is divided into 16 lines; each line has 64 locations. As illustrated on the video display worksheet (page C/7 of the TRS-80 Manual), the locations on line 1 are numbered 0 to 63, on line 2, 64 to 127, . . . , on line K, 64*(K–1) to 64*K – 1, where K ranges from 1 to 16.

The number of the first location of each of the 16 lines are, in decimal:

(1)	0	(2)	64	(3)	128	(4)	192
(5)	256	(6)	320	(7)	384	(8)	448
(9)	512	(10)	576	(11)	640	(12)	704
(13)	768	(14)	832	(15)	896	(16)	960

and in hex:

(0)	0	(1)	40	(2)	80	(3)	C0
(4)	100	(5)	140	(6)	180	(7)	1C0
(8)	200	(9)	240	(A)	280	(B)	2C0
(C)	300	(D)	340	(E)	380	(F)	3C0

Since the first location is in memory location $3C00_H$ (15360_H), the memory location corresponding to location #N (counting is started with N = 0) is $3C00_H$ + N (15360_D + N).

We can POKE at these locations to speed up graphics. For instance,

```
POKE 15510, 131
```

and

```
PRINT @150, CHR$(131)
```

both print a bar at location 33 of line 3, but the POKE is about twice as fast! (For speed in drawing horizontal lines use STRING$.)

POKEs speed up graphics. However, real speed is achieved with machine language subroutines. This is discussed in Chapter 11 and Appendix 1.

THE KEYBOARD

Switches

The keyboard arrangement is shown in Figure 5.1. In this figure, D0 to D7 are the eight lines of the data bus and A0 to A7 are the eight low-order lines of the address bus. There are 64 switches at the intersections of these lines; if a key is pressed, the corresponding switch is closed.

	D0	D1	D2	D3	D4	D5	D6	D7
A0	@	A	B	C	D	E	F	G
A1	H	I	J	K	L	M	N	O
A2	P	Q	R	S	T	U	V	W
A3	X	Y	Z					
A4	0	! 1	" 2	# 3	$ 4	% 5	& 6	' 7
A5	(8	) 9	* :	+ ;	< ,	= -	> .	? /
A6	ENT	CLR	BRK	UA	DA	LA	RA	SBR
A7	SHFT							

ENT = ENTER   CLR = CLEAR   BRK = BREAK
UA = UP ARROW   DA = DOWN ARROW   LA = LEFT ARROW
RA = RIGHT ARROW   SBR = SPACE BAR   SHFT = SHIFT

FIGURE 5.1. Keyboard Switches

In looking at Figure 5.1 we see that pressing D connects the address line A0 with the data line D4. Pressing J, K, L at the same time connects A1 with three data lines: D2, D3, and D4. Pressing SHIFT A (lowercase a) connects A0 with D1 and A7 with D0.

Decoding

Three rules explain how to figure out which keys have been pressed using PEEK.

First Rule

PEEK at an address whose MSB is 38_H. If the MSB is 38_H, this gives a signal to the address decoder to connect the CPU with the keyboard switches.

There are 256 addresses with 38_H as MSB: 3800_H to $38FF_H$ (14336_H to 14591_D). Of these, 255 are utilized.

Second Rule

PEEKing at an address with MSB 38_H, we obtain information about row i of the keyboard switches, if bit i of the LSB is set (Figure 5.1): We start numbering the rows at 0; Ai heads row i.

Here is a simple example: PEEK at 14337_D. Since 14337_D is 3801_H the MSB is 38_H and the LSB is 01_H. By the first rule, this address should give us information about the switches. The LSB, 01_H, is $0000\ 0001_B$; thus bit 0 is set. By the second rule we can sense the switches on the address line A0.

Third Rule

The value returned by PEEK (at an address with MSB 38_H) is the decimal conversion of the 8-bit binary number in which bit j is set if a key is pressed in column j of *any* row sensed (see second rule) by that address.

Continuing the example, the value returned by PEEK(14337) is the decimal conversion of the 8-bit binary number in which bit j is set if the key in column j of row 0 is pressed. For instance, if PEEK(14337) returns 2, then A is pressed. Thus PEEK(14337) = 0 if no key in the first row is being pressed. If @ is pressed, we get PEEK(14337) = 1; A gives 2, B gives 4, C gives 8, D gives 16, E gives 32, F gives 64, and G gives 128. The value returned for a single row is additive. If D and G are both pressed, we get 144.

We see from the second rule that we have to use an address with one 1 and seven 0's in the LSB to determine what happens in a single row. Such addresses are 3801_H, 3802_H, 3804_H, 3808_H, 3810_H, 3820_H, 3840_H, 3880_H (in decimal, 14337, 14338, 14340, 14344, 14352, 14368, 14400, 14464). Hence these addresses have to be used to test whether a key on a given row has been pressed.

Examples: Is T pressed (and nothing else)?
Check: PEEK(14340) = 16.
Is % pressed?
Check: PEEK(14352) = 32 and PEEK (14464) = 1, the second PEEK checks the SHIFT key.
Are J, K, L simultaneously pressed?
Check: PEEK(14338) = 28.

The decoding scheme for these eight addresses is given in Figure 5.2. Figure 5.2 is sufficient to handle any single key using the following rule.

Single-Key Decoding Rule

We pick an address from the first column of Figure 5.2 (in decimal form). This fixes the row with which we are working. PEEKing at this address returns the decimal form of the 8-bit binary number in which bit i is set if the key in column i of this row is pressed.

	bit 0	bit 1	bit 2	bit 3	bit 4	bit 5	bit 6	bit 7
3801	@	A	B	C	D	E	F	G
3802	H	I	J	K	L	M	N	O
3804	P	Q	R	S	T	U	V	W
3808	X	Y	Z					
3810	0	1	2	3	4	5	6	7
3820	8	9	:	;	,	-	.	/
3840	ENT	CLR	BRK	UA	DA	LA	RA	SBR
3880	SHFT							

FIGURE 5.2. Single-Row Decoding for Keyboard

However, to answer the following questions, we have to use the three rules and Figure 5.1.

Is any letter (including @) pressed (shifting is not permitted)? We check for this at the address that can sense A0, A1, A2, and A3 but not A4, A5, A6, or A7. Thus the LSB of this address in binary is 0000 1111 = $0F_H$. This address is $380F_H$ (14351_D). Check: PEEK(14351) <> 0.

Is any key being pressed? The required address has $1111\ 1111_B = FF_H$ as its LSB, so the address is $38FF_H$ (14591_D). Check: PEEK(14591) < > 0.

Repeat Key

Let us utilize our knowledge of the keyboard to add a repeat key to a program. Repeat keys may be useful in graphics input or for the space bar and the period in text input.

Program 5.1. Repeat A

```
10 FOR I = 1 TO 20 : NEXT
20 IF PEEK(14591) = 0 THEN 20
30 IF PEEK(14337) = 2 THEN PRINT "A"; : GOTO 30
40 IF PEEK(14337) = 2 OR PEEK(14591) = 0 THEN GOTO 20
50 REM PROGRAM CONTINUES HERE
```

This will repeat PRINTing "A" as long as the A key is pressed; this can be done again and again. If any other key is pressed, control transfers to line 50.

In Program 5.1 line 10 was added so that this segment could be RUN independently; without line 10 PEEK (14591) will catch the ENTER key we pressed after RUN, and control transfers to line 50. Note that PEEK(14337) = 2 is repeated in line 40 in case A is pressed and released while line 30 is being executed. Using PEEK instead of INKEY$ ensures that fewer input attempts are lost.

THE CASSETTE

Port 255 is used to communicate with the cassette. When we are sending a byte to the port (OUT 255, X where X is 0 to 255) the 4 high-order bits are disregarded. Bit 3 has nothing to do with the cassette; it is 1 to choose the 32-character-per-line display format on the video display and 0 for the regular display. Bit 2 is 1 to turn the cassette motor on; it is 0 to turn the motor off. Bits 0 and 1 send signals to the cassette recorder: 00_B is no signal, 11_B and 10_B are low signal, and 01_B is high signal. Input from this port uses only 2 bits: bit 7 for cassette input and bit 6 for the video display format.

You may be interested in knowing how programs are recorded on tape. A byte is represented as 8 consecutive bits. A bit is recorded on the tape as a beep with a pause (a high signal followed by a low signal), followed by another beep for bit 1 or by more erased tape for bit 0.

A BASIC program starts with 256 00_H bytes (the "leader"), followed by the byte $A5_H$; then $D3_H$ three times followed by the 1-byte-long program name (e.g., "A" in ASCII). The program text now follows, byte by byte, in the same way as described in Chapter 4.

Data are recorded in a similar way by PRINT#-1. The 257 bytes start off as above, followed by the data—an ASCII string of up to 256 characters. Within this string commas can separate independent items. Numeric information is also recorded as an ASCII string with leading and trailing blanks. $0D_H$ terminates the data block.

An immediate conclusion is that, when storing data, most of the tape contains blanks. We can try to optimize data storage by using strings that are about 256 bytes long (concatenate numbers and shorter strings). This can speed up data transmission by 10 to 15 times. Nevertheless, even at the best of times half the tape is wasted.

DEVICE PROGRAMMING

It is easy to learn how to communicate with the devices discussed so far. Through the port or address port the device sends a "status word." When the status word indicates that the device is ready to receive, we send a character.

Lineprinter

Let us illustrate this with the lineprinter. The address port is $37E8_H$ (14312_D). We read the status word by PEEK(14312). Actually, we are mainly interested in bit 7. If bit 7 is 1, the printer is busy; if bit 7 is 0, the printer is available. We loop until bit 7 becomes 0 and then POKE 14312, X where X is the ASCII of the character to be printed. Then again we wait until bit 7 becomes 0 before sending the next character.

Interrupts

To understand how to interact with the floppy drives, we must discuss interrupts first.

An "interrupt" is a signal coming into the computer. It indicates that something of importance has happened that requires the immediate attention of the CPU. There are two kinds of interrupts:

1. An "unmaskable interrupt" means that the work of the CPU is interrupted. Pressing the reset button or the power-up button gives an unmaskable interrupt. [Pressing the reset button

starts executing (the program in ROM) at 0066_H,] whereas powering-up starts executing at 0000_H.]

2. A "maskable interrupt" tells the CPU that an interrupt signal came in, *provided* that the interrupts have not been disabled. CMD "T" disables interrupts and CMD "R" enables interrupts.

Thus unmaskable interrupts are beyond the control of the programmer and they cannot be altered. You cannot change the fact that pressing the reset button starts program execution at 0066_H. However, maskable interrupts can be "disconnected," that is, disabled.

When a maskable interrupt is received (and the interrupts are enabled) the CPU interrupts the program it is running, stores all the information needed to resume execution later, and turns its attention to "servicing the interrupt."

The Z-80 can support three types of maskable interrupts. Of these only one is available in the TRS-80 computer—interrupt mode 1. The interrupt causes the interrupt address port (location $37E0_H$, see Table 3.2) to record what caused the interrupt and the CPU calls a special subroutine (RST 38H).

Clock

The TRS-80 disk system uses maskable interrupts for only two tasks: an internal clock that interrupts every 25 milliseconds to update the time, and disk input/output. The clock uses the following locations (Table 3.2)

4041 – 4046	16449 – 16454	Time area (seconds, minutes, hours, year, day, month)

It is important to know when interrupts can occur. When we are running a time-sensitive program (for instance, writing data on a cassette tape), we certainly do not want to be interrupted. So start such a program by disabling the interrupt; for example, before CLOAD or CSAVE, in a disk system we execute CMD "T" (disable interrupt).

Similarly, many disk routines are time sensitive; these automatically turn the clock off for the duration of the input/output. This explains why the clock runs too slowly when we do a lot of disk input/output.

Disk

Communication with the disk uses six addresses as shown in Table 3.2.

37E0	14304	Interrupt address port: bit 7 is set for clock, bit 6 is set for disk
37E1	14305	Disk drive select
37EC	14316	Disk command/status
37ED	14317	Disk track select
37EE	14318	Disk sector select
37EF	14319	Disk data

The disk drive i (i can be 0, 1, 2, or 3) to be used is selected by setting bit i of disk drive select. Thus POKE 14305, 1; POKE 14305, 2; POKE 14305, 4; POKE 14305, 8 will select drives 0, 1, 2, or 3 respectively. (We can select more than one drive at a time. This means that data can be written onto up to four disks simultaneously.) We have to pause for one second to wait for the disk drive to get ready, and then we write the track and sector numbers in the appropriate locations, and we are ready to issue a command. The byte to be sent is placed in the disk data address port; the byte received is also found there.

Commands are issued by POKEing them into the disk command/status address port. Fifty microseconds after a command is issued the location contains the status word: bit 0 is set (= 1) for busy; bit 6 is the write-protect flag; bit 7 is set if the motor stopped, and is reset otherwise. (All the other bits are also used.)

An Application

A typical CONTROLLED BASIC application is the following. If a program requires a lot of disk input/output, long delays in the program execution can be introduced by the one-second delay between a drive selection and the first read or write on the drive. A POKE 14305, 2 will keep drive 1 from stopping. Inserting such a POKE where necessary may speed up a program by 40 to 50 percent. Disk input/output is discussed further in Appendix 1.

A word of caution: If the timing of the POKE is wrong, it may happen that the disk drive had already stopped before the POKE was done. The POKE will start up the drive. Now if the disk in that drive is used before it achieves full speed, then the read or write may be incorrect. To avoid this use the POKE only to keep the drive running. The BASIC line

```
100 IF PEEK(14316) < 128 THEN POKE 14305, 2
```

will accomplish this.

Disk Status Read

Program 5.2 is a subroutine by B. Fred* that utilizes some of the information about the disk address ports.

The Alternate Source, Vol. 1, No. 5. © 1980 The Alternate Source, 1806 ADA, Lansing, MI. 48910, Reprinted with permission.

Program 5.2. Reading the Disk Status in BASIC

```
10000 IF DN < 0 OR DN > 3 THEN DS = 3 : RETURN
10001 SV% = 1 : IF DN > 0 THEN FOR X% = 1 TO DN : SV% = SV% + SV%
      : NEXT
10002 POKE 14316, 208 : FOR X% = 1 TO 100 : POKE 14305, SV% :
      NEXT : PV% = PEEK(14316) AND 2
10003 FOR X% = 1 TO 100 : POKE 14305, SV% : CV% = PEEK(14316) :
      IF (CV% AND 2) <> PV% THEN 10005
10004 NEXT : DS = 2 : IF CV% AND 2 THEN 10006 ELSE DS = 3 : GOTO
      10006
10005 DS = 0 : IF CV% AND 64 THEN DS = 1
10006 RETURN
```

This subroutine is called with DN containing the drive number (0 to 3). On return, DS is the disk status: DS is 0 if the drive is ready and it contains a disk that is not write protected; DS is 1 if the drive is ready and it contains a write-protected disk; DS is 2 if the drive does not contain a disk; finally, DS is 3 if there is no such drive or the door of the drive is open.

Devices

It seems appropriate to conclude this chapter by discussing what a device is. From a theoretical point of view a "device" is anything that is capable of receiving information from or transmitting information to the CPU. A device is a "read device" if the CPU can read it, and a "write device" if the CPU can write to it. The keyboard is a read device and the video display is a write device; the cassette is a read device in the play mode and a write device in the record mode. Disk files are also devices; they have device control blocks (see the TRS-DOS Manual) and drivers.

The model of all small computer operating systems, the OS-8 of DEC, handles all devices in the same way. A typical command may be

```
COPY DEV1 < DEV2
```

where DEV1 is any write device and DEV2 is any read device. Thus this one command unifies the following: print on a lineprinter; list on the video display; rename a file; copy a file to another disk; store on tape; type in data from the keyboard; send file to another computer; etc.

A number of TRS-80 operating systems use this logical system, for instance, CP/M (Control Program Monitor) of Digital Research. CP/M is available for most computers using an 8080 or Z-80 microprocessor. Programs written under CP/M BASIC are transportable to all computers using CP/M.

Review and Programming Practice

1. Define the following terms.
   (a) CPU
   (b) Bus
   (c) Address decoder
   (d) Memory-mapped device
   (e) Port
2. Explain how the CPU sends the number $0B_H$ to the address $7E00_H$.
3. Can you replace the BASIC command LPRINT "HAPPY" by POKEs? Can you see the application of this in machine language programming?
4. Write a "screen print" subroutine for a BASIC program. It should print on the printer each printable character on the video display and print a "." for an unprintable character.
5. Improve on the previous program. If from a character to the end of the line we have only blanks on the video display, then send the code for the carriage return to the printer and proceed with the next line.
6. Finally, write a variant for the above program. You are inputing text that is displayed on the screen; if the keys J, K, L are pressed at the same time, we get screen print.
7. In BASIC games it is often necessary to have simultaneous keyboard input. Here is an example. In a car race the first driver controls the direction of the first car with the up and down arrow keys whereas the second driver uses the left and right arrow keys to control the second car. The two players are permitted to press one of their assigned keys simultaneously. Write a BASIC program that accepts such input and prints out the names of the keys that have been pressed.
8. Write a BASIC program to check whether or not your computer has a lowercase conversion installed. (*Hint:* Clear screen, PRINT @0, lowercase a. PEEK to see whether it is lowercase.)
9. Program 5.1 has a slight defect: Check to see what happens if A and I are pressed simultaneously.

Answers

There are many correct answers to the programming questions. The answers provided here are only guidelines by which to judge your own answers.

1. (a) CPU: central processing unit.
   (b) Bus: 8 or 16 lines of wire connecting the CPU to the rest of the computer.

(c) Address decoder: analyzes the address on the address bus to decide to what the data bus should be connected.
(d) Memory-mapped device: a device wired to one or more memory addresses.
(e) Port: 256 devices can be directly wired to the Z-80 through the ports. Each port can input or output a single byte.

2. The CPU puts $0B_H$ on the data bus and $7E00_H$ on the address bus. The CPU then sends signals through the control group that cause $0B_H$ to be sent to $7E00_H$.

3.

```
10 A$ = "HAPPY"
20 FOR I = 1 TO LEN(A$)
30 POKE 14312, ASC(MID$(A$,I))
40 NEXT
50 POKE 14312, 13 : REM THIS IS CARRIAGE RETURN
```

4.

```
1000 FOR I = 0 TO 15 : REM THERE ARE 16 LINES
1010 FOR J = 0 TO 63 : REM AND 64 CHARACTERS EACH LINE
1020 AS = PEEK(15360 + J + I*64) : REM TAKE NEXT CHARACTER
1030 IF 31 < AS OR AS < 128 THEN LPRINT CHR$(AS); : ELSE LPRINT
     ".";
1040 NEXT
1050 LPRINT CHR$(13); : REM END OF LINE CARRIAGE RETURN
1060 NEXT
1070 RETURN
```

5. Add the following lines.

```
1025 IF AS = 32 THEN GOTO 1080
1080 FOR Z = J + 1 TO 63
1090 IF PEEK(15360 + Z + I*64) <> 32 THEN Z = 64 : NEXT :
     GOTO 1030
1100 NEXT
1110 J = 64 : GOTO 1040
```

6.

```
10 X$ = INKEY$
20 IF PEEK(14338) = 28 THEN GOSUB 1000
30 PRINT X$
40 GOTO 10
```

7.

```
10  X% = PEEK(14502)
20  IF X% = 8 THEN PRINT "UP ARROW"
30  IF X% = 16 THEN PRINT "DOWN ARROW"
40  IF X% = 32 THEN PRINT "LEFT ARROW"
50  IF X% = 64 THEN PRINT "RIGHT ARROW"
60  IF X% = 40 THEN PRINT "UP AND LEFT ARROW"
70  IF X% = 72 THEN PRINT "UP AND RIGHT ARROW"
80  IF X% = 48 THEN PRINT "DOWN AND LEFT ARROW"
90  IF X% = 80 THEN PRINT "DOWN AND RIGHT ARROW"
100 GOTO 10
```

8.

```
10 CLS : POKE 15360, 97 REM 97 IS THE ASCII FOR LOWER CASE A
20 IF PEEK(15360) = 97 THEN PRINT "LOWER CASE CONVERSION"
   ELSE PRINT "NO LOWER CASE CONVERSION"
```

9. The program does not know whether A is pressed alone or in combination with any other key not in the first row in Figure 5.2.

PART III
Background for FAST BASIC

CHAPTER SIX

The Z-80 Register Set

And I am rich with little store.

—E. Dyer in *My Mind to Me a Kingdom Is*

In FAST BASIC we rewrite the time-consuming lines of a BASIC program into machine language with the use of ROM routines, and in this way we increase the speed of execution. But to be able to write FAST BASIC programs, we have to know CONTROLLED BASIC, especially the memory organization of TRS-80 BASIC. In addition, we have to become somewhat familiar with the Z-80 microprocessor. This is accomplished in Part III.

THE REGISTERS

We start this chapter by discussing the memory of the Z-80 microprocessor.

Eight-Bit Registers

The central processing unit (CPU) of the TRS-80 computer is a Z-80 microprocessor. The Z-80 microprocessor is a microcomputer with a very limited set of memory: a set of 8-bit "registers" and a set of 16-bit registers. We start with the 8-bit registers.

```
A   F   A'  F'
B   C   B'  C'
D   E   D'  E'
H   L   H'  L'
I   R
```

Registers A, B, C, D, E, H, L are just like memory locations containing 1 byte each. Register F is special; it contains the flags (explained soon). I is the interrupt register and R is refresh register; these play no role in FAST BASIC.

We manipulate the registers by moving the contents of one into another, by moving a byte from memory into a register, and so on. This is discussed in Chapter 7.

Alternate Register Set

The registers A'–L' are called the "alternate register set." At any given time we have access only to registers A–L but not to A'–L'. We can interchange A–L with the alternate register set A'–L'. After the interchange A–L becomes A'–L' and A'–L' becomes A–L.

For instance, if A contains 02_H and A' contains 23_H, then after the interchange A contains 23_H and A' contains 02_H.

We interchange the register sets if A–L contain some information we want to save for future use. In the next chapter we learn how to effect the interchange.

Sixteen-Bit Registers

The 16-bit registers are

IX IY
SP PC

Recall that an address is a 16-bit binary number (or 4 hex digits). The four 16-bit registers are most often used for storing addresses. However, they play different roles:

1. IX and IY are the "index registers"; they are mostly pointers to memory areas (tables) where useful information is stored. (See "Memory Addressing.")
2. SP is the "stack pointer"; it points to the stack, the most important storage space of a machine language program, similar in role to the BASIC stack discussed in Chapter 4. (See Figure 7.1 for an illustration of how the stack works.)
3. PC is the "program counter"; it points in memory at the *next* machine language instruction. (See the section below on The Program Counter for a detailed discussion.)

Register Pairs

From the 8-bit registers we can form eight register pairs:

AF AF'
BC BC'
DE DE'
HL HL'

AF is A and F; AF' is A' and F', and so on. Paired together, BC, DE, HL, and their primed counterparts (ignore for this use AF and AF') can be used as 16-bit registers. To remember which registers can be paired: BC is *byte counter*, DE is *decrement*, and HL is *high low*.

For instance, let register B contain 23_H and C contain $A5_H$; then BC contains $23A5_H$.

Memory Addressing

Register pairs and 16-bit registers play a dominant role in memory addressing. If register B contains $2A_H$ and register C contains 15_H, then BC contains the 16-bit integer $2A15_H$. Thus BC can be regarded as a memory pointer; it points at the memory location $2A15_H$. (See Table 6.1.) The contents of the memory location $2A15_H$, usually denoted by $(2A15_H)$, can also be represented by (BC).

To illustrate memory addressing let us assume that the registers contain the following values:

BC	= $2A15_H$	DE	= $2A00_H$	HL	= $3BBC_H$
IX	= $3C10_H$	IY	= $3C20_H$	SP	= $4FFF_H$

These registers can point at a number of memory locations; some of these are shown in Table 6.1.

TABLE 6.1. Memory Addressing

Pointer	→	Memory Location (in hex)	Memory Contents
			Low memory
DE	→	2A00	(DE) = (2A00)
BC	→	2A15	(BC) = (2A15)
HL	→	3BBC	(HL) = (3BBC)
IX–1	→	3C0F	(IX–1) = (3C0F)
IX+0	→	3C10	(IX+0) = (3C10)
IY+5	→	3C25	(IY+5) = (3C25)
...			
		Stack	
SP	→	4FFF	Bottom of stack
...			
		Top of stack	
...			
			High memory

An inspection of Table 6.1 shows that:

1. IX and IY can be modified by adding an 8-bit signed integer called "offset"; the range is from IX – 128 to IX + 127 and the same for IY.
2. It is advisable to write IX + 0 for IX (e.g., the Radio Shack Editor/Assembler does not accept IX).
3. The top of the stack is set in the program; the bottom of the stack is in SP.

The Flag Register

Finally, we come to register F. We cannot use register F for storing a byte. This register contains the flags: the carry flag, the zero flag, the sign flag, and the P/O flag. These 1-bit flags are set automatically by the results of machine language operations.

In FAST BASIC we use only two flags. The "carry flag" (bit 0 of F) holds the carry from bit 7 in arithmetic operations. The "zero flag" (bit 6 of F) is set if the result of an arithmetic or logical operation is 0.

The status of the flags may be important in a machine language program. Subroutine calls, as a rule, change the flags. So we have to save the flags before a subroutine call and then restore them after the subroutine.

THE PROGRAM COUNTER

To discuss the role of PC we need a machine language program. We start with a very simple program: It loads into register A the contents of the memory location $5A19_H$ and then loads register A into register B. (We end up with the contents of $5A19_H$ in register B.)

Program 6.1. A Machine Language Program

Address	Contents
7E00	3A
7E01	19
7E02	5A
7E03	47

We execute this program by setting PC = $7E00_H$. (For instance, in all the examples in the book we call a machine language program from BASIC with a USR, a user subroutine. Before we call the USR we have to POKE in the starting address. This is the step that sets PC to the required value.)

Now we follow step by step what happens to PC as this program is executed.

PC = $7E00_H$

7E00	3A	The CPU reads the byte pointed at by PC: 3A (all these numbers are, of course, hex). The CPU concludes that this is the first byte of a 3-byte instruction; it adds 3 to PC (now PC = $7E03_H$) and the CPU carries out the 3-byte instruction: It loads into register A the contents of memory location $5A19_H$. (Observe, 5A19 in the second and third byte of the instruction, first the LSB, 19, then the MSB, 5A.)
7E01	19	
7E02	5A	

PC = $7E03_H$

7E03	47	Again, the CPU reads the byte PC is pointing at: 47. This is a 1-byte instruction, so PC is incremented to $7E04_H$. The instruction loads register A into register B.

This shows the role of PC. At the beginning it points to the start of the machine language program; it is continually updated to point to the instruction following the one that is being executed.

ASSEMBLY LANGUAGE

We would be, of course, in difficulty if we had to write programs such as Program 6.1. But this is the only kind of program the CPU can understand! Even a BASIC program has to be translated into one like this by the Interpreter. Assembly language programming solves the problem. Program 6.2 is the same program written in assembly language.

Program 6.2. An Assembly Language Program

```
100          ORG     7E00H
110          LD      A,(5A19H) ;LOAD INTO A (5A19H)
120          LD      B,A       ;LOAD A INTO B
130          END
```

The Radio Shack Editor/Assembler was used to write this program. For simple programs this assembler is completely satisfactory (although a macro assembler—see Appendix 7—is preferable). As you can see, mysterious hex numbers are replaced by mnemonics, such as LD for load.

In each line the text following ";" is a comment ignored by the assembler. The role of ";" in assembly language is the same as that of "REM" in BASIC. However, keep in mind that comments are even more important in assembly language than in BASIC.

After we finish writing the assembly language program we use the ASSEMBLE command of the assembler (command A for the Radio Shack Editor/Assembler). Here is the output of the assembler (to save space we omitted the comments).

```
7E00          100    ORG     7E00H
7E00  3A195A  110    LD      A,(5A19H)
7E03  47      120    LD      B,A
0000          130    END

00000 TOTAL ERRORS
```

The machine language listing is the second column; this was used in Program 6.1.

Please read your assembler manual carefully. In this book we use the mnemonics of the Radio Shack Assembler (your assembler may use a different set). If you have a more advanced assembler, use its capabilities to simplify the implementation of FAST BASIC.

Review and Programming Practice

1. Define the following terms: 8-bit register, 16-bit register, register pair, and flag.
2. Name the 8-bit registers.
3. Name the 16-bit registers.
4. Name the register pairs.
5. What are the names for the registers SP, PC, and IX?
6. If the registers contain the numbers shown:

A	B	C	D	E
02_H	$2A_H$	DD_H	$F0_H$	$0F_H$

and

$(2ADD_H) = 35_H$ $(F00F_H) = 6_H$ $(DDF0_H) = FF_H$

(a) What does register A contain?
(b) What does register C contain?
(c) What does the register pair BC contain?
(d) What does (BC) contain?
(e) What does (CD) contain?

7. What does SP point to?
8. PC points to $7E00_H$. What will PC point to after a 3-byte load instruction is executed?
9. What is the purpose of assembly language?
10. What is the assembly language mnemonics (a) for origin; (b) for load; (c) for end?
11. Name the flags we use in FAST BASIC.

Answers

1. 8-bit register: memory location of the CPU containing 1 byte; 16-bit register: memory location of the CPU containing 2 bytes;

register pair: one of eight pairs of 8-bit registers that can be used as 16-bit registers (AF and AF' can be used as 16-bit registers only for PUSH and POP);

flag: a bit of register F.

2. 8-bit registers:

A F B C D E H L
A' F' B' C' D' E' H' L'
I R

3. 16-bit registers:

IX IY SP PC

4. Register pairs:

AF AF' BC BC' DE DE' HL HL'

5. Stack pointer, program counter, and index register.
6. (a) 02_H; (b) DD_H; (c) $2ADD_H$; (d) 35_H; (e) there is no such register pair.
7. SP points to the bottom of the stack.
8. PC will point to $7E03_H$.
9. Assembly language is a readable form of machine language.
10. (a) ORG; (b) LD; (c) END.
11. The carry flag and the zero flag.

CHAPTER SEVEN

Some Z-80 Instructions

My only difficulty is to choose and reject . . .
—J. Dryden in Preface to *Fables*

In this chapter we continue to lay the groundwork for FAST BASIC. We discuss 18 machine language instructions and some assembly language conventions.

We start writing FAST BASIC programs in Chapter 8. For the programs of that chapter we need only eight machine language instructions.

DATA MOVEMENT

In BASIC we move data in memory by statements such as LET X = Y. The assembly language mnemonics for data movements are LD (for load) to overwrite; POP and PUSH for stack operations; and EX and EXX (for exchange) to interchange.

Eight-Bit Loads

A load operation always overwrites: It takes a piece of data and overwrites with it the data at a given location. For instance,

```
LD A,B
```

loads the contents of register B into register A. Note that the contents of B are unchanged.

We can also load numbers:

```
LD A,5H
```

places the byte 05_H into register A.

And we can use pointers. Let HL point at a byte in memory that we want to load into register D; the instruction

LD D,(HL)

will effect this load. This last load is the only one we use in Chapter 8.

For instance, let the registers contain the following numbers:

A	B	D	H	L
12_H	31_H	08_H	56_H	AB_H

Then HL is $56AB_H$. Let $(56AB_H) = FF_H$. (Recall, this means that memory location $56AB_H$ contains FF_H.) Then performing the three load instructions one after another changes the registers as follows:

	A	B	D	H	L
	12_H	31_H	08_H	56_H	AB_H
LD A,B	31_H	31_H	08_H	56_H	AB_H
LD B,5H	31_H	05_H	08_H	56_H	AB_H
LD D,(HL)	31_H	05_H	FF_H	56_H	AB_H

The memory location $56AB_H$ remains unchanged.

These are all examples of 8-bit loads. In general, an 8-bit load has the following form:

LD named location, named location or number

where "named location" is any register A, B, C, D, E, H, L or any location named as in Table 6.1: (nm), (BC), (DE), (HL), (IX+d), (IY+d). "Number" is any 8-bit integer *n*.

In our descriptions of assembly language instructions we use the following notation: nm is a 16-bit integer, n is an 8-bit integer, and d is an 8-bit signed integer (used as the offset in IX + d and IY + d).

Not all the load instructions that follow the prescribed format can be used in the Z-80. (For a complete list see Appendices 2 and 3.) It is quite difficult to remember which ones are permitted; for instance, LD A,B is permitted but LD (1234H),5H is not.

Luckily, in FAST BASIC we need only a few types of 8-bit loads (r and r' are 8-bit registers, n is an 8-bit integer, and d is an 8-bit signed integer):

Load	Examples	
LD r,r'	LD A,B	LD H,D
LD r,(HL)	LD A,(HL)	LD H,(HL)
LD r,(IX+d)	LD A,(IX–3)	LD H,(IX+0)
LD (HL),r	LD (HL),A	LD (HL),L
LD (IX+d),r	LD (IX+3),B	LD (IY–100),E
LD r,n	LD A,0	LD D,0DEH

Sixteen-Bit Loads

Sixteen-bit loads are very similar to 8-bit loads. We only have to keep in mind, however, that a memory pointer is always to a single byte of data, whereas for a 16-bit load we need 2 bytes of data. In FAST BASIC we use only the following types of 16-bit loads (nm stands for a 16-bit integer).

Load	Examples	
LD HL,nm	LD HL,12A5H	LD HL,0A5AFH
LD HL,(nm)	LD HL,(12A5H)	LD HL,(0A5AFH)
LD (nm),DE	LD (72A5H),DE	LD (0A5AFH),DE
LD (nm),HL	LD (72A5H),HL	LD (0A5AFH),HL

The first example is easy: LD HL,12A5H loads 12_H into H and $A5_H$ into L. LD HL,(12A5H) is trickier: (12A5H) is loaded into L and (12A5H + 1) is loaded into H! (Note the use of 0 in 0A5AFH; without the 0 the assembler would regard A5AFH as a label, as explained at the end of this chapter.) Similarly, LD (72A5H),HL will load L into $72A5_H$ and H into $72A6_H$.

In Chapter 8 only the first type of 16-bit load is used.

Exchange

The exchange operations are of two kinds: They either exchange the register set with the alternate register set or they swap the contents of two register pairs. In FAST BASIC, we use only three exchange instructions (only the first is used in Chapter 8).

Exchange	Explanation
EX DE,HL	Swaps DE and HL
EX AF,AF′	Interchanges A with A′ and F with F′
EXX	Interchanges B through L by B′ through L′

Note that the 16-bit registers IX, IY, SP, PC have no primed counterparts. Thus to bring in the complete alternate register set we need two instructions: EX AF,AF' and EXX.

Stack

We left the stack to the last. The stack is a temporary storage area. We store a register pair (including AF) or a 16-bit register in the stack by PUSH and restore it by POP. Every PUSH makes the stack 2 bytes larger with the 2 new bytes at the bottom; every POP shrinks the stack by 2 bytes. SP is the pointer to the bottom of the stack.

As an example, suppose that we are in the middle of a program, and the 8-bit registers contain information needed at a later stage. Then we save the registers by PUSHing them to the stack. Later, when they are needed, we restore them by POPping them from the stack. Remember: The sequence of PUSHes must be inverted to get the sequence of POPs. So to save all the registers we do PUSH AF, PUSH BC, PUSH DE, and PUSH HL; to restore them all we do POP HL, POP DE, POP BC, and POP AF.

Although it is not necessary in FAST BASIC programming to understand how the stack works, we present a detailed description of the stack operations for the curious reader.

At the beginning of the assembly language program the stack is set up by assigning a value to SP. SP has the following default values.

1. In a machine language program started by the SYSTEM? command the default value is 4288_H (17032_D). This does not leave room for a very large stack.
2. In a machine language subroutine of a BASIC program (that is, a USR) we continue to use the BASIC stack. (Caution: At the end of a USR call the stack must be identical to the state it was in when the machine language subroutine was entered!)

Figure 7.1 may help you visualize PUSH HL and POP HL. In the example SP was initialized at $90A5_H$ and its present value is $904F_H$; so the stack is the area $904F_H$ to $90A5_H$. Let HL = $AF0B_H$. The left side of Figure 7.1 shows the present situation. The right side shows the situation after PUSH HL.

As you can see in Figure 7.1, the value of HL is not changed by PUSH HL. HL is copied into the stack: First the MSB is copied and SP is decremented by 1 and then the LSB is copied and SP is again decremented by 1. As a

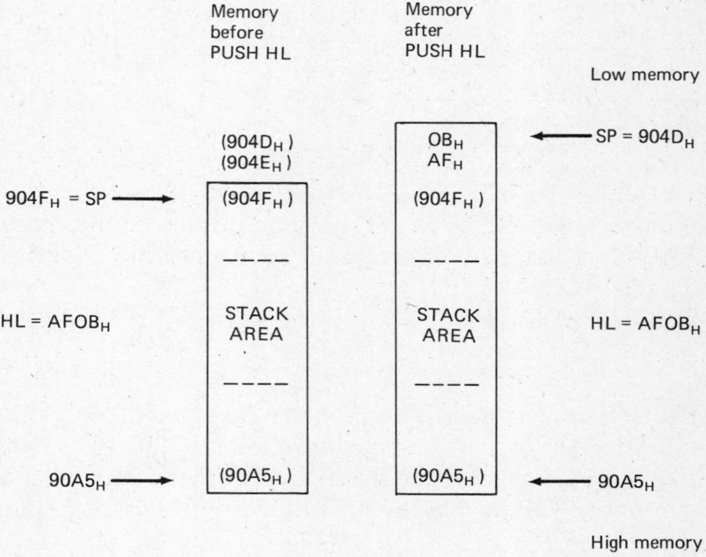

FIGURE 7.1 PUSH HL

result the stack area is increased by 2 bytes and SP is decremented by 2.
POP is the inverse of PUSH. Start with the right side of Figure 7.1, except now HL is unspecified. Then POP HL will bring about the left side of the figure: The stack shrinks by 2 bytes, SP is incremented by 2, and the 2 bytes of the stack, AF and 0B, are copied into HL.

We can PUSH and POP the register pairs AF, BC, DE, and HL, and the 16-bit registers IX and IY.

BRANCHING, INCREMENT, AND DECREMENT

Branching Instructions

To control the flow of the program we need instructions that correspond to the BASIC GOTO, GOSUB, and RETURN. In assembly language they are called JP (jump), CALL, and RET (return).

Jump (JP) is just like the BASIC GOTO. In BASIC, GOTO 200 transfers execution to line 200. In assembly language JP 45A7H transfers the execution of the program to memory location $45A7_H$. In effect this instruction loads $45A7_H$ into PC.

In BASIC we call a subroutine located at line 200 by GOSUB 200. In assembly language we call a subroutine starting at $45A7_H$ by CALL 45A7H. In BASIC the address from which we call the subroutine is recorded in the BASIC stack. A CALL PUSHes PC to the stack (remember, PC points at the instruction following the CALL), loads $45A7_H$ into PC, and continues program execution from the instruction starting at $45A7_H$.

RET ends the subroutine CALLed; it is the same as the BASIC RETURN. It POPs the stack into PC and resumes the program execution at the location in PC, that is, at the instruction following the CALL.

The same warning applies to RET as was mentioned in connection with machine language subroutine calls from BASIC. At the end of the subroutine the stack should be the same as it was at the beginning! This ensures that we shall indeed return to the appropriate instruction.

There are also conditional jumps (IF THEN in BASIC). For instance,

JP C,45A7H

jumps to location $45A7_H$ if there is a carry (the carry flag is set). The general form of a conditional jump is

JP condition,address

In FAST BASIC we need only four conditions (only one of these, C, is used in Chapter 8):

C carry, NC no carry, Z zero, NZ nonzero

Examples:

JP C,45A7H	JP NC,45A7H
JP Z,45A7H	JP NZ,45A7H

The mnemonic refers to the actual condition signified by the flag, so we do not even have to remember whether the condition sets or resets the flag. (RETurns can also be made conditional: RET Z, RET NZ, RET C, RET NC, and so on. However, these are not used in FAST BASIC.)

Increment and Decrement

Increment adds 1 and decrement subtracts 1. Increment (INC) and decrement (DEC) can be applied to A, B, C, D, E, H, L, BC, DE, HL, SP, IX, IY, (HL), (IX + d), and (IY + d). The 8-bit increments and decrements affect the zero and carry flags; the 16-bit versions affect no flags.

Examples: Let A contain 55_H, B contain 255_D, DE contain $5A5A_H$, and HL contain 65535_D. Then INC A increases A to 56_H, INC B adds 1 to B, but 256_D is 0 (and C is set), so after INC B register B contains 0. Similarly, INC HL makes HL 0. DEC DE puts $5A59_H$ in DE. As a last example, let IX contain 0. Then DEC IX puts $FFFF_H$ in IX.

PSEUDO OPERATIONS AND LABELS

These are all the Z-80 instructions we need. But remember, we are writing the machine language programs in assembly language; what we write has to be translated (assembled) into machine language by an assembler. So we have to learn a few words, called "pseudo-ops" (pseudo operations), to send instructions to the assembler.

Pseudo-Ops

The most important pseudo-op is

ORG

(origin). For instance, ORG 7E00H has to be the first line of an assembly language program producing Program 6.1. This pseudo-op instructs the assembler to start assembling at address $7E00_H$.

The pseudo-op

END

tells the assembler that it has reached the *physical* end of the assembly language program. Other often-used pseudo-ops are DEFB, DEFW, and DEFM. For instance,

DEFB 15H

DEFines the byte to be 15_H; the line assembles as 15_H. DEFW (here W stands for *w*ord, meaning 2 bytes) is used for numbers that require 2 bytes, for example,

DEFW 1000D

Finally,

DEFM 'I WIN'

DEFines the Message 'I WIN'; it assembles into as many bytes as there are characters in the message, in this case five, and gives the ASCIIs of the characters. Pseudo-ops may change from assembler to assembler.

Labels

One of the most important convenience features of assembly language is the use of "labels." A label is a string of up to six characters; the first character has to be a letter. Examples: LOOP, EXIT1, START, A1234.

Check the manual of your assembler for a more detailed definition; the length of a label and the characters that can be used vary greatly.

A label always stands for an address. The following example shows the most important use of labels.

Program 7.1. Illustrating Labels

```
100             ORG     7E00H    ;PROGRAM TO BE ASSEMBLED AT 7E00H
110   INIT:     LD      HL,3000D;INIT STANDS FOR INITIALIZATION
120   LOOP:     DEC     HL       ;THE START OF THE DELAY LOOP
130   CHECK:    LD      A,H      ;THE START OF THE CHECK FOR ZERO
140             OR      L        ;FORM H OR L
150             JP      NZ,LOOP  ;IF NOT ZERO, JUMP BACK TO LOOP
160   DONE:     RET              ;OTHERWISE DONE
170             END
```

Line 100 will not be assembled; it is only a directive to start assembly at $7E00_H$. Line 110 is initialization: We place 3000_D in HL. (The assembler will convert 3000_D to hex.) Line 120 starts the loop. The program will do lines 120 to 150 3000_D times. Line 120 decrements HL.

Since the 16-bit decrement does not affect flags, we have to find a tricky way to test whether HL is zero. Recall from Chapter 1 that HL = 0 can be tested by checking whether H OR L is 0. This we accomplish by loading H into A (line 130) and ORing A with L (line 140). If the result of the OR is 0, condition Z holds (flag Z is set) and so line 150 is not executed; we "fall through" to line 160 and the routine is finished. Otherwise (on NZ) we jump back to LOOP (line 120).

Here is an assembled version of this program.

```
7E00           100              ORG     7E00H
7E00 21B80B    110    INIT:     LD      HL,3000D
7E03 2B        120    LOOP:     DEC     HL
7E04 7C        130    CHECK:    LD      A,H
7E05 B5        140              OR      L
7E06 C2037E    150              JP      NZ,LOOP
7E09 C9        160    DONE:     RET
0000           170              END
00000 TOTAL ERRORS


CHECK    7E04 130
DONE     7E09 160
INIT     7E00 110
LOOP     7E03 120   150
```

The table at the end identifies the labels with hex addresses; for instance, LOOP is $7E03_H$. The numbers 120 and 150 following 7E03 identify the lines in which the label LOOP occurs.

Another way of defining labels is with the EQU (equate) pseudo-op. Examples:

```
VIDEO    EQU      3000H

BASIC    EQU      1A19H
```

These define the label VIDEO as 3000_H and the label BASIC as $1A19_H$. We can use these labels in a program in place of the numbers, which are difficult to remember. All such labels used in this book are listed in Appendix 6.

As an illustration of the use of labels we present Program 7.2, the program promised in Chapter 3.

Program 7.2. Slowing Down LIST

```
100               ORG     7F00H       ;THIS IS THE ORIGIN FOR THE POKE
110      BASIC    EQU     1A19H       ;THE ENTRY POINT OF TRS-80 BASIC
111      POKE:    LD      A,7FH       ;THE NEXT FOUR LINES POKE INTO
112               LD      (401FH),A   ;THE VIDEO DRIVER BLOCK THE NEW
113               LD      A,10H       ;DRIVER ADDRESS: 7F10H
115               LD      (401EH),A
```

```
116             JP      BASIC       ;EXIT TO TRS-80 BASIC
117             ORG     07F10H      ;THE START OF THE NEW DRIVER
118     INIT:   PUSH    HL          ;SAVE THE REGISTERS USED: H,L
120             PUSH    AF          ;AND A
130             LD      HL,(TIME)   ;LOAD HL WITH THE TIME DELAY
140     LOOP:   DEC     HL          ;THE DELAY LOOP
150             LD      A,H
160             OR      L
170             JP      NZ,LOOP
172             POP     AF          ;RESTORE REGISTERS
175             POP     HL
178             JP      0488H       ;JUMP TO VIDEO DRIVER
190     TIME:   DEFW    1000D
200             END
```

Note that we PUSH and POP in the reverse order. The assembled version follows.

```
7F00            100          ORG     7F00H
1A19            110 BASIC    EQU     1A19H
7F00 3E7F       111 POKE:    LD      A,7FH
7F02 321F40     112          LD      (401FH),A
7F05 3E10       113          LD      A,10H
7F07 321E40     115          LD      (401EH),A
7F0A C3191A     116          JP      BASIC
7F10            117          ORG     07F10H
7F10 E5         118 INIT:    PUSH    HL
7F11 F5         120          PUSH    AF
7F12 2A207F     130          LD      HL,(TIME)
7F15 2B         140 LOOP:    DEC     HL
7F16 7C         150          LD      A,H
7F17 B5         160          OR      L
7F18 C2157F     170          JP      NZ,LOOP
7F1B F1         172          POP     AF
7F19 C1         175          POP     BC
7F1A C38804     180          JP      0488H
7F1D E803       190 TIME:    DEFW    1000D
0000            200          END
00000 TOTAL ERRORS

BASIC   1A19 110    116
INIT    7F10 118
LOOP    7F12 140    170
POKE    7F00 111
TIME    7F1D 190
```

Note, in particular, the location of the loop counter, TIME. If you want to slow down LIST more, POKE into $7F1E_H$ (the MSB, in decimal, 32542) a number larger than 3.

Review and Programming Practice

In the first four review questions let the registers contain the following numbers.

A	B	C	D	E	H	L	IX
20_H	05_H	03_H	$0F_H$	35_H	23_H	01_H	7221_H

1. Explain the result of the following load operations. (a) LD B,A; (b) LD B,L; (c) LD (HL),A; (d) LD (IX+5),H; (e) LD H,23H; (f) LD L,0FH.
2. What is the result of the following three loads carried out one after another?

```
LD A,B
LD B,H
LD H,A
```

3. Let (7021_H) = 21_H, (7022_H) = 22_H. Describe the result of (a) LD HL,7021H; (b) LD HL,(7021H); (c) LD (7021H),HL
4. What are the contents of D, E, H, L after EX DE,HL?
5. We want to load into register B the contents of location 5103_H. If DE contains 5103_H, how many instructions do we need to carry out the load?
6. We want to load BC into DE. How do we do it?
7. How many memory locations are affected by (a) LD HL,(2131H); (b) LD (2131H),HL?
8. What is the difference between LD HL,2131H and LD HL,(2131H)?
9. How many instructions does it take to exchange all 8-bit registers with their primed counterparts?
10. Let the stack pointer contain $78A0_H$. Describe what happens after we execute:

```
PUSH HL
PUSH DE
POP HL
```

11. Sometimes we shall do:

```
POP HL
PUSH HL
```

Can you explain what this could be useful for?

12. What are the assembly language mnemonics for return, carry, no carry, zero, nonzero.
13. Write the assembly language form of: jump on nonzero to 2032_H and jump on carry to 2032_H.
14. Give the assembly language mnemonics for increment and decrement. Which one affects the flags: INC A or INC HL?
15. Define the pseudo-ops: ORG, END, DEFB, DEFW, DEFM, EQU.
16. Does DEFM 'TRICKY QUESTION' assemble into 14 or 15 bytes?
17. Which of the following labels are legal? (a) LOOP; (b) 2LOOP; (c) THREELOOP.
18. In Program 7.2 we find the lines:

```
POKE:   LD      A,7FH       ;THE NEXT FOUR LINES POKE INTO
        LD      (401FH),A   ;THE VIDEO DRIVER BLOCK THE NEW
```

These lines load $7F_H$ into memory location $401F_H$. Why did we not do this load in a single line with the following instruction?

```
LD (401FH),7FH
```

19. We have three versions of an assembly language program.

(a)		(b)		(c)	
	EQU		ORG		ORG
	ORG		EQU		. . .
	. . .		. . .		END
	END		END		EQU

Which of these schemes is correct?

Answers

1. (a) B becomes 20_H.
   (b) B becomes 01_H.
   (c) $(2301_H) = 20_H$.
   (d) $(7226_H) = 23_H$.
   (e) H becomes 23_H.
   (f) L becomes $0F_H$.

2. A becomes 5_H, H becomes 5_H, and B becomes 23_H.
3. (a) HL contains 7021_H.
   (b) HL contains 2221_H.
   (c) $(7021_H) = 01_H$ and $(7022_H) = 23_H$.
4. D contains 23_H, E contains 01_H, H contains $0F_H$, and L contains 35_H.
5. Two instructions, for instance:

```
EX DE,HL
LD B,(HL)
```

6. One solution is

```
PUSH BC
POP DE
```

and another one is

```
LD D,B
LD E,C
```

7. (a) None; (b) two.
8. Executing LD HL,2131H will place 2131_H in HL. After executing LD HL,(2131H), L contains (2131_H) and H contains (2132_H).
9. Two instructions:

```
EXX
EX AF,AF'
```

10. SP = $789E_H$, HL is placed in the bottom of the stack and DE is copied into HL.
11. A number is saved in the stack. During the program, when it is needed, it is POPped out. At the same time it is PUSHed to save it for future reference.
12. RET, C, NC, Z, NZ.
13. JP NZ,2032H, JP C,2032H.
14. INC and DEC. INC A affects the flags.
15. ORG: origin
    END: end
    DEFB: define byte
    DEFW: define a 2-byte number
    DEFM: define message
    EQU: equate.
16. 15 bytes (space is a character too).

17. (a) legal; (b) illegal—a label must start with a character; (c) illegal—a label cannot be longer than six characters in most assemblers.

18. There is no such load instruction.

19. Only (c) is incorrect. Since END designates the physical end of the program the EQU lines falls outside the program. The assembler will give an "undefined symbol" message.

PART IV
FAST BASIC

CHAPTER EIGHT

FAST BASIC Introduced

Our primary purpose in this book is to teach you how to cook, so that you will understand the fundamental techniques and gradually be able to divorce yourself from a dependence on recipes.

—J. Child *et al.* in *Mastering the Art of French Cooking**

FAST BASIC is a hybrid language: It mixes BASIC with machine language subroutines.

FAST BASIC uses BASIC primarily for handling variables, for communication with the keyboard, video display, cassettes, and disks, and for anything else that BASIC can do efficiently.

FAST BASIC uses machine language routines (mainly CALLs to the ROM) to speed up the execution of those parts of the program (FOR NEXT loops) that require a great deal of computation or string manipulation.

How you mix the two ingredients should depend on your needs and ingenuity.

In this chapter we learn how to write machine language subroutines (USRs) that can be called from a BASIC program, a shorthand for such programs, and how to locate and move BASIC variables from a USR. We list and name the most important JPs and CALLs to the ROM needed to replace BASIC lines with machine language routines. Several examples illustrate the replacement procedure.

USR: USER SUBROUTINE

TRS-80 BASIC provides a very convenient way to call a user-written machine language subroutine. Let us take Program 7.1 as an example and see how we call it as a USR.

*Julia Child, Simone Beck, and Louisette Bertholle, *Mastering the Art of French Cooking*, Vol 1. © 1961 Alfred A. Knopf, Inc. Reprinted with permission.

Loading a USR

The assembler you use has the ability to store the machine language version of Program 7.1 on cassette tape or disk. How do we get it into the computer?

If the program was recorded on tape, first make sure to protect enough memory for the USR. All our example programs start at $7E00_H$ (32256_D). So answer the MEMORY SIZE? question with 32255. Now type SYSTEM, and respond to the *? prompt with the name you assigned to the program at assembly. When the loading is complete the prompt *? appears again. Press the BREAK key, and you are back in BASIC and the USR has been loaded.

In Disk BASIC, at the DOS READY prompt, type LOAD filename, where filename is the name you gave to the machine language program when it was assembled to disk. Then type BASIC and answer the HOW MANY FILES? question by pressing ENTER and the MEMORY SIZE? question by 32255. In Part IV we always assume that the BASIC MEMORY SIZE? was set at 32255.

A third way to load our machine language program is by POKEing it in. The assembled listing of Program 7.1 shows (in hex): 21, B8, 0B, 2B, 7C, B5, C2, 03, 7E, C9. We can POKE the byte 21_H by POKE 32256, 33; the byte $B8_H$ by POKE 32257, 184; and so on. This tedious procedure is simplified by the program VIEW/MOD (listed in Appendix 8) or by writing a BASIC program to do the POKEs. (See Program 10.3.)

Invoking a USR

First we have to tell BASIC where the USR starts. In TRS-80 BASIC this is done by POKEing the starting address into $408E_H$ and $408F_H$ (16526_D and 16527_D). For instance, we POKE the starting address $7E00_H$ by

```
100 POKE 16526, 0 : POKE 16527, 126
```

In Disk BASIC this takes the form:

```
100 DEFUSR = &H7E00
```

Then we call the USR by

```
110  X = USR(A)
```

In this, A can be any integer (range: -32768 to 32767) or any expression evaluating to an integer. This A can be passed *to* the USR if desired. X is a variable that may receive an integer *from* the USR.

Returning from a USR

We may terminate a machine language subroutine with RET. Table 8.1 lists some other possibilities.

TABLE 8.1.

Label	Value	Type	Explanation
BSCPAR	0A9A	JP	Return to the BASIC program with parameter
BASIC	1A19	JP	Return to BASIC and display the BASIC READY prompt (if you have difficulty with $1A19_H$, try $6CC_H$ or 72_H instead)
DOS	402D	JP	Return to DOS; do not initialize
DOSCLD	0000	JP	Reinitialize DOS; "cold" entry to DOS
GETPAR	0AF7	CALL	Load the parameter A in USR(A) into HL; it must be the first instruction of the user subroutine
DELAY	0060	CALL	Load BC with n; loop n times

In subsequent assembly language programs we write, for example, JP BSCPAR and include the necessary EQUates.

The table entry "type" identifies how the ROM routine is to be called. CALL refers to a subroutine and JP to a jump. For instance, JP BASIC returns to BASIC. It is a safe practice to return from a USR with JP BSCPAR (not with RET), because some USR calls (namely, the ones that do not use SA, see the section on Arithmetic below) will give an error message if terminated by RET.

We may exit from a machine language program with JP BASIC to get the BASIC prompt, with JP DOS to enter DOS (which is in memory) without reinitializing it, or with JP DOSCLD to reinitialize DOS.

Table 8.1 contains two labels not yet mentioned: CALL GETPAR has to be the first line of a USR if we wish to pass the integer A (appearing in USR(A)) to the USR. After CALL GETPAR, the integer A will be in the register pair HL. Finally, CALL DELAY illustrates how a ROM call can ease programming. LD BC,3000D and CALL DELAY can replace lines 110 to 150 of Program 7.1

A very important warning: *The machine language programs we are going to write will run only if they are called from BASIC.* These programs rely heavily not only on the ROM but also on those portions of the RAM that are initialized by BASIC. If this initialization does not take place, these programs may not work.

ARITHMETIC

Software and Register Accumulator

The ROM subroutines perform arithmetic operations on numbers in special locations. The most important location of this kind is the "software accumulator" (SA) shown in Table 8.2.

At $40AF_H$ (16559_D) we find the "typeflag." If it is 2, the number is an integer occupying 4121_H (16673_D) and 4122_H (16674_D). The typeflag for single

TABLE 8.2.

40AF	411D	411E	411F	4120	4121	4122	4123	4124
Typeflag			Number					
2					LSB	MSB		
4					LSB	BYTE 2	MSB	EXP
8	LSB	BYTE 2	BYTE 3	BYTE 4	BYTE 5	BYTE 6	MSB	EXP

precision is 4; for double precision it is 8. Single- and double-precision numbers are placed in SA as shown. An alternate software accumulator, SA_1, is located at 4127_H to $412E_H$ (16679_D to 16686_D). SA_1 is used only for double-precision numbers.

Integers and single-precision numbers are also stored in registers. Integers are stored in DE and HL. Single-precision numbers are often kept in the registers E, D, C, and B (LSB, BYTE 2, MSB, EXP), called the (single-precision) "register accumulator," or RA.

ROM Subroutines

Table 8.3 gives the most important arithmetic ROM subroutines. The mnemonics should be self-explanatory: INT is integer, SP is single precision, DP is double precision. The arithmetic operations are ADD, DIV(ide), SUB(tract), M(u)LT(iply), raise to the POWER. CP stands for compare.

Under the table entry "type" we find a new classification, RST; it stands for *restart*. It signifies a special type of subroutine call that should be invoked by RST 16H rather than CALL 16H.

As we saw in Chapter 2 the integers in DE and HL are in 16-bit two's complement form. When these are added, subtracted, or multiplied and the result is an integer the result is placed in HL and also in SA with flag = 2. If the result is too large or too small to be an integer, it is stored in SA in single-precision form with flag = 4.

FINDING VARIABLES

We find a BASIC variable using the ROM routine VARPTR:

VARPTR	260D	CALL	Get variable address in DE; HL points at variable name

For example, if we need to know the location of the BASIC variable HI# in the variable table, we include in the assembly language subroutine the following code.

```
VARPTR  EQU     260DH
VARHI:  DEFM    'HI#'
DEFB    0
```

TABLE 8.3. Arithmetic ROM Routines

Label	Value	Type	Explanation
ADDINT	0BD2	CALL	Add DE and HL; result in HL and in SA if no overflow; result in SA if overflow (flag = 4)
ADDSP	0716	CALL	Add RA and SA; result in SA
ADDDP	0C77	CALL	Add SA and SA_1; result in SA
CPINT	0A39	CALL	Compare DE and HL*
CPDP	0A78	CALL	Compare SA and SA_1*
CPSP	0A0C	CALL	Compare RA and SA*
CP16	0018	RST	Compare DE and HL as 16-bit unsigned integers*
DIVINT	2490	CALL	Divide DE by HL; result in SA in single-precision format
DIVSP	08A2	CALL	Divide RA by SA; result in SA
DIVDP	0DE5	CALL	Divide SA by SA_1; result in SA
MLTINT	0BF2	CALL	Multiply DE with HL; result in HL and in SA if no overflow (flag = 2); result in SA if overflow (flag = 4)
MLTSP	0847	CALL	Multiply RA and SA; result in SA
MLTDP	0DA1	CALL	Multiply SA and SA_1; result in SA
POWER	13F7	CALL	Raise RA to the power SA; result in SA
SUBINT	0BC7	CALL	Subtract HL from DE; result in HL and in SA if no overflow (flag = 2); result in SA if overflow (flag = 4)
SUBSP	0713	CALL	Subtract SA from RA; result in SA
SUBDP	0C70	CALL	Subtract SA_1 from SA; result in SA

*Result of compares:
If the two numbers are equal, the zero flag is set (= 1).
If the two numbers are unequal, the zero flag is reset (= 0).
If the first number is smaller, the carry flag is reset (= 0).
If the second number is smaller, the carry flag is set (= 1).

And when we need the address:

```
LD      HL,VARHI
CALL    VARPTR
```

After this call DE will contain the address of HI#. The "address of HI#" is the address returned by the VARPTR function of BASIC (see Tables 4.1 and 4.2).

Type in, assemble, and load Program 8.1.

Program 8.1. USR to Locate a Variable

```
80      BSCPAR  EQU     0A9AH
90      VARPTR  EQU     260DH
100             ORG     7E00H
110             LD      HL,VARHI
120             CALL    VARPTR
130             EX      DE,HL
140             JP      BSCPAR
150 VARHI2:     DEFM    'HI#'
160             DEFB    0
170             END
```

In Program 8.1 line 140 assures that the value in HL is passed on to A# in the BASIC program when returning from the USR (invoked by A# = USR(0)). The CALL in line 120 places the address of HI# in DE; line 130 copies it into HL.

Now type in and RUN Program 8.2.

Program 8.2. BASIC Program to Locate a Variable

```
10 HI# = 5 : A# = 10
20 PRINT "THE ADDRESS OF HI# DETERMINED BY THE VARPTR FUNCTION
   OF BASIC IS: "; VARPTR(HI#)
30 POKE 16526, 0 : POKE 16527, 126
40 A# = USR(0)
50 PRINT "THE ADDRESS OF HI# DETERMINED BY THE USR CALL
   IS: "; A#
```

In Disk BASIC substitute line 30 by DEFUSR = &H7E00.

It is reassuring that Programs 8.1 and 8.2 find the same address for HI#.

MOVING VARIABLES

Before we can show you examples of how to do arithmetic and compares, we have to learn how to move numbers into DE, HL, RA, SA, and SA_1.

Single-Precision Variables

Table 8.4 lists CALLs for moving single-precision variables. In the table LD stands for load and ST for the stack; DE, HL, SA, and RA need no explanation. The labels are modeled after the load instructions: LD followed by "where to" and then "where from."

Figure 8.1 should help visualize these loads.

TABLE 8.4. Single-Precision Loads

Label	Value	Type	Explanation
LDDEHL	09D2	CALL	Load single-precision number pointed to by HL into area pointed to by DE; needs FLAGSP
LDRAHL	09C2	CALL	Load single-precision number pointed to by HL into RA
LDRASA	09BF	CALL	Load SA into RA
LDHLDE	09D3	CALL	Load single-precision number pointed to by DE into area pointed to by HL; needs FLAGSP
LDHLSA	09CB	CALL	Load SA into area pointed to by HL
LDSTSA	09A4	CALL	Load SA into stack
LDSARA	09B4	CALL	Load RA into SA
LDSAHL	09B1	CALL	Load single-precision number pointed to by HL into SA

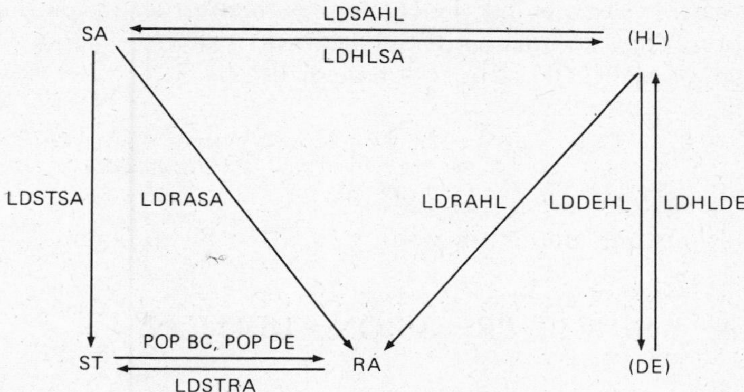

FIGURE 8.1 Single-Precision Loads

For instance, let us assume that we have located the single-precision variable X with a CALL VARPTR and we want to move X into SA:

```
EX      DE,HL
CALL    LDSAHL
```

will accomplish that. Now load SA into the stack: CALL LDSTSA. Next load the stack into RA:

```
POP     BC
POP     DE
```

Double-Precision Variables

The few ROM subroutines moving double-precision numbers are listed in Table 8.5.

TABLE 8.5. Double-Precision Moves

Label	Value	Type	Explanation
FLAGDP	0AEC	CALL	Set typeflag of SA to double precision
MVALT	09FC	CALL	Move SA into alternate software accumulator (SA_1); needs FLAGDP
MVDEHL	09D3	CALL	Move the number pointed to by HL to the area pointed to by DE; needs FLAGDP
MVHLDE	09D2	CALL	Move the number pointed to by DE to the area pointed to by HL; needs FLAGDP
MVSAHL	09F7	CALL	Move the number pointed to by HL into the software accumulator; needs FLAGDP
SA	411D	EQU	The first byte of the software accumulator
SA1	4127	EQU	The first byte of the alternate software accumulator (SA_1)
SAFLAG	40AF	EQU	Contains the typeflag of the software accumulator (SA)

Under "type" we find a new entry—EQU. These entries are used to define a memory location. They do not signify subroutines.

A slight variant of MVHLDE is the following call.

MVVAR	0982	CALL	Move the number of bytes shown by the typeflag from the area pointed to by DE to the area pointed to by HL; needs typeflag

This completes our preparation for writing FAST BASIC programs.

CONVERTING A SINGLE-PRECISION ADDITION

Now that we have the most important CALLs and JPs, we are ready to start writing FAST BASIC programs. We take some simple BASIC lines and practice converting them to assembly language.

Keep in mind that the conversion of a single line may require the same amount of overhead as converting ten lines. Therefore, these examples may call into question whether such conversions are worthwhile. We ask the readers to reserve judgment until the next chapter, where the first real conversion is discussed.

Single-Precision Addition

In Program 8.3 we replace line 20 by a machine language subroutine.

Program 8.3. Single-Precision Addition in BASIC

```
10 X = 2.5 : Y = 3.5 : Z = 0
20 Z = X + Y
30 PRINT Z
```

To add two single-precision numbers we need the following labels.

BSCPAR	0A9A	JP	Return to the BASIC program with parameter
VARPTR	260D	CALL	Get variable address in DE; HL points at variable name
ADDINT	0BD2	CALL	Add DE and HL; result in HL and in SA if no overflow; result in SA if overflow (flag = 4)
ADDSP	0716	CALL	Add RA and SA; result in SA
LDRAHL	09C2	CALL	Load single-precision number pointed to by HL into RA
LDHLSA	09CB	CALL	Load SA into area pointed to by HL

First we move X and Y into RA and SA, respectively, and then CALL ADDSP. The result is in SA.

Program 8.4. Single-Precision Addition

```
VARPTR  EQU     260DH
ADDSP   EQU     0716H
LDSAHL  EQU     09B1H
LDRAHL  EQU     09C2H
LDHLSA  EQU     09CBH
BSCPAR  EQU     0A9AH
        ORG     7E00H
        LD      HL,VARX     ;LOOKING FOR X
        CALL    VARPTR      ;DE POINTS AT X
        EX      DE,HL       ;NOW HL POINTS AT X
        CALL    LDSAHL      ;LOAD X INTO SA
        LD      HL,VARY     ;LOOKING FOR Y
        CALL    VARPTR      ;ADDRESS IN DE
        EX      DE,HL       ;NOW HL POINTS AT Y
        CALL    LDRAHL      ;Y INTO RA
        CALL    ADDSP       ;CALL SINGLE PRECISION ADDITION
        LD      HL,VARZ     ;LOOKING FOR Z
        CALL    VARPTR      ;ADDRESS IN DE
        EX      DE,HL       ;HL POINTS AT Z
        CALL    LDHLSA      ;LOAD RESULT INTO VARIABLE TABLE
        JP      BSCPAR
VARX:   DEFM    'X'
        DEFB    0
VARY:   DEFM    'Y'
        DEFB    0
VARZ:   DEFM    'Z'
        DEFB    0
        END
```

Now assemble and load the subroutine (remember we responded to the BASIC MEMORY SIZE? querry with 32255). After Program 8.4 is in the memory, RUN Program 8.5.

Program 8.5.

(Disk BASIC)

```
10 X = 2.5 : Y = 3.5 : Z = 0
20 PRINT "RESULT FROM BASIC: "; X + Y
30 POKE 16526, 0 : POKE 16527, 126      (DEFUSR = &H7E00)
40 N = USR(0)
50 PRINT "RESULT FROM MACHINE LANGUAGE SUBROUTINE: "; Z
```

Verify that the machine language subroutine and the BASIC calculation obtain the same result.

A SHORTHAND FOR ASSEMBLY LANGUAGE PROGRAMS

There is much repetition in the code of Program 8.4, and this makes it difficult to follow the flow of the program. In Program 8.6 we rewrite Program 8.4 in a "shorthand."

Program 8.6. Shorthand Version of Program 8.4

```
100             EQUATES:VARPTR,ADDSP,LDSAHL,LDRAHL,LDHLSA,BSCPAR
140     LOAD    MACRO   WHAT, INTO, FROM
150             LD      HL,VAR&WHAT
160             CALL    VARPTR
170             EX      DE,HL
180             CALL    LD&INTO&FROM
190             ENDM
200             ORG     7E00H
210             LOAD    X,SA,HL
300             LOAD    Y,RA,HL
400             CALL    ADDSP
500             LOAD    Z,HL,SA
540             JP      BSCPAR
600             DEFINE VARIABLE NAMES: X, Y, Z
610             END
```

The shorthand employs three conventions: EQUATES (in line 100), MACRO (in line 140), and DEFINE VARIABLE NAMES (in line 600). We now discuss these in detail.

EQUATES

Instead of defining the labels (such as VARPTR) with a list of EQUates, we simply wrote EQUATES: VARPTR, ... Each label in this list needs a separate line in the full assembly language listing. All labels listed after EQUATES can be found in Appendix 6.

Most disk-based macro assemblers—see Appendix 7—have a command to look up labels in a file. If you use such a macro assembler, then type all the labels from Appendix 6 into a file. Then, indeed, you can define in a single line all the labels you need in a program.

DEFINE VARIABLE NAMES

At the end of the program DEFINE VARIABLE NAMES: X, Y, Z instructs you to write two assembly language lines (as in Program 8.4) for each variable listed. For X we write

```
VARX:   DEFM    'X'
        DEFB    0
```

and the same for Y and Z. Thus the shorthand condenses six lines of Program 8.4 into a single line of Program 8.6.

Most macro assemblers have commands (IRP—indefinite repeat, or some version thereof) that make it possible to condense such repetitive coding. There is one problem with this shorthand. What if we need a variable name such as A$? Since no assembler permits $ in a label, we have to use some substitute for the label VARX$. Say, we agree to use VARX2 for VARX$. We express this in our shorthand by

```
DEFINE VARIABLE NAMES: X$ AS X2
```

This substitutes for the assembly language lines:

```
VARX2:   DEFM     "X$"
         DEFB     0
```

MACRO

The most important feature of this shorthand is the macro in lines 150 to 190. A "macro" is a subprogram with labels (called "parameters") that are repeated in the program; the labels in the subprogram may change at each repetition.

In the example the macro has three parameters: WHAT, INTO, and FROM. WHAT is the name of a variable, INTO is the loading address, and FROM is the present address. The macro is named LOAD. It can be called by that name; any time it is called we have to specify the labels: WHAT, INTO, and FROM.

The macro occurs first in line 210:

```
LOAD X,SA,HL
```

To understand what is happening, let us compare the macro definition with the assembly language program lines.

```
140 LOAD   MACRO WHAT, INTO, FROM          210       LOAD   X,SA,HL

150        LD    HL,VAR&WHAT               210       LD     HL,VARX
160        CALL  VARPTR                    220       CALL   VARPTR
170        EX    DE,HL                     230       EX     DE,HL
180        CALL  LD&INTO&FROM              240       CALL   LDSAHL
190        ENDM
```

On the left side we repeat the macro definition, lines 140 to 190 of Program 8.6. Every macro definition starts with a line introducing the name of the macro (LOAD) and the parameters (WHAT, INTO, FROM). The last line is ENDM (end of macro).

On the right you see line 210 of Program 8.6, the first invocation of the macro. Below it you find lines 210 to 240 of Program 8.4. This is what the macro represents! Let us look at this line by line.

```
140 LOAD   MACRO WHAT, INTO, FROM          210          LOAD  X,SA,HL
```

Line 210 is the macro invocation. This tells us that WHAT = X, INTO = SA, and FROM = HL.

```
150        LD    HL,VAR&WHAT               210          LD     HL,VARX
```

On the left side, & stands for string concatenation, and so VAR&WHAT becomes VARX, since WHAT is X.

Lines 160 and 170 contain no parameters, so they are simply copied. Finally,

```
180        CALL  LD&INTO&FROM              240          CALL  LDSAHL
```

Since INTO = SA and FROM = HL, the label LD&INTO&FROM becomes LDSAHL.

A macro assembler will assemble line 210 of Program 8.6 and lines 210–240 of Program 8.4 in the same way. To gain some practice in translating macro calls to assembly language, verify that the macro calls in line 300 and line 500 of Program 8.4 will give lines 300–330 and lines 500–530 of Program 8.4.

We repeat, for emphasis, that we do not need a macro assembler to use FAST BASIC. If you do not have a macro assembler, then make the macro replacements as you type the programs in.

Macros make the programs much easier to read and understand. If the macros are properly commented when defined, they need little explanation in the program listing itself.

THREE EXAMPLES OF SINGLE-PRECISION ARITHMETIC

Multiplication

What if we want to change X + Y to X * Y in line 20 of Program 8.3 (line 20 of Program 8.5)? In other words, we want to learn how to multiply two single-precision numbers. This is easy. In Table 8.3 we learned:

MLTSP	0847	CALL	Multiply RA and SA; result in SA

So we just replace line 110 of Program 8.4 by

```
110     MLTSP    EQU     0847H
```

and in line 400 we CALL MLTSP.

Converting Two BASIC Lines

Now let us convert two BASIC lines. We add to Program 8.3 the line:

```
25 Z = Z * X
```

Thus we want to convert the lines:

```
20 Z = X + Y
25 Z = Z * X
```

We start out as in Program 8.6, except now we also include MLTSP in the list of labels.

Program 8.7. Two-Line Conversion

```
                EQUATES: VARPTR,ADDSP,LDSAHL,LDRAHL,LDHLSA
                EQUATES: MLTSP,BSCPAR
        LOAD    MACRO   WHAT, INTO, FROM
                LD      HL,VAR&WHAT
                CALL    VARPTR
                EX      DE,HL
                CALL    LD&INTO&FROM
                ENDM
                ORG     7E00H
                LOAD    X,SA,HL     ;CONVERTING LINE 20
                LOAD    Y,RA,HL
                CALL    ADDSP
                LOAD    X,RA,HL     ;CONVERTING LINE 25
                CALL    MLTSP
                LOAD    Z,HL,SA
                JP      BSCPAR
                DEFINE VARIABLE NAMES: X,Y,Z
                END
```

The additional line of BASIC code needs only two more lines of (macro) code. Observe that the result of the addition, stored in SA, was not sent back to the variable table because we needed it again in the conversion of line 25.

In subsequent programs we shall store the address of a variable that is used many times. This minimizes the use of the VARPTR subroutine.

Converting a Conditional Statement

Now let us do a conditional statement. Change line 20 of Program 8.3 to

```
20 IF Y < X THEN Z = 0 ELSE Z = X
```

Program 8.8 is the Assembly Language version.

Program 8.8. Conditional Statement

```
100 to 190 as in Program 8.6
200              ORG     7E00H
210              LOAD    X,SA,HL
300              LOAD    Y,RA,HL
400              CALL    CPSP       ;CALL SINGLE PRECISION COMPARE
410              JP      NC,FINISH  ;IF Y < X GOTO FINISH
500              LOAD    Z,HL,SA
540     FINISH:  JP      BSCPAR
600              DEFINE VARIABLE NAMES: X, Y, Z
610              END
```

Again, this program changes very little from the previous ones. In line 400 we do a compare. If Y < X, then there is no carry, so on NC we jump to FINISH, that is, return to BASIC. Otherwise we LOAD X, which is already in SA, into the address of Z.

RUN the BASIC program with different values of X and Y to see how CPSP works.

INTEGER AND DOUBLE-PRECISION ARITHMETIC

Integers and double-precision numbers are harder to move around, thus making the arithmetic operations more cumbersome to write. Study the next two programs, which repeat Z = X + Y in integer and double-precision formats.

Integer Addition

For integer addition we use two important macros. The macro ADDR finds the location of the variable "WHAT". Now if HL points to an integer variable, the macro SHOVE will move the integer in the register pair REG1,REG2. If we want to move the integer into BC, then we invoke SHOVE B,C; moving it into DE is SHOVE D,E.

Program 8.8. Integer Addition

```
100              EQUATES: VARPTR, ADDINT, BSCPAR
120     ADDR     MACRO    WHAT
130              LD       HL,VAR&WHAT
140              CALL     VARPTR
150              EX       DE,HL
160              ENDM
```

```
SHOVE   MACRO   REG1,REG2
        LD      REG2,(HL)
        INC     HL
        LD      REG1,(HL)
        ENDM
        ORG     7E00H
        ADDR    X          ;GET ADDRESS OF X
        SHOVE   B,C        ;PUT X INTO BC
        PUSH    BC         ;SAVE IT IN STACK
        ADDR    Y          ;GET ADDRESS OF Y
        SHOVE   D,E        ;PUT Y IN DE
        POP     HL         ;X BACK IN HL
        CALL    ADDINT     ;ADD X AND Y
        PUSH    HL         ;SAVE RESULT
        ADDR    Z          ;GET ADDRESS OF Z
        POP     BC         ;PUT RESULT IN BC
        LD      C,(HL)     ;AND LOAD RESULT
        INC     HL         ;INTO VARIABLE TABLE
        LD      B,(HL)
        JP      BSCPAR
        DEFINE VARIABLE NAMES: X, Y, Z
        END
```

This program can be tested with Program 8.9.

Program 8.9.

(Disk BASIC)

```
5 DEFINT A - Z
10 X = 2 : Y = 3 : Z = 0
20 PRINT "RESULT FROM BASIC: "; X + Y
30 POKE 16526, 0 : POKE 16527, 126          (DEFUSR = &H7E00)
40 N = USR(0)
50 PRINT "RESULT FROM MACHINE LANGUAGE SUBROUTINE: "; Z
```

Double-Precision Addition

Owing to the cumbersome format of the double-precision moves, the MOVE macro now has four parameters: WHAT is the variable name; INTO and FROM are HL and DE pointing to the areas we want to move from and into; finally, ACC is the accumulator, namely, SA or SA_1.

Program 8.10.

```
100             EQUATES: VARPTR,ADDDP,MVHLDE,MVDEHL,SA,SA1,BSCPAR
150     MOVE    MACRO   WHAT, INTO, FROM, ACC
160             LD      HL,VAR&WHAT
170             CALL    VARPTR
180             LD      HL,ACC
190             CALL    MV&INTO&FROM
200             ENDM
210             ORG     7E00H
220             CALL    FLAGDP   ;SETS FLAG OF SA
230             MOVE    X,HL,DE,SA ;PUTS X IN SA
270             MOVE    Y,HL,DE,SA1;PUTS Y IN SA1
310             CALL    ADDDP    ;CALL DOUBLE PRECISION ADDITION
320             MOVE    Z,DE,HL,SA ;PUTS RESULT INTO TABLE
360             JP      BSCPAR
370             DEFINE VARIABLE NAMES: X, Y, Z
380             END
```

This program can be tested with Program 8.11, the double-precision version of Program 8.5.

Program 8.11.

(Disk BASIC)

```
5 DEFDBL A - Z
10 X = 2.51234 : Y = 3.59908765 : Z = 0
20 PRINT "RESULT FROM BASIC: "; X + Y
30 POKE 16526, 0 : POKE 16527, 126      (DEFUSR = &H7E00)
40 N = USR(0)
50 PRINT "RESULT FROM MACHINE LANGUAGE SUBROUTINE: "; Z
```

This completes the FAST BASIC arithmetic. Now we are ready to write some meaningful FAST BASIC programs.

Review and Programming Practice

1. What is the assembly language listing for the following?

```
EQUATES: BSCPAR, VARPTR, ADDINT
```

2. What is the assembly language listing for the following?

```
DEFINE VARIABLE NAMES: X% AS X, Y, Z$ AS Z2
```

3. What is a "macro"? How is a macro called?

4. Write a portion of an assembly language program that will locate (a) the integer variable XR; (b) the single-precision variable XR!; (c) the double-precision variable XR#.
5. The call to VARPTR returns the same address as was explained with the BASIC VARPTR function in Chapter 4. Write a segment of an assembly language program that finds where the string XR$ is stored.
6. DE points at a memory location that contains a single-precision number. Load that number into RA.
7. HL points at an integer variable X. Load the integer into DE.
8. Move a single-precision number from SA to RA and from RA to SA.
9. Move the single-precision number starting at 4121_H to the area starting with $90A5_H$.
10. Move a double-precision number from SA_1 into SA.
11. Z is a single-precision variable. Turn into FAST BASIC the line:

```
100 Z = Z * Z
```

12. Convert into FAST BASIC the following BASIC line:

```
100 Z = X1 + X2 + X3
```

where all the variables are single precision. (*Hint*: Do the conversion in two steps: Z = X1 + X2, Z = Z + X3.)

13. Convert into FAST BASIC (Z, X, Y, and U are single-precision variables, U = 3):

```
100 Z = (X + 3) * Y * (X + 3)
```

14. Let X, Y, Z be single-precision variables. Convert the conditional statement:

```
100 IF Y < 2 * X THEN Z = X * Y ELSE X = Z * Y
```

into FAST BASIC. [*Hint*: Use a variable U = 2 to have 2 at hand in single-precision format. (1) Compute U * X, result stays in SA. (2) Place Y in RA. (3) Compare. (4) If Y < 2*X fails, the carry flag is set.]

Answers

There are many correct answers to the programming questions. The answers provided here are only guidelines by which to judge your own answers.

1.

```
100     BSCPAR  EQU     0A9AH
110     VARPTR  EQU     260DH
120     ADDINT  EQU     0BD2H
```

2.

```
600     VARX:   DEFM    'X%'
610             DEFB    0
620     VARY:   DEFM    'Y'
630             DEFB    0
640     VARZ2:  DEFM    'Z$'
650             DEFB    0
```

3. A macro is a program segment with parameters starting with "name MACRO parameters" and ending with ENDM. The macro is invoked by its name and a list corresponding to the parameters.

4. (a)

```
200             LD      HL,VARXR
210             CALL    VARPTR      ;NOW DE POINTS AT XR
    ...
400     VARXR:  DEFM    'XR'
410             DEFB    0
```

(b) Change XR in line 400 to XR!
(c) Change XR in 400 to XR#.

5.

```
200             LD      HL,VARXR
210             CALL    VARPTR
220             PUSH    DE
230             POP     IX
240             LD      L,(IX+1)
250             LD      H,(IX+2)    ;NOW HL POINTS AT XR$
    ...
400 VARXR:      DEFM    'XR$'
410             DEFB    0
```

6.

```
200             EX      DE,HL
210             CALL    LDRAHL
```

7.

```
        LD      E,(HL)
        INC     HL
        LD      D,(HL)
```

8. CALL LDRASA and CALL LDSARA.

9.

```
        LD      H,41H
        LD      L,21H
        LD      D,90H
        LD      E,A5H
        CALL    LDDEHL
```

10.

```
        LD      HL,SA1
        CALL    FLAGDP
        CALL    MVSAHL
```

11.

```
                EQUATES: VARPTR, MLTSP, LDSAHL, LDRASA, LDHLSA
        LOAD    MACRO   WHAT, INTO, FROM
                LD      HL,VAR&WHAT
                CALL    VARPTR
                EX      DE,HL
                CALL    LD&INTO&FROM
                ENDM
                ORG     7E00H
                LOAD    Z,SA,HL     ;GET Z INTO SA
                CALL    LDRASA      ;COPY IT OVER TO RA
                CALL    MLTSP       ;Z * Z IN SA
                LOAD    Z,HL,SA     ;SEND BACK TO VARIABLE TABLE
        VARZ:   DEFM    'Z'
                DEFB    0
```

12.

```
050            EQUATES: BSCPAR, LDRAHL, LDSAHL, ADDSP, VARPTR
060            EQUATES: LDHLSA
070     LOAD   MACRO    WHAT, INTO, FROM
080            LD       HL,VAR&WHAT
085            CALL     VARPTR
090            EX       DE,HL
095            CALL     LD&INTO&FROM
098            ENDM
100            ORG     7E00H
110            LOAD    X1, SA, HL
200            LOAD    Z, RA, HL
240            CALL    ADDSP
250            LOAD    X3, RA, HL
290            CALL    ADDSP
300            LOAD    Z, HL, SA
340            JP      BSCPAR
350            DEFINE VARIABLE NAMES: X1, X2, X3, Z
400            END
```

13.

```
050            EQUATES: VARPTR, LDSAHL, LDRAHL, ADDSP, MLTSP
060            EQUATES: LDHLSA, BSCPAR, LDSTSA
070     LOAD   MACRO    WHAT, INTO, FROM
080            LD       HL,VAR&WHAT
085            CALL     VARPTR
090            EX       DE,HL
095            CALL     LD&INTO&FROM
098            ENDM
100            ORG     7E00H
150            LOAD    X, SA, HL
200            LOAD    U, RA, HL
250            CALL    ADDSP      ;X + 3 IN SA
260            CALL    LDSTSA     ;SAVE IN STACK
300            LOAD    Y, RA, HL ;LOAD Y
310            CALL    MLTSP      ;Y*(X + 3) IN SA
320            POP     BC
330            POP     DE         ; X + 3 FROM STACK TO SA
340            CALL    MLTSP      ;RESULT IN SA
350            LOAD Z, HL, SA     ;MOVE RESULT INTO VARIABLE TABLE
390            JP      BSCPAR
400            DEFINE VARIABLE NAMES: X, Y, Z, U
410            END
```

14.

```
050          EQUATES: VARPTR, LDHLSA, LDSAHL, LDRAHL
060          EQUATES: ADDSP, MLTSP, CPSP, BSCPAR
070  LOAD    MACRO   WHAT, INTO, FROM
080          LD      HL,VAR&WHAT
085          CALL    VARPTR
090          EX      DE,HL
095          CALL    LD&INTO&FROM
098          ENDM
100          ORG     7E00H
110          LOAD    X, SA, HL
150          LOAD    U, RA, HL
190          CALL    MLTSP       ;2 * X IN SA
200          LOAD    Y, RA, HL ;Y IN RA
240          PUSH    BC
250          PUSH    DE          ;SAVE Y IN STACK
260          CALL    CPSP        ;COMPARE Y AND 2 * X
270          JP      C,ELSE      ;CONDITION FAILS, DO ELSE
300          LOAD X, SA, HL      ;CONDITION HOLDS, PUT X IN SA
320          POP     DE
330          POP     BC          ;Y IN RA
340          CALL    MLTSP       ;MULTIPLY
350          LOAD    Z, HL, SA ;RESULT MOVED TO VARIABLE TABLE
390          JP      BSCPAR
400  ELSE:   LOAD    Z, SA, HL ;Z TO SA
440          POP     DE
450          POP     BC          ;Y TO RA
460          CALL    MLTSP       ;MULTIPLY
500          LOAD    X, HL, SA ;RESULT TO VARIABLE TABLE
510          JP      BSCPAR
520          DEFINE VARIABLE NAMES: U, X, Y, Z
600          END
```

CHAPTER NINE

Special Techniques: Loops and Strings

The height of
technical felicity
is to combine
sublime simplicity
with sufficient
ingenuities
to show how difficult
to do it is.

—P. Hein in *Grooks 4**

Most FAST BASIC programming is as simple as the examples in Chapter 8. Call the variables in with the appropriate subroutine calls, perform the necessary operations, and then store the result in the BASIC variable tables. However, in two situations this method should not be followed: implementing FOR NEXT loops and manipulating string variables.

We investigate how FOR NEXT loops can be implemented in machine language. A little care in the implementation of the FOR NEXT loops can result in very fast loop structures, exceeding the speed of the BASIC loop structure by a factor of 100.

Next we consider string variables. We have seen in Chapter 4 how TRS-80 BASIC uses a very time-consuming method to keep the string space in order. This can cause unacceptable delays in string sorts and similar programs. In this chapter we learn how to avoid this problem. In one sample program this technique improves the 49-minute execution time of a BASIC program to 3 seconds.

THE MOST IMPORTANT LOOP

There are many types of loops. We start with the type that is most often used:

```
FOR I = 1 TO 100
NEXT I
```

where I is an integer variable.

In agreement with our policy to let BASIC handle our numbers and variables, we use two variables: LO and UP to contain the lower and upper boundaries of the loop. In our example LO = 1 and UP = 101. Note that both LO and UP are integer variables and that UP is one more than the upper boundary of the loop. The loop now takes the form:

```
FOR I = 1 TO UP - 1

NEXT I
```

First Variant

Recall that in TRS-80 BASIC the loop first is executed and then the loop counter is tested. Thus we plan the loop according to the following steps.

1. Find the address of the two variables we need for the loop (LO, UP); we store the values of LO and UP at SAVELO and SAVEUP.
2. Do a NOP (nothing) in the loop.
3. Increment LO; store the new value; compare it with UP. If they are equal, then RETurn; otherwise go back to 2.

Program 9.1. Loop

```
100           EQUATES: VARPTR,CPINT,BSCPAR
120   LOAD    MACRO    WHAT          ; THIS MACRO  TAKES THE
130           LD       HL,VAR&WHAT   ; VARIABLE WHAT, GETS ITS
140           CALL     VARPTR        ; ADDRESS INTO DE
150           EX       DE,HL         ; THEN INTO HL
160           LD       C,(HL)        ; LOADS LSB OF WHAT INTO C
170           INC      HL
180           LD       B,(HL)        ; LOADS MSB OF WHAT INTO B
190           LD       (SAVE&WHAT),BC ; STORES WHAT INTO
200           ENDM                   ; RESERVED SPACE
300           ORG      7E00H         ;START OF STEP 1
310           LOAD     LO            ;LOAD LO INTO SAVELO
320           LOAD     UP            ;LOAD UP INTO SAVEUP
400   LOOP:   NOP                    ;DO NOTHING
500   TEST:   LD       DE,(SAVELO)   ;STEP 3: LOAD LO INTO DE
510           INC      DE            ;LO = LO + 1 THE NEW LO
520           LD       (SAVELO),DE   ;PUT NEW LO BACK TO SAVELO
530           LD       HL,(SAVEUP)   ;LOAD UP INTO HL
540           CALL     CPINT         ;COMPARE LO AND UP
550           JP       NZ,LOOP       ;IF UNEQUAL (NZ) GOTO LOOP
560   FINISH: JP       BSCPAR
600           DEFINE VARIABLE NAMES: LO,UP
610   SAVELO: DEFM     'LO'
620   SAVEUP: DEFM     'UP'
630           END
```

In Program 9.1 we saved 2 bytes at SAVELO and SAVEUP for the variables LO and UP. At LOOP we used a new instruction, NOP, which does nothing. In implementing a real loop the work of the loop is coded at this label.

Second Variant

An alternative arrangement is to keep LO and UP permanently in DE and HL. When these registers are needed we use EXX to keep them out of the way. This arrangement works well if we do not need LO and UP within the loop. If we do, we should PUSH them to the stack for easy access. Program 9.2 uses the new arrangement.

Program 9.2. Loop: Variant 2

```
100             EQUATES: VARPTR,CPINT,BSCPAR
120     LOAD    MACRO   WHAT,REG1,REG2 ; THIS MACRO  TAKES THE
130             LD      HL,VAR&WHAT  ; VARIABLE WHAT, GETS ITS
140             CALL    VARPTR       ; ADDRESS INTO THE REGISTER
150             EX      DE,HL        ; PAIR DE, THEN INTO HL
160             LD      REG2,(HL)    ; LOADS LSB OF WHAT INTO REG2
170             INC     HL
180             LD      REG1,(HL)    ; LOADS MSB OF WHAT INTO REG1
190             ENDM
300             ORG     7E00H
310             LOAD    LO,B,C       ;LOAD LO INTO BC
320             PUSH    BC           ;SAVE LO IN STACK
330             LOAD    UP,D,E       ;LOAD UP INTO DE
340             POP     HL           ;LO NOW IN HL
400     LOOP:   EXX                  ;LO AND UP IN ALT. REG. SET
410             NOP                  ;DO NOTHING
600     TEST:   EXX                  ;STEP 3: BRING IN ALT. REG.
610             INC     HL           ;LO = LO + 1 THE NEW LO
620             PUSH    DE           ;SAVE DE
630             PUSH    HL           ;AND HL IN STACK
640             CALL    CPINT        ;COMPARE LO AND UP
650             POP     HL           ;RECOVER HL
660             POP     DE           ;AND DE
670             JP      NZ,LOOP      ;IF UNEQUAL (NZ) GOTO LOOP
680     FINISH: JP      BSCPAR
700             DEFINE VARIABLE NAMES: LO,UP
710             END
```

In Program 9.2 there is a small change in TEST. Since LO and UP "live" in the registers, we PUSH them into the stack before CALL CPINT. (This is very important! ROM subroutines use the registers, and so we must save all registers that we need later on.)

Third Variant

An alternative approach to the TEST segment is to write it ourselves. CALL CPINT is too powerful a tool to use here; we only want to test as to whether LO and UP are equal. The instruction CP r compares the registers A and r and sets the appropriate flags exactly as the CP subroutines (Table 8.3).

Program 9.3. Modified TEST

```
TEST:   EXX                 ;STEP 3: BRING IN ALT. REG.
        INC     DE          ;LO = LO + 1 THE NEW LO
        LD      A,D         ;LOAD D INTO A
        CP      H           ;COMPARE A WITH H
        JP      NZ,LOOP     ;IF UNEQUAL, CONTINUE LOOP
        LD      A,E         ;LOAD E INTO A
        CP      L           ;COMPARE A WITH L
        JP      NZ,LOOP     ;IF UNEQUAL, CONTINUE LOOP
FINISH: JP      BSCPAR
```

Other Loops

Now you should be ready to do any kind of loop. Try a FOR I = A TO B STEP C where A, B, and C are double-precision variables, a loop not permitted in TRS-80 BASIC. If you are familiar with it, try a structured construct such as WHILE X < 3.14159 DO . . . ENDWHILE.

Run Times

Table 9.1 compares the run time of various BASIC loops with the FAST BASIC variants using Programs 9.1, 9.2, and 9.3. We always set LO = 1. We tabulate the times for four kinds of BASIC loops:

1. All variables are integer variables; we use NEXT and not NEXT I.
2. Same as 1 with NEXT I.
3. Single-precision I, LO, UP; we use NEXT.
4. Same as 3 with NEXT I.

Table 9.1 shows that the third machine language version ran under 0.5 second even for UP = 30,000. It is interesting to notice the effect of I in the NEXT I. At the very least, we should learn from this table *never* to use

TABLE 9.1. Loop Timing

UP =	10,000	20,000	30,000
BASIC 1	16	32	48
BASIC 2	24	47	71
BASIC 3	25	50	75
BASIC 4	33	66	99
Machine language 1	1	2	3
Machine language 2	1	2	3
Machine language 3	0	0	0

NEXT I instead of I and to use, whenever possible, integer variables as loop counters.

The FAST BASIC implementation of FOR NEXT loops require some study and practice. However, from Table 9.1 we see that this extra effort does result in a considerable saving in execution time.

The Fastest Loop

Finally, let us mention the fastest loop. If we put the counter in register B, the instruction DJNZ LOOP decrements B and tests for 0; if B is not 0, then it jumps (relative) to LOOP. Thus this one instruction carries out all three functions needed to test a loop: (1) decrement, (2) test, and (3) jump if not finished.

ONE MORE LOOP IMPLEMENTATION

A Benchmark Program

The following BASIC program asks for an integer input and tests as to whether the input is a prime number. (A "prime number" is an integer > 1 with the property that the only smaller integer dividing it is 1.) The test is very primitive. However, programs of this type (called "benchmarks") are often used to compare speeds of various language implementations because they use many arithmetic operations.

Program 9.4. Testing Primes

```
10 DEFINT J, P, U, X
20 J = 2 : P = 0 : U = 0 : UP = 0
30 INPUT "INPUT NUMBER TO BE TESTED FOR BEING PRIME"; UP
40 IF UP < 2 THEN 10
50 P = 0
60 FOR J = 2 TO UP - 1
70 X = INT(UP/J)
80 X = X * J
90 IF X = UP THEN P = 1 : J = UP
100 NEXT
110 IF P = 1 THEN PRINT X; "IS NOT PRIME" : GOTO 30
120 PRINT X; "IS PRIME" : GOTO 30
```

J goes from 2 to UP – 1. For each value of J we check whether J divides UP. In lines 70 and 80 we form INT(UP/J) * J; if this expression equals UP, we found a divisor, set the flag P to 1, and jump out of the loop.

FAST BASIC Conversion

We shall implement one more variant of the FOR NEXT loop: We use IX and IY to store J and UP. (We can safely use IX and IY because no subroutine mentioned so far uses them. But one must be careful because some input/output subroutines use IX.) Program 9.5 replaces lines 60–100 of Program 9.4 with P = USR(0).

Program 9.5.

```
100            EQUATES: BSCPAR, DIVINT, MLTINT, VARPTR, INT
120   LOAD     MACRO    INTO,FROM ;THIS MACRO LOADS A 16-BIT
130            PUSH     FROM      ;REGISTER OR REGISTER PAIR
140            POP      INTO      ;"FROM" INTO THE 16-BIT REGISTER
150            ENDM               ;OR REGISTER PAIR "INTO"
200            ORG      7E00H
210            LD       IX,2H     ;J IN IX
220            LD       HL,VARUP  ;GETTING
230            CALL     VARPTR    ;ADDRESS OF UP
240            LOAD     IY,DE     ;IN IY
250            LD       E,(IY+0)  ;NOW PUTTING UP
260            LD       D,(IY+1)  ;IN DE
270            LOAD     IY,DE     ;STORE IT IN IY
300   LOOP:    LOAD     DE,IY     ;PLACE UP IN DE
320            LOAD     HL,IX     ;AND J IN HL
340            CALL     DIVINT    ;UP/J IN SA
350            CALL     INT       ;INT(UP/J) IN HL
360            LOAD     DE,IX     ;NOW PLACE J IN DE
380            CALL     MLTINT    ;INT(UP/J) * J IN HL
390            LOAD     DE,IY     ;NOW WE COMPARE HL WITH UP SO WE
410            LD       A,D       ;PUT UP IN DE. WE USE THE
420            CP       H         ;COMPARE OF PROGRAM 9.4
430            JP       NZ,TEST   ;IF NOT EQUAL CONTINUE LOOP
440            LD       A,E
450            CP       L
460            JP       NZ,TEST   ;IF THEY ARE EQUAL WE FOUND
470            JP       NOTPRM    ;A DIVISOR, UP IS NOT A PRIME
500   TEST:    INC      IX        ;J = J + 1
510            LOAD     HL,IX     ;PLACE NEW J IN HL (UP IS STILL
530            LD       A,D       ;IN DE) WE COMPARE NEW J
540            CP       H         ;WITH UP AS IN PROGRAM 9.4
550            JP       NZ,LOOP   ;IF NOT EQUAL
560            LD       A,E
570            CP       L
580            JP       NZ,LOOP   ;CONTINUE LOOP
590   PRIME:   LD       HL,0      ;IF J = UP, LOOP IS COMPLETE
600            JP       BSCPAR    ;UP NOT PRIME SO SET P = 0
610   NOTPRM:  LD       HL,1      ;UP NOT PRIME SO SET P = 1
```

```
620                 JP      BSCPAR
700     VARUP:      DEFM    'UP'
710                 DEFB    0
```

Some timing comparisons are shown in Table 9.2. Let us emphasize again that very much faster programs to test primes can be written. As Table 9.2 shows, we can expect a speed-up by a factor of 3 to 4 in programs with a lot of computation.

STRINGS

The examples so far did not include string variables. There is a good reason for this. In all the previous examples we handled the variables in BASIC and we carried out the arithmetic in assembly language. Unfortunately, the string storage method of TRS-80 BASIC precludes the use of the same technique for string variables.

Plans

We suggest the following techniques to handle string variables.

1. If the program only requires the inspection of strings, then there is no difficulty. Programs 9.6 and 9.7 will illustrate this.
2. When sorting strings we swap them by replacing the pointers to the strings. In this way no new strings are created in the string space. See Programs 9.8 and 9.9.
3. If we have to manipulate strings, we create our own string buffers. In Program 9.10 we create a buffer as follows: We add 258 to the current starting address of the BASIC program (stored at $40A4_H = 16548_D$), and then LOAD the BASIC program. This creates a buffer of 258 bytes under the BASIC program. We store the length of the string in the first byte of the buffer and the string follows; there should be a byte 00_H to terminate the string and a byte 00_H at the end of the buffer. (There has to be a byte 00_H to precede the first line of BASIC text.) A string placed in this buffer can be moved to the string space with MVSTR. Programs 9.11 and 9.12 illustrate this with a simple string concatenation.

TABLE 9.2. Timing the Arithmetic Benchmark Program

	Input			
	547	1607	3571	
BASIC	14	41	82	(in seconds)
FAST BASIC	5	13	25	

ROM Routines

The labels in Table 9.3 are useful in handling strings.

Counting Letters

Program 9.6 is a BASIC program that takes a line of text and counts the number of occurrences of the letter "E" in the text.

Program 9.6. Counting E's

```
10 CLEAR 300
20 DEFINT C, J
30 DEFSTR T
40 INPUT "PLEASE TYPE IN ONE LINE OF TEXT (0 - 255 CHARACTERS)"; TX
50 C = 0 : J = 0
60 FOR J = 1 TO LEN(TX)
70 IF MID$(TX,J,1) = "E" THEN C = C + 1
80 NEXT J
90 PRINT "TEXT CONTAINS "; C; " OCCURRENCES OF THE LETTER E"
```

Program 9.6 inspects a string variable; the string variable is not manipulated in a way that disturbs the string space. Thus in FAST BASIC we let BASIC handle the string variable. As a result it is easy to convert lines 60 to 80 into an assembly language subroutine; see Program 9.7.

TABLE 9.3.

Label	Value	Type	Explanation
BSCTXT	40A4	EQU	The start of the BASIC program (text) is at this address
CPSTR	25A1	CALL	Compare two strings; HL and BC point at the strings, D and E contain the lengths*
MOVEA	09D6	CALL	Move data; DE points at source, HL points at destination, A contains the count—how many bytes to move
MOVEB	09D7	CALL	Same as MOVEA but B contains the count
MVSTR	21E3	CALL	Move string into string space; HL points at the first byte of the buffer and BC points at the variable name

*Result of compare:
If the two strings are equal, the zero flag is set (= 1).
If the two strings are unequal, the zero flag is reset (= 0).
If the first string is smaller, the carry flag is reset (= 0).
If the second string is smaller, the carry flag is set (= 1).

Program 9.7. Counting E's in Assembly Language

```
100              EQUATES: BSCPAR,VARPTR
200              ORG      7E00H
210              LD       HL,VARTX
220              CALL     VARPTR
230              EX       DE,HL
240              LD       B,(HL)     ;LOAD INTO B THE LENGTH OF TX
250              INC      HL         ;NOW HL POINTS AT ADDRESS OF TX
260              LD       E,(HL)     ;TRANSFER ADDRESS
270              INC      HL
280              LD       D,(HL)     ;TO DE
290              EX       DE,HL      ;THEN TO HL
300              LD       A,'E'      ;ASCII OF E INTO REGISTER A
310              LD       DE,0       ;DE IS USED AS COUNTER
400      LOOP:   CP       (HL)       ;COMPARE CHARACTER OF TX WITH A
410              JP       NZ,SKIP    ;IF EQUAL, INCREMENT DE
414              INC      DE
418      SKIP:   INC      HL         ;INCREMENT POINTER TO TEXT
420              DJNZ     LOOP       ;DECREMENT B, IF NOT ZERO
430                                  ;CONTINUE LOOP
440              EX       DE,HL      ;PLACE COUNTER INTO HL
450              JP       BSCPAR     ;PASS IT BACK TO BASIC
500      VARTX:  DEFM     'TX'
510              DEFB     0
520              END
```

After assembling and loading Program 9.7, RUN Program 9.6 with lines 60–80 replaced by

```
60 C = USR(0)
```

Programs of this type are very useful. For instance, frequency counts are often used in text compression (storing English text in as few bytes as possible).

STRING SORTING

Binary Sorting

We test the string-handling capabilities of FAST BASIC by the benchmark program called binary sort. We are given n strings $X_1, \ldots, X_n$ to sort. We repeat the following step: Compare two strings X and Y; if $X > Y$, then swap them. We do this for X_1 and X_2, X_1 and X_3, . . . , X_1 and X_n. We go on with X_2 and X_3, . . . , X_2 and X_n. The process continues until X_{n-1} and X_n are compared.

This procedure is illustrated with four strings in Table 9.4.

TABLE 9.4. Binary Sort

				Compare	Action
JONES	SMITH	ALBERT	GEORGE	1 and 2	None
JONES	SMITH	ALBERT	GEORGE	1 and 3	Swap
ALBERT	SMITH	JONES	GEORGE	1 and 4	None
ALBERT	SMITH	JONES	GEORGE	2 and 3	Swap
ALBERT	JONES	SMITH	GEORGE	2 and 4	Swap
ALBERT	GEORGE	SMITH	JONES	3 and 4	Swap
ALBERT	GEORGE	JONES	SMITH		

BASIC Implementation

Program 9.8 implements the binary sort in BASIC.

Program 9.8. Binary String Sort in BASIC

```
10 CLEAR 700
20 CLS
30 PRINT "NOT MORE THAN 50 CHARACTERS IN STRINGS"
40 DEFINT I, J, N
50 INPUT "NUMBER OF STRINGS (NOT MORE THAN 100)"; N
60 IF N <= 0 STOP
70 DIM A$(N)
80 FOR I = 1 TO N
90 PRINT "STRING# "; I;
100 INPUT A$(I-1)
110 NEXT
120 IF N = 1 GOTO 180
130 FOR I = 0 TO N - 2
140 FOR J = I + 1 TO N - 1
150 IF A$(I) > A$(J) THEN C$ = A$(J) : A$(J) = A$(I) : A$(I) = C$
160 NEXT
170 NEXT
180 PRINT : PRINT
190 PRINT "SORTED STRINGS:"
200 FOR I = 1 TO N
210 PRINT "STRING# "; I, A$(I - 1)
220 NEXT
```

FAST BASIC Plan

Now we convert lines 130–170 into assembly language. Our plan is the following.

1. *Initialize.* We put the VARPTR of A$(0) into BC and the VARPTR of A$(N – 1) into HL. We locate A$(0) through a VARPTR call. However, finding A$(N – 1) is more difficult. We include a line

```
115 OF% = 3 * (N - 1)
```

   Adding OF% (the offset) to the VARPTR of A$(0), we obtain the VARPTR of A$(N – 1).
2. *Initialize pointers.* We place BC in IX and BC + 3 in IY. Then IX and IY will point to the first pair of strings to be tested.
3. *Compare.* Interchange the register sets. Load in the lengths and addresses of the strings singled out by IX and IY. CALL CPSTR. If the first is the bigger string, then we have a carry, and so on C call in the SWAP subroutine swapping the two strings.
4. *Test.* Bring back the other register set. Compare IY with HL. If they are different, increment IY three times and continue with step 3. If IY = HL, then move the pointer to the first string. Increment BC three times. If now BC = HL, then we are finished. If not, continue with initializing the pointers for the next round with step 2.

Finally, we use the SWAP subroutine to interchange the 3 bytes pointed to by IX with the 3 bytes pointed to by IY.

The Assembly Listing

Program 9.9 implements this plan.

Program 9.9. Machine Language Subroutine for FAST BASIC Binary Sort

```
                EQUATES: VARPTR,ADDINT,CPSTR,BSCPAR
        INC3    MACRO   RP              ;INCREMENT THE REGISTER PAIR
                INC     RP              ;RP THREE TIMES
                INC     RP
                INC     RP
                ENDM
        LOAD    MACRO   PTR,LENGTH,ADDMSB,ADDLSB; PTR IS IX OR IY
                LD      LENGTH,(PTR+0);PTR POINTS AT A STRING
                LD      ADDLSB,(PTR+1);ENTRY IN THE VARIABLE TABLE;
                LD      ADDMSB,(PTR+2);LOAD THE LENGTH AND THE
                ENDM                    ;ADDRESS INTO THE REGISTERS.
        SW      MACRO   N               ;INTERCHANGE THE BYTE
                LD      A,(IX+N)        ;(IX+N) WITH THE BYTE
                LD      B,(IY+N)        ;(IY+N)
                LD      (IY+N),A
                LD      (IX+N),B
                ENDM
        EQUAL   MACRO   R1,R2,OUT       ;R1R2 IS A REGISTER PAIR
```

```
290            LD      A,R1          ;IF IT DOES NOT EQUAL HL
300            CP      H             ;THEN JUMP TO OUT
310            JP      NZ,OUT
320            LD      A,E
330            CP      L
340            JP      NZ,OUT
350            ENDM
400            ORG     7E00H
410   INIT:    LD      HL,VARA       ;INITIALIZE
420            CALL    VARPTR        ;DE = VARPTR OF A$(0)
430            PUSH    DE            ;SAVE IT
440            LD      HL,VAROF      ;GET OFFSET
450            CALL    VARPTR
460            EX      DE,HL
470            LD      E,(HL)
480            INC     HL
490            LD      D,(HL)        ;OFFSET IN DE
500            POP     HL            ;VARPTR OF A$(0) IN HL
510            PUSH    HL
520            CALL    ADDINT        ;HL = VARPTR OF A$(N - 1)
530            POP     BC            ;BC = VARPTR OF A$(0)
600   SETUP:   PUSH    BC
610            POP     IX            ;IX = VARPTR OF CURRENT A$(I)
620            PUSH    BC
630            POP     IY
640            INC3    IY            ;IY = VARPTR OF A$(I + 1)
650            EXX
700   COMP:    LOAD    IX,D,H,L      ;LOAD A$(I) AND
710            LOAD    IY,E,B,C      ;A$(J) INTO REGISTERS
720            CALL    CPSTR
730            CALL    NC,SWAP       ;IF A$(I) > A$(J) THEN SWAP
800   TEST:    EXX
810            PUSH    IY
820            POP     DE
830            EQUAL   D,E,INCIY     ;IS IY = VARPTR OF A$(N - 1)?
840            INC3    BC            ;YES, UPDATE CURRENT A$(I)
850            EQUAL   B,C,SETUP     ;IS IT A$(N - 1)?
860            JP      BSCPAR        ;YES, WE ARE FINISHED
900   INCIY:   INC3    IY            ;IY <> VARPTR A$(N - 1)
910            EXX                   ;THEN INCREMENT IT
920            JR      COMP
950   SWAP:    SW      0
960            SW      1
970            SW      2
980            JP      BSCPAR
1000           DEFINE VARIABLE NAMES: A$(0)AS A, OF% AS OF
1010           END
```

Timing

In a test run we took 100 strings of five characters each (in a worst case situation). These were sorted in BASIC by Program 9.8 in 49:12 minutes. Then we replaced lines 120–170 of Program 9.8 by a USR call to Program 9.9. The resulting FAST BASIC program sorted the strings in 3 seconds, that is, 984 times faster!

CONCATENATING STRINGS

Register Arithmetic

To implement string concatenation we have to do some arithmetic with the lengths of the strings. We can do this, of course, with ADDINT and SUBINT, but it is much more convenient to do it with the Z-80 instructions: ADD A,r, which adds register r to A (result in A); ADD HL,BC, which adds HL and BC (result in HL); ADD IX,BC, which adds IX and BC (result in IX); and SBC HL,BC (result in HL), which subtracts BC from HL.

Program 9.12 converts the BASIC line A$ = B$ + C$.

Plan

We proceed as follows: We set up a string buffer by loading the BASIC program 258 bytes higher in memory than usual. We accomplish this by calling in the BASIC program STRING/BAS by Program 9.10, another BASIC program.

Program 9.10.

```
10 A% = PEEK(16548) + PEEK(16549)*256
20 A% = A% + 258
30 POKE 16548, A% - (INT(A%/256)*256) : POKE 16549, INT(A%/256)
40 RUN "STRING/BAS"
```

Program 9.10 is the Disk BASIC version. In a cassette system replace line 40 by CLOAD "S" (where "S" is the name of the BASIC program) and at BASIC READY type RUN.

Program 9.10 increments the pointer at BSCTXT by 258. The BASIC program, STRING/BAS, loads 258 bytes higher, leaving a buffer of 258 bytes. Line 40 calls the BASIC program STRING/BAS, which concatenates two strings.

Program 9.11. STRING/BAS

(Disk BASIC)

```
10 CLEAR 600
20 POKE 16526, 0 : POKE 16527, 254        (DEFUSRO = &H7E00)
30 INPUT B$
40 INPUT C$
50 A% = USR(A%)
60 PRINT A$
70 GOTO 30
```

Buffer

The USR utilizes the buffer as follows: The first byte is the length of the string (IX points at this); this is followed by the string. HL is the pointer to the first available byte (HL points at the byte after the string). The string is terminated by a 00_H byte (this is needed by MVSTR). The last byte of the buffer is a 00_H also (otherwise the BASIC program will not run).

USR

Our plan is implemented in Program 9.12.

Program 9.12. String Concatenation

```
                EQUATES: BSCPAR,BSCTXT,MVSTR,MOVEA,VARPTR
        LOAD    MACRO    WHAT           ;THIS MACRO LOOKS UP THE
                LD       HL,VAR&WHAT    ;VARPTR OF WHAT$
                CALL     VARPTR         ;AND PLACES THE ADDRESS OF
                EX       DE,HL          ;WHAT$ INTO DE
                LD       A,(HL)         ;AND LENGTH INTO A
                INC      HL
                LD       E,(HL)
                INC      HL
                LD       D,(HL)
                ENDM
                ORG      7E00H
                LD       IX,BSCTXT      ;NEW BASIC START
                LD       (IX-1),0       ;PLACES 00H BEFORE IT
                LD       L,(IX+0)       ;IX = IX - 258
                LD       H,(IX+1)
                XOR      A              ;THIS RESETS THE CARRY FLAG
                LD       BC,258         ;SO C DOES NOT INTERFERE
                SBC      HL,BC          ;WITH THE SUBTRACTION
                PUSH     HL             ;PLACE BUFFER POINTER
                POP      IX             ;IN IX
                INC      HL             ;POINTER FOR FIRST AV. BYTE
                PUSH     HL             ;POINTER SAVED
                LOAD     B              ;SETS UP B$
```

```
430      LD       (IX+0),A     ;LENGTH PLACED IN BUFFER
440      POP      HL           ;POINTER TO FIRST AV. BYTE
450      PUSH     HL           ;POINTER SAVED
460      CALL     MOVEA        ;MOVES B$ INTO BUFFER
470      POP      HL           ;RESTORE FIRST AV. BYTE POINTER
480      LD       C,(IX+0)
490      LD       C,A
500      XOR      B
510      ADD      HL,BC        ;POINTER UPDATED
520      PUSH     HL           ;AND SAVED
530      LOAD     C            ;SET UP C$
540      PUSH     AF           ;SAVE LENGTH OF C$
550      ADD      A,(IX+0)     ;COMPUTE NEW LENGTH
560      LD       (IX+0),A     ;PLACE IT IN BUFFER
570      POP      AF           ;GET LENGTH OF C$ BACK
580      POP      HL           ;GET FIRST AV. BYTE POINTER
590      CALL     MOVEA        ;MOVE C$ INTO BUFFER
600      PUSH     IX           ;SAVE BUFFER POINTER
610      LD       C,(IX+0)     ;BC = CONCATENATED LENGTH
620      XOR      B
630      ADD      IX,BC        ;STRING TERMINATOR 00H
640      LD       (IX+1),0
650      POP      HL           ;SETTING UP STRING MOVE
660      LD       BC,VARA
670      CALL     MVSTR
680      JP       BSCPAR
690      DEFINE VARIABLE NAMES: A$ AS A,B$ AS B,C$ AS C
700      END
```

Other Applications

It is now easy to see that Program 9.12 can be adjusted to do any string manipulation. For instance, if

```
A$ = B$ + LEFT$(C$,5)
```

then after line 530 (register A contains the length of C$) we compare: CP 5; if LEN(C$) is greater than 5, we do a LD A,5, and proceed as above. RIGHT$ and MID$ are handled similarly.

Observe also that we can have strings of arbitrary length. Simply leave 2 bytes for the length and do not try to move strings that are too long into the string space.

Review and Programming Practice

1. Look up the instructions CP r and DJNZ in Appendix 2.
2. Look up in Appendix 2 the arithmetic instructions used in string handling.
3. In Program 9.5 replace lines 410–460 and 530–580 by a macro.
4. Rewrite the following BASIC program in FAST BASIC using the loop structure of Program 9.1 (I and J are integer variables; in addition, we also have the integer variables LO = 1 and UP = 101).

```
10 J = 0 : LO = 1 : UP = 101
20 FOR I = 1 TO 100
30 J = J + I
40 NEXT I
50 PRINT J
```

5. Use DJNZ to rewrite the previous program in FAST BASIC.
6. Rewrite in FAST BASIC (J and X(I) are single-precision variables; LO = 1 and UP = 101 are integer variables):

```
10 J = 0 : LO = 1 : UP = 101
20 FOR I = 1 TO 1000
30 J = J + X(I)
40 NEXT I
50 PRINT J
```

[*Hint:* Use VARPTR to find X(0); let HL point at the first byte of X(0). Use LDRAHL to move X(0) into RA. Place J into SA. Carry out the addition. Increment HL four times. Now HL points at X(1). Continue. Use the loop structure of Program 9.2.]

7. Rewrite Program 9.5 using CPINT. Is there a measurable difference in the timing?
8. Line 550 of Program 9.12 computes the length of B$ + C$. Add a test to detect when B$ + C$ is too long.
9. The following BASIC program is an improved version of Program 9.4. It tests that 3571 is a prime in less than 0.5 second. Can you explain how the program works?

```
10 DEFINT A - Z
20 INPUT "INPUT NUMBER TO BE TESTED FOR BEING PRIME"; UP
30 IF UP < 2 THEN 20
40 P = 0
50 IF UP = 2 OR UP = 3 THEN GOTO 100
60 IF UP = 2 * INT(UP/2) THEN P=1  : GOTO 100
70 FOR J = 3 TO INT(SQR(UP)) STEP 2
80 IF UP = J * INT(UP/J) THEN P = 1 : J = UP
90 NEXT
100 IF P = 1 THEN PRINT UP; "IS NOT PRIME" : GOTO 20
110 PRINT UP; "IS PRIME" : GOTO 20
```

Answers

There are many correct answers to the programming questions. The answers provided here are only guidelines by which to judge your own answers.

1. We find CP r in the "Eight-bit Arithmetic and Logical Operations" group:

CP r	(2.25)	CP n	(3.95)	CP (HL)	(3.95)
CP (IX+d)	(10.71)	CP (IY+d)	(10.71)		

   CP is compare. The flags are set by CP as by the compare ROM routines (see Table 8.3).

   DJNZ label (7.89 if B not 0, 4.51 if B is 0)

   The numbers in parentheses are the execution times in microseconds (one millionth of a second).

2. We find ADD A,r in the "Eight-bit Arithmetic and Logical Operations" group: The operation ADD A,r adds register A to another register, r; the result is in register A:

   ADD A,r (2.25)

   All flags are affected.

   We find ADD HL,BC, ADD IX,BC, and SBC HL,BC in the "Sixteen-bit Arithmetic Operations" group: ADD HL,BC stores the result in HL. Only the carry flag works as in the 8-bit case; it contains the overflow. ADD IX,BC stores the result in IX. SBC HL,BC subtracts with carry (borrow) with the result in HL. The carry flag works for both.

   ADD HL,BC (6.2)   ADD IX,BC (8.46)

Flags affected: H is set if there is a carry from bit 11, reset otherwise; N is reset; C contains the carry from bit 15.

SBC HL,BC (8.46)

Flags affected: S, Z, O, C, N; H has the carry (borrow) from bit 12.

3.

```
10    EQUAL   MACRO   OUT
20            LD      A,D
30            CP      H
40            JP      NZ,OUT
50            LD      A,E
60            CP      L
70            JP      NZ,OUT
80            ENDM
```

Lines 410 to 460 can be replaced by

```
410           EQUAL   TEST
```

and lines 530 to 580 by

```
530           EQUAL   LOOP
```

4. Note that the macro we use, LOAD1, is one line shorter than the macro of Program 9.1. This change is attributable to the fact that in the first invocation we store J in the stack.

```
100           EQUATES: VARPTR, CPINT, ADDINT, BSCPAR
120   LOAD1   MACRO   WHAT          ; THIS MACRO  TAKES THE
130           LD      HL,VAR&WHAT   ; VARIABLE WHAT, GETS ITS
140           CALL    VARPTR        ; ADDRESS INTO DE
150           EX      DE,HL         ; THEN INTO HL
160           LD      C,(HL)        ; LOADS LSB OF WHAT INTO C
170           INC     HL
180           LD      B,(HL)        ; LOADS MSB OF WHAT INTO B
190           ENDM
200           ORG     7E00H
210           LOAD1   J             ;J IN BC
220           PUSH    BC            ;SAVE IT IN STACK
230           LOAD1   LO            ;LO IN BC
270           LD      (SAVELO),BC   ;STORE IT AT SAVELO
280           LOAD1   UP            ;UP IN BC
340           LD      (SAVEUP),BC   ;STORE IT AT SAVEUP
350   LOOP:   LD      HL,(SAVELO)   ;PUT LO IN HL
360           POP     DE            ;J IN DE
```

```
        CALL    ADDINT       ;LO + J IN HL
        PUSH    HL           ;SAVE NEW J
TEST:   LD      DE,(SAVELO)  ;LO IN DE
        INC     DE           ;LO = LO + 1
        LD      (SAVELO),DE  ;STORE NEW LO
        LD      HL,(SAVEUP)  ;UP INTO HL
        CALL    CPINT        ;COMPARE UP AND LO
        JP      NZ,LOOP      ;IF NOT EQUAL, CONTINUE
        LD      HL,VARJ      ;LOAD RESULT
        CALL    VARPTR       ;BACK INTO
        EX      DE,HL        ;THE VARIABLE TABLE
        POP     DE           ;FOR J
        LD      (HL),E
        INC     HL
        LD      (HL),D
FINISH: JP      BSCPAR
        DEFINE VARIABLE NAMES: J, LO, UP
SAVELO: DEFM    'LO'
SAVEUP: DEFM    'UP'
        END
```

5. Note: We add 100 first, then 99, and so on.

```
        EQUATES: VARPTR, ADDINT, BSCPAR
        ORG     7E00H
        LD      HL,VARJ
        CALL    VARPTR
        PUSH    DE
        POP     IX          ;ADDRESS OF J% IN IX
        LD      L,(IX+0)
        LD      H,(IX+1)    ;J% IN HL
        LD      B,100D      ;100D IN B (COUNTER)
        PUSH    HL          ;SAVE J%
LOOP:   LD      E,B
        LD      D,0H        ;COPY B INTO DE
        POP     HL          ;J% IN HL
        PUSH    BC          ;SAVE B (COUNTER)
        CALL    ADDINT      ;J% + COUNTER IN HL
        POP     BC          ;GET COUNTER BACK IN B
        PUSH    HL          ;SAVE RESULT
        DJNZ    LOOP
        LD      HL,VARJ
        CALL    VARPTR
        PUSH    DE          ;ADDRESS OF J%
        POP     IX          ;INTO IX
        POP     HL          ;RESULT IN HL
        LD      (IX+0),L
        LD      (IX+1),H    ;RESULT IN VARIABLE TABLE
```

```
        JP      BSCPAR
VARJ:   DEFM    'J%'
        DEFB    0
        END
```

6.

```
EQUATES: CPINT, VARPTR, BSCPAR, ADDSP, LDRAHL, LDHLSA
ADDRSS  MACRO   WHAT
        LD      HL,VAR&WHAT
        CALL    VARPTR
        ENDM
        ORG     7E00H
        ADDRSS  X0
        PUSH    DE          ;ADDRESS OF X(0) SAVED IN STACK
        ADDRSS  J
        EX      DE,HL
        CALL    LDSAHL      ;J IN SA
        ADDRSS  LO
        EX      DE,HL
        LD      C,(HL)
        INC     HL
        LD      B,(HL)      ;LO IN BC
        PUSH    BC          ;SAVED IN STACK
        ADDRSS  UP
        EX      DE,HL
        LD      E,(HL)
        INC     HL
        LD      D,(HL)      ;UP IN DE
        POP     HL          ;LO IN HL
LOOP:   EXX
        POP     HL          ;ADDRESS OF CURRENT X(LO) IN HL
        PUSH    HL          ;KEEP IT SAVED
        CALL    LDRAHL      ;AND LOAD X(LO) INTO RA
        CALL    ADDSP       ;X(LO) + PREVIOUS RESULT IN SA
        POP     HL          ;ADDRESS OF X(LO)
        INC     HL
        INC     HL
        INC     HL
        INC     HL          ;ADDRESS OF X(LO + 1)
TEST:   EXX                 ;GET LO AND UP BACK
        INC     HL          ;LO = LO + 1
        PUSH    DE
        PUSH    HL          ;SAVE LO AND UP IN STACK
        CALL    CPINT       ;COMPARE LO AND UP
        POP     HL
        POP     DE          ;GET LO AND UP BACK FROM STACK
        JP      NZ,LOOP     ;IF UNEQUAL, CONTINUE
```

```
500   FINISH: ADDRSS  J          ;ADDRESS OF J IN DE
510           EX      DE,HL      ;NOW IN HL
520           CALL    LDHLSA     ;PUT RESULT IN VARIABLE TABLE
530           JP      BSCPAR
540           DEFINE VARIABLE NAMES: J, X(0) AS X0, UP, LO
600           END
```

7.

```
500   TEST:   INC     IX         ;J = J + 1
510           LOAD    HL,IX      ;PLACE NEW J IN HL (UP IS STILL
530           CALL    CPINT      ;IN DE) COMPARE HL AND DE
580           JP      NZ,LOOP    ;CONTINUE LOOP
```

There is no measurable difference in the timing.

8. Add to Program 9.12 the following lines.

```
555           JP      C,LONG
672           LD      HL,0
682   LONG:   LD      HL,1       ;RETURN IF STRING TOO LONG
684           JP      BSCPAR
```

Add to Program 9.11 the line:

```
52 IF A% = 1 THEN PRINT "CANNOT CONCATENATE, STRING TOO LONG"
```

9. If UP is not a prime, then there is a smallest prime number K that divides UP. Thus UP can be written as UP = K *K1. Since K is the smallest number dividing UP, K1 cannot be smaller than K, and hence UP >= K * K. In other words, K does not exceed INT(SQR(UP)).

We take the case UP = 2 and UP = 3 separately in line 50. Then we check to see whether 2 divides UP; if it does, UP is not a prime. The real work starts in line 70: We look for a number dividing UP starting with 3 but taking only the odd numbers. We go up to INT(SQR(UP)).

The moral is clear: FAST BASIC is not much help if the BASIC program is not well thought out.

CHAPTER TEN

Step by Step

You press the button,
and we'll do the rest.
—Advertisement for the first Kodak camera

We have a BASIC program that runs too slowly. We want to rewrite it in FAST BASIC. What should we do?

In this chapter we summarize many of the common sense rules of Chapter 4 about speeding up BASIC programs. Then we learn how to rewrite the time-consuming parts in SIMPLE BASIC, a simplified form of BASIC that helps in the conversion to FAST BASIC. Finally, we look at various options about the placement of the machine language segments.

PRELIMINARY STEPS

The first two steps presented in this section should be carried out for every BASIC program. In Chapter 4 we discussed the reasons why these are effective.

Step 1. *Variable maintenance.* Minimize the use of single- and double-precision variables. Quite often loop counters are single precision by default; if they take only integer values, make them integer variables.

Initialize all variables at the beginning of the program. This accomplishes two goals: first, it avoids variable table reorganization during program execution; second, by initializing often used variables (primarily, loop counters) first, this minimizes the time spent on scanning variable tables.

Step 2. *Program organization.* Heavily used subroutines should be located close after the lines from which they are called, or they should be close to the beginning of the program. This suggests that line 1 should be a GOTO NN; lines 2 to NN –1 contain the subroutines that are called from many parts of the program. These subroutines should be listed in order of frequency—those that are called more often should come first. Initialize your variables starting at line NN. For instance, the BASIC disassembler (see the listing in Appendix 8) starts with GOTO 160 and variable initialization takes place in lines 164 to 182.

CONVERSION TO SIMPLE BASIC

Step 3. *Determine the parts of the BASIC program that have to be rewritten in assembly language. In these parts eliminate compound expressions, compound conditions, and compound statements.* (Such simplified program lines are said to be in SIMPLE BASIC.)

Let us pause here for a minute. Steps 1 and 2 were demonstrated in previous chapters. These are steps that should be carried out in every BASIC program. They conflict to a small extent with advice you may have been reading (some stylists prefer to place the commonly used subroutines at the end of the program) but they are effective rules based on the structure of the BASIC program.

Step 3 is different. Here it is suggested that we give up the many conveniences offered by TRS-80 BASIC and rewrite the program in a primitive BASIC. This is a very important step; *after the rewriting, the BASIC lines will correspond to small standard groups of assembly language statements.* As a result the assembly language program is debugged in BASIC!

A BASIC line is in SIMPLE BASIC if it performs a single command: It performs an arithmetic operation; it evaluates a BASIC function; it tests a single condition.

Arithmetic Expressions

Converting to SIMPLE BASIC is not too difficult. The task is completely mechanical. We are already familiar with reducing compound expressions. The line

```
10    X = (X + Y) * Z
```

is the same as the SIMPLE BASIC lines:

```
10    X = X + Y
11    X = X * Z
```

Sometimes it may be necessary to use an auxiliary variable. Hence

```
10    X = (Y1 + Y2) * (SQR(Y1) + SQR(Y2))
```

can be reduced to the SIMPLE BASIC lines:

```
10    W1 = Y1 + Y2
11    W2 = SQR(Y1)
12    W3 = SQR(Y2)
```

```
13    W2 = W2 + W3
14    X  = W1 * W2
```

In actual practice most of these auxiliary variables will not be used in the FAST BASIC version.

Compound Conditions

We continue with some examples of compound conditions.

```
10 IF X = 2 AND Y > 3 GOTO 100
20 ...
```

In SIMPLE BASIC:

```
10 IF X = 2 GOTO 15
11 GOTO 20
15 IF Y > 3 GOTO 100
20 ...
```

We have two conditions. If both are satisfied, we want program execution to be continued with line 100. The pattern is clear. We test the first condition in line 10; if it is holds, we go to line 15 and test the second condition. If either condition fails, we proceed with 20.

Consider:

```
10 IF X = 2 OR Y > 3 GOTO 100
20 ...
```

In SIMPLE BASIC:

```
10 IF X = 2 GOTO 100
11 IF Y > 3 GOTO 100
20 ...
```

This again is very simple: Two conditions connected with OR are separately tested.

Finally, we consider the NOT. Since

NOT(cond1 AND cond2)

is the same as

NOT(cond1) OR NOT(cond2)

and

NOT(cond1 OR cond2)

is the same as

NOT(cond1) AND NOT(cond2)

the rules we have so far can handle any compound conditions.

Examples

Let us practice this. X$ is a single character. We want to test whether it is a hexadecimal digit. If it is, we continue with the program; if not, we go to line 100 (error message):

```
10 IF ASC(X$) < 48 OR (ASC(X$) > 57 AND ASC(X$) < 65) OR
   ASC(X$) > 70 THEN GOTO 100
20 ...
```

In SIMPLE BASIC:

```
10 IF ASC(X$) < 48 GOTO 100 : REM FIRST TEST
12 IF ASC(X$) > 57 GOTO 14 : REM SECOND TEST, PART 1
13 GOTO 16
14 IF ASC(X$) < 65 GOTO 100 : REM SECOND TEST, PART 2
16 IF ASC(X$) > 70 GOTO 100 : REM THIRD TEST
20 ...
```

We have three conditions connected by OR, and so we have three tests. The second required three lines because it included an AND.

Observe the bad programming practice in this example. The function ASC is called four times. (See Appendix 1 for the FAST BASIC version of ASC.) We can increase the efficiency of the program by defining X% = ASC(X$) and then work with X%.

As our next example, we take

```
10 IF (X < 1 OR Y = 6) AND (Z$ = "GO" OR Z$ = "SLOW") THEN GOTO
   100
20 ...
```

In SIMPLE BASIC:

```
10 IF X < 1 GOTO 15 : REM FIRST TEST, PART 1
11 IF Y = 6 GOTO 15 : REM FIRST TEST, PART 2
12 GOTO 20
15 IF Z$ = "GO" GOTO 100 : REM SECOND TEST, PART 1
16 IF Z$ = "SLOW" GOTO 100 : REM SECOND TEST, PART 2
20 ...
```

Conditions as Expressions

There is an alternative way to handle compound conditions. To illustrate this we rewrite line 10 of the last example:

```
10 X% = (X < 1 OR Y = 6) AND (Z$ = "GO" OR Z$ = "SLOW")
11 IF X% THEN GOTO 100
```

and handle line 10 as a compound expression.

Compound Statements

Compound statements are easier to handle:

```
10 IF X > 3 THEN PRINT X : X = X + 1 : RETURN
20 ...
```

In SIMPLE BASIC:

```
10 IF X > 3 GOTO 15
11 GOTO 20
15 PRINT X
16 X = X + 1
17 RETURN
20 ...
```

In an IF . . . THEN . . . ELSE statement the commands following the ELSE should be put in the next line; this eliminates the ELSE.

It is suggested that the conversion from BASIC to SIMPLE BASIC be done one step at a time. With a little practice converting to SIMPLE BASIC becomes a routine task. Take care to number the lines of the BASIC program to leave room for the additional lines of SIMPLE BASIC.

A Complex Example

It is a dangerous practice to put conditional statements within conditional statements; the Interpreter follows some undocumented rules, thus making the outcome somewhat unpredictable. (See Review Question 1 for some examples.)

However, we may have to unravel such BASIC lines when we translate into FAST BASIC a program we find in some magazines or books. The following example is from Appendix H of the Level II BASIC Manual (lines are renumbered).

```
100 IF W$ <> CHR$(8) THEN 200 ELSE IF WL% = 0 THEN 80 ELSE PRINT
    CHR$(24); : IF FL > 0 THEN 180 ELSE IF PEEK(16418) = 43 THEN
    190
150 ...
```

First, we get rid of the first ELSE:

```
100 IF W$ <> CHR$(8) THEN 200
110 IF WL% = 0 THEN 80 ELSE PRINT CHR$(24); : IF FL > 0 THEN 180
    ELSE IF PEEK(16418) = 43 THEN 190
```

Now we get rid of the second ELSE, which is a compound statement:

```
100 IF W$ <> CHR$(8) THEN 200
110 IF WL% = 0 THEN 80
120 PRINT CHR$(24); : IF FL > 0 THEN 180 ELSE IF PEEK(16418) = 43
    THEN 190
```

Next we break up the compound statement in line 120 and eliminate the ELSE:

```
100 IF W$ <> CHR$(8) THEN 200
110 IF WL% = 0 THEN 80
120 PRINT CHR$(24);
130 IF FL > 0 THEN 180
140 IF PEEK(16418) = 43 THEN 190
150 ...
```

If you can understand this conversion, you are already an expert.

CONVERSION FROM SIMPLE BASIC TO MACHINE LANGUAGE

Step 4. *Rewrite the SIMPLE BASIC lines into assembly language.* The comments in the assembly language program should reference the SIMPLE BASIC line numbers.

As a rule each SIMPLE BASIC line becomes a small group of assembly language lines. There are some exceptions: FOR NEXT loops change into one of the schemes discussed in Chapter 9. Another exception surfaced in Chapter 9: Three consecutive BASIC lines of the type

```
100 C = Y
110 Y = X
120 X = C
```

swap the variables X and Y; the FAST BASIC translation swaps the values of X and Y for numeric variables and the lengths and addresses for string variables (C is not used).

Some other techniques for improving the FAST BASIC program have been demonstrated in the examples. For instance, do not put the result of a computation back into the variable table if it is needed in the next line. The address of a variable used often should be located only once and then stored for future use.

Macros as Building Blocks

In most programs we find that there is a limited number of types of SIMPLE BASIC lines. By introducing the appropriate macros, the assembly language listing will not be much longer than the SIMPLE BASIC listing. And remember, once you have worked out these macros they can be used in any future FAST BASIC program.

Here is an example borrowed from Chapter 8. In Program 8.4 the following lines add two variables and store the result in the variable table.

```
210          LD      HL,VARX    ;LOOKING FOR X
220          CALL    VARPTR     ;DE POINTS AT X
230          EX      DE,HL      ;NOW HL POINTS AT X
240          CALL    LDSAHL     ;LOAD X INTO SA
300          LD      HL,VARY    ;LOOKING FOR Y
310          CALL    VARPTR     ;ADDRESS IN DE
320          EX      DE,HL      ;NOW HL POINTS AT Y
330          CALL    LDRAHL     ;Y INTO RA
400          CALL    ADDSP      ;CALL SINGLE PRECISION ADDITION
500          LD      HL,VARZ    ;LOOKING FOR Z
510          CALL    VARPTR     ;ADDRESS IN DE
520          EX      DE,HL      ;HL POINTS AT Z
530          CALL    LDHLSA     ;LOAD RESULT INTO VARIABLE TABLE
```

We can easily make a macro out of this.

```
200   ADD    MACRO   A1, A2, R ;ADDS A1 AND A2, R IS THE RESULT
210          LD      HL,VAR&A1 ;LOOKING FOR A1
220          CALL    VARPTR    ;DE POINTS AT A1
230          EX      DE,HL     ;NOW HL POINTS AT A1
240          CALL    LDSAHL    ;LOAD A1 INTO SA
300          LD      HL,VAR&A2 ;LOOKING FOR A2
310          CALL    VARPTR    ;ADDRESS IN DE
320          EX      DE,HL     ;NOW HL POINTS AT A2
330          CALL    LDRAHL    ;Y INTO RA
400          CALL    ADDSP     ;CALL SINGLE PRECISION ADDITION
500          LD      HL,VAR&R  ;LOOKING FOR R
510          CALL    VARPTR    ;ADDRESS IN DE
520          EX      DE,HL     ;HL POINTS AT R
530          CALL    LDHLSA    ;LOAD RESULT INTO VARIABLE TABLE
540          ENDM
```

Once we have this macro, the BASIC line

```
Z = X + Y
```

translates into

```
ADD X,Y,Z
```

and the BASIC line

```
U = U + W2
```

becomes

```
ADD U,U,W2
```

Of course, we can have many variants of such a macro handy. For instance, we may not want to put the result back in the variable table. So we can have a macro ADD1 A1,A2 that leaves the result in SA. ADD1 can be obtained from ADD by deleting lines 500 to 530.

The important thing is that, as a rule, we need rather few of these macros, and each macro has to be thought out only once.

PACKING MACHINE LANGUAGE PROGRAMS INTO VARIABLES

Step 5. *Decide where to put the machine language programs.*

In all the examples we placed the machine language programs starting at $7E00_H$. In a 48K computer we may start them at $FE00_H$. To change the starting address we only have to change the ORG statement and we can assemble the required version.

Changing the ORG

If you recall, Program 7.1 was a simple loop. The listing of Program 10.1 shows Program 7.1 assembled twice, once with ORG 7E00H and once with ORG 0FE00H.

Program 10.1.

```
7E00 21B80B      INIT   LD    HL,3000D    FE00 21B80B
7E03 2B          LOOP   DEC   HL          FE03 2B
7E04 7C          CHECK  LD    A,H         FE04 7C
7E05 B5                 OR    L           FE05 B5
7E06 C2037E             JP    NZ,LOOP     FE06 C203FE
7E09 C9          DONE   RET               FE09 C9
0000                    END
00000 TOTAL ERRORS


CHECK  7E04 130                           FE04
DONE   7E09 160                           FE09
INIT   7E00 110                           FE00
LOOP   7E03 120  150                      FE03
```

The assembly at $7E00_H$ is the first two columns; the assembly at $FE00_H$ is the last two columns. The assembly of lines 110 to 140 does not change at all. But the old assembly of line 150 is C2037E whereas that of the new is C203FE. This is easy to understand; the first byte of the two assemblies is the same — C2, the code for jump on nonzero (JP NZ). The next 2 bytes tell where to jump: 037E is the address 7E03 and 03FE is the address FE03. And this is the only difference between the two assemblies.

We can summarize this as follows. Changing the ORG in line 100 effects two changes:

1. It changes the address where the first byte is to be loaded (this information is utilized by the loader that moves the machine language program from cassette or disk to memory).
2. It changes all labels (not defined by an EQU) that represent locations and, as a result, it changes all jumps (JP), subroutine calls (CALL), and all other instructions utilizing such a label (or a reference to the current location, $ in most assemblers) such as LD HL, VARTX in line 210 of Program 9.7.

If we can devise our own "loader" (the program that loads the machine language program into memory), then the first change is unimportant. The second change can be minimized by replacing jump (JP) by "jump relative" (JR). This is very simple. Replace in all lines

JP label   JP C,label   JP NC,label   JP Z,label   JP NZ,label

by

JR label   JR C,label   JR NC,label   JR Z,label   JR NZ,label

Such an instruction is coded by telling PC how far ahead or back it has to jump (the "displacement"). This information is stored as an 8-bit signed integer, so we cannot jump too far. The range of a signed integer is –128 to 127. All jump relatives are 2-byte instructions, and so when they are executed PC has already been incremented by 2. Thus the furthest we can go back is $-128 + 2 = -126$, and the furthest we can go ahead is $127 + 2 = 129$. This is more than enough for FAST BASIC.

Relocatability

A machine language program is "relocatable" if it excludes all instructions using a label (not defined by an EQU) that refer to a location in the program, with the exception of jump relative. Program 10.2 shows the relocatable version of Program 10.1 (Program 7.1) assembled at $7E00_H$ and $FE00_H$. Notice that, apart from the loading addresses, the two programs are identical.

Program 10.2.

```
7E00 21B80B    110    INIT:    LD      HL,3000D     FE00 21B808
7E03 2B        120    LOOP:    DEC     HL           FE03 2B
7E04 7C        130    CHECK:   LD      A,H          FE04 7C
7E05 B5        140             OR      L            FE05 B5
7E06 20FB      150             JR      NZ,LOOP      FE06 20FB
7E08 C9        160    DONE:    RET                  FE08 C9
0000           170             END
00000 TOTAL ERRORS


CHECK    7E04 130                                   FE04
DONE     7E08 160                                   FE08
INIT     7E00 110                                   FE00
LOOP     7E03 120    150                            FE03
```

Program 10.3 gives us the loader in BASIC.

Program 10.3.

```
90 X# = 32256
100 FOR I = 0 TO 8
110 READ X% : POKE X# + I, X%
120 NEXT
200 DATA 33, 184, 11, 43, 124, 181, 32, 251, 201
```

In line 90, 32256 is $FE00_H$. In line 210 the statement DATA 33, 184, 11, . . . was read from the hex conversion table (Appendix 5) as the decimal equivalent of the program 21, B8, 0B, . . . We can add the lines of Program 10.3 to any BASIC program and it will POKE into memory the machine language program.

Now comes the fun. Let us agree that we call BASIC protecting enough memory for this program. Replace line 90 of Program 10.3 by

```
90 X# = PEEK(16562)*256 + PEEK(16561) + 1 : IF X# > 32267 THEN
   X# = -1*(65536 - X#)
```

This computes (see Table 3.2) where it is safe to load the program and will load it there. [Remember: (1) Use the same X# when defining the starting address of the USR! (2) Test X# as to whether there is enough room to POKE in the program.]

Now we have achieved true relocatability!

Variable Packing

The way we have been implementing FAST BASIC has a disadvantage: We must protect memory and load a machine language program into the protected area. An alternative is to POKE the machine language program into some other areas we can protect: a string variable, an array variable, or the BASIC program text.

The 9 bytes of Program 10.2 can easily be POKEd into a string variable. First we define the string by adding to Program 10.3 a new line:

```
80 A$ = "123456789"
```

The length of A$ is the number of bytes in the machine language program. And we replace in Program 10.3 line 90 by

```
90 X1# = VARPTR(A$) : X# = PEEK(X1# + 2)*256 + PEEK(X1# + 1) :
   IF X# > 32267 THEN X# = -1*(65536 - X#)
```

This BASIC line uses the formula we learned in Chapter 4 to locate the string A$.

This method has one disadvantage: If we POKE 00_H or 22_H into a string, BREAK the program, and RUN it again, we get a syntax error message when the line containing the string is executed. (Reason: For the Interpreter 00_H and 22_H indicate the end of the string. The bytes following the terminator cannot be interpreted properly, thus causing the syntax error.) This trouble does not arise if the line containing the string follows the END of the program.

If a string variable does not have enough room, dimension an integer array, say W%, to (number of required bytes)/2. The corresponding line 90 in Program 10.3 is

```
90 X# = VARPTR(W%(0)) : IF X# > 32267 THEN X# = -1*(65536 - X#)
```

In fact, one integer array can contain any number of USRs, one starting at 0, the next at 12, and so on.

Remember (see Chapter 4) that variables may move during program execution, if they are not *all* initialized at the beginning of the program (as suggested in Step 1). So, to be on the safe side, POKE the starting address (DEFUSR) before *each* call to the USR.

Storing machine language programs into a string variable or into a numeric variable array has a big advantage for disk users: The machine language program can easily be saved into a disk file. When needed, recover it from the disk. The POKEing routine is no longer needed and can be deleted from the BASIC program.

Packing into the Text

Finally, let us put the machine language program in the BASIC text. Let us start the BASIC program with

```
10  REM JUST FILLING IN
```

As we discussed in Chapter 4,

```
X1# = PEEK(16548) + PEEK(16549)*256
```

is the starting address of the BASIC program (see also Table 3.1) and PEEK(X1#), PEEK(X1# + 1) are the LSB and MSB of the start of the next line. Thus in Program 10.3 replace line 90 by

```
90 X1% = PEEK(16548) : X2% = PEEK(16549) : X# = X1% + X2%*256 :
   IF X# > 32267 THEN X# = -1*(65536 - X#) : POKE 16548, PEEK(X#)
   : POKE 16459, PEEK(X# + 1)
```

This will make the address that designates the start of the BASIC program point at the second line. X1% and X2% should be POKEd into $408E_H$ (16526_D) and $408F_H$ (16527_D, see Table 3.2) as the start of the USR.

Conclusion

As you see, there are many places you can put the machine language programs needed to run a FAST BASIC program. Which one should you choose?

If the machine language programs are long, LOAD (CLOAD) them first. POKEing in a long program is time consuming. There are two disadvantages to loading machine language programs:

1. In Disk BASIC we have to get out of BASIC to do it and in a cassette system the procedure is time consuming.
2. We have to remember to reserve space at power-up (or when BASIC is called).

Various remedies are available for these, for instance, operating systems that let you load a machine language program in BASIC and that set up a reserved area automatically. (The Model III disk system has these features. Programs that modify the Model I to have these features are widely available.)

If the machine language programs are short, you should consider packing them into a string variable or in a REM in the text. This has the advantage that after the program is packed, you can delete the lines that did the POKEing and SAVE (CSAVE) the program, and you do not have to POKE ever again.

FINAL HINTS

The hints in this final section call your attention to a few things that a FAST BASIC programmer should always keep in mind.

Variables

In a FAST BASIC program we often store variables in the stack, in special areas set up for storing variables, in RA, and so on. Always remember to send all the variables back to the BASIC tables before returning to BASIC.

Debugging

If your machine language routine needs debugging, proceed as follows: Put a STOP in your BASIC program just before the USR is called. When the program STOPs call in your machine language monitor (for a discussion of monitors see Appendix 7). For instance, DEBUG in a disk system is activated by CMD "D". Now you can single-step the machine language program in the exact environment in which it is supposed to be running.

Syntax Error

Suppose you call the USR in line 100 of the BASIC program. On return from the USR the BASIC program is aborted with the ERROR message:

```
SYNTAX ERROR IN LINE 100
```

Most embarrassing! Line 100 is only A = USR(0), and so how could there be a syntax error?

The most likely explanation is that you returned to BASIC with RET and not with JP BSCPAR. However, other errors in a machine language program can cause a syntax error on return. Thus, if you get a SYNTAX ERROR on return, check your machine language program and not the BASIC program.

No Return

Quite often, after the call to the USR the program hangs up, and it never returns to BASIC. The following checklist shows some of the causes of a no return.

1. Typing error in an EQU. If your program does not return, first check the EQUs with the listing in Appendix 6. A single typing error in an EQU will send the machine language program beyond recovery.
2. Stack not restored. Make sure that, when concluding a sub-

routine CALL, the stack is in the same condition as it was when the CALL was made. We discussed this with the USR itself: When returning to BASIC the BASIC stack should be the same as it was at entry. The same care should be observed with all CALLs.

3. Save registers. CALLs may change registers. Make sure you save all needed registers before a CALL is made. Restore the registers after the CALL. Remember, the order of POPs is the reverse of the order of the PUSHes.
4. USR not found. The USR is stored in a variable (array) and the starting address is POKEd in (DEFUSR). If a new variable is encountered during program execution before the USR is invoked, then the variable (array) containing the USR is not where we assume it to be. Execution will transfer to an area of the memory that contains data and not the USR.

   The same trouble will occur if we store the USR in the program text and the starting address of the USR is defined as a number. Any change in the program text or the use of a different operating system will cause a "USR not found." Always use pointers to the text as a reference point for the starting address to the USR.

Review and Programming Practice

1. If you think that you understand how IF THEN is handled by the Interpreter, try the following test. Type in the following three short BASIC programs.

   (a)

```
10 A = 1
20 IF A = 0.1.0 THEN HANAHAAH ELSE PRINT "WHOOPS!"
30 STOP
```

   (b)

```
10 A = 1
20 Y = 3
30 IF A = 1 THEN IF Y = 2 PRINT "WRONG" ELSE PRINT "RIGHT ELSE":
   ELSE PRINT "WRONG ELSE"
```

   (c)

```
10 A$ = "X"
20 IF A$ = "Y"Z THEN GOTO 50 ELSE GOTO 50
30 PRINT "LINE 20 IS IGNORED"
40 END
50 PRINT "LINE 20 NOT IGNORED"
```

RUN these programs. Can you predict the computer's responses?

2. Modify a BASIC program to print a report on the frequency of subroutine use.
3. Rewrite in SIMPLE BASIC (next line is line 20):

```
10 X = (X1 * X2) * (X1 + X3) - X1
```

4. Rewrite in SIMPLE BASIC (next line is line 20):

```
10 X = (SQR(X1) + X2) * (X1 - X2)
```

5. Rewrite in SIMPLE BASIC (next line is line 20):

```
10 IF X1 + X2 > X1 * X2 THEN X1 = X1 * X2 ELSE X1 = X1 + X2
```

6. Rewrite in SIMPLE BASIC (next line is line 20):

```
10 IF X > 0 THEN GOSUB 90 : PRINT X : ELSE GOSUB 100 :
   PRINT X * X
```

7. Rewrite in SIMPLE BASIC (next line is line 20):

```
10 IF X1 * X2 > 5 OR X1 * X2 < 6 THEN GOTO 50
```

8. Rewrite in SIMPLE BASIC (next line is line 20):

```
10 IF X1 * X2 > 5 AND X1 * X2 < 6 THEN GOTO 50
```

9. Rewrite in SIMPLE BASIC: (next line is line 20):

```
10 IF PEEK(16418) = 46 THEN WD = 0 : GOTO 135 ELSE IF PEEK(16418)
   = 43 OR PEEK(16418) = 45 THEN WS = 0
```

Answers

There are many correct answers to the programming questions. The answers provided here are only guidelines by which to judge your own answers.

1. (a) WHOOPS!
   (b) RIGHT ELSE
   (c) LINE 20 IS IGNORED
2. At the beginning of each subroutine put in a counter. At the end of the program print out the counters.
3.

```
10 Y = X1 + X2
11 X = X1 + X3
12 X = Y * X
13 X = X - X1
```

4.

```
10 X = SQR(X1)
11 X = X + X2
12 Y = X1 - X2
13 X = X * Y
```

5.

```
10 Y = X1 + X2
11 Z = X1 * X2
12 IF Y > Z THEN 14
13 X1 = X1 + X2
14 GOTO 20
15 X1 = X1 * X2
```

6.

```
10 IF X > 0 THEN 14
11 GOSUB 100
12 Y = X + X
13 PRINT Y
14 GOSUB 90
15 PRINT X
```

7.

```
10 Y = X1 * X2
11 IF Y > 5 THEN GOTO 50
12 IF Z < 6 THEN GOTO 50
```

8.

```
10 Y = X1 * X2
11 IF Y > 5 THEN GOTO 13
12 GOTO 20
13 IF Y< 6 THEN GOTO 50
```

9.

```
10 Y = PEEK(16418)
11 IF Y = 46 THEN GOTO 15
12 IF Y = 43 THEN GOTO 18
13 IF Y = 45 THEN GOTO 18
14 GOTO 20
15 WD = 0
16 GOTO 135
17 GOTO 20
18 WS = 0
```

CHAPTER ELEVEN

Enhancing FAST BASIC

There are more things
in heaven and earth, Horatio,
Than are dreamt of
in your philosophy.

—W. Shakespeare in *Hamlet*

We have to learn very few machine language instructions to be able to convert from BASIC to FAST BASIC. We should remember, however, that the Z-80 microprocessor has a large and powerful set of instructions. In this chapter we show how the power of some additional instructions can be utilized to enhance FAST BASIC.

By enhancing FAST BASIC we can carry out tasks that *cannot* be done, practically, in BASIC, and we can further speed up FAST BASIC programs.

BLOCK TRANSFER AND BLOCK SEARCH

The Z-80 instructions we learn in this chapter help greatly in keeping the machine language routines short; some of them also make these routines very fast. Two stars of the Z-80 instruction set—the block transfer, LDIR, and the block search, CPIR—illustrate both the brevity and the speed they can lend to a routine.

Block Transfer

The block transfer instruction moves a whole block of data to a new location. We have to specify the start address of the block (load it into HL), the start address of the location where the block is to be moved (load this into DE, the *d*estination address), and the number of bytes to be transferred (load this into BC, the *b*yte *c*ounter). Here is a simple illustration of the use of LDIR (in the next two examples we assume a 32K system, and BASIC MEMORY SIZE is 45000; this leaves more than 3,000 bytes for storage).

We stored at the address SAVE, in 1024_D bytes, a picture or text we want to put on the video display (which starts at VIDEO = $3C00_H$). Program 11.1 does this.

Program 11.1. Show

```
100     VIDEO   EQU     3C00H
110     SAVE    EQU     0B100H
120     BSCPAR  EQU     0A9AH
130             ORG     0B000H
140             LD      HL,SAVE    ;HL POINTS TO START OF BLOCK TO
150                                ;BE TRANSFERRED
160             LD      DE, VIDEO  ;DE POINTS WHERE TO TRANSFER
170             LD      BC, 1024D  ;BC COUNTS HOW MANY BYTES TO
180                                ;TRANSFER
190             LDIR
200             JP      BSCPAR
210             END
```

LDIR will transfer the picture to the video display in 12.12 milliseconds! Thus we can execute more than 82 such transfers in a second. The reverse procedure is done by Program 11.2. It stores, at the address SAVE, what is shown on the video display.

Program 11.2. Stash

```
100     VIDEO   EQU     3C00H
110     SAVE    EQU     0B100H
120     BSCPAR  EQU     0A9AH
130             ORG     0B0A0H
140             LD      HL,VIDEO
150             LD      DE,SAVE
160             LD      BC,1024D
170             LDIR
180             JP      BSCPAR
190             END
```

Both of these routines can be used very effectively to display a company logo, to store (or recall) a drawing made on the video display, etc. A useful application is to combine Programs 11.1 and 11.2; USR(1) to USR(6) should store the video display to SAVE1 through to SAVE6, and USR(7) through USR(12) should call these back.

Here is our program plan. We start the assembly language program with JP GETPAR; this will put the parameter, the integer 1 to 12, in register L. We use the instruction CP L to compare register A with L. First, load 6 in A and CP L; if 6 is smaller than the contents of L, then the flag C is set. On C we jump to Program 11.2; otherwise we continue with Program 11.1.

One more detail needs attention: If SAVE2 = SAVE1 + 1024D, etc., then we test whether L is 1; if not, then we add (L) – 1 times 1024D to SAVE1. Since we cannot add to DE, SAVE first has to be loaded into HL, 1024D in BC, and then we perform ADD HL,BC as many times as necessary. Now EX DE,HL and proceed as in Program 11.2. When we proceed to Program 11.1 we have to subtract 6 from L. The instruction SUB 6 subtracts 6 from register A (there is no subtract instruction for L).

Scrolling

An alternative use of LDIR is to scroll only a portion of the video display. Here is a typical example.

The user of the program has to answer a series of questions. The questions are displayed on line 9 of the video display. Responding by "HELP" provides useful information in lines 1 to 8. However, eight lines are not always enough to display this text. Pressing @ scrolls lines 1 to 8, that is, moves lines 2 to 8 up to lines 1 to 7, and displays the next line of information on line 8.

Program 11.3 does the scrolling.

Program 11.3. Scrolling

```
VIDEO    EQU     3C00H
BSCPAR   EQU     0A9AH
         ORG     7E00H
         LD      HL,VIDEO
         LD      DE,VIDEO + 64D
         LD      BC, 448D   ;7 X 64 = 448
         LDIR
         JP      BSCPAR
         END
```

After Program 11.3 does the scrolling, we do

```
PRINT @448, CHR$(30)
```

in the BASIC program (this clears line 8) and then print on line 8 a line of text. Do not forget to close the BASIC print statement with ";" to avoid unintended scrolling.

Although this scrolling could still be done in BASIC, the machine language version is much faster. Moreover, the same technique can be applied to scroll any portion of the video display or to scroll many portions independently. This is almost impossible to accomplish in BASIC.

Block Search

The search version of LDIR is CPIR. It searches through a block of memory for the byte in register A. HL points to the start of the area to be searched and BC contains the number of bytes to be searched. The instruction is terminated if the byte is found or if the search is finished. If the byte is found, the zero flag is set (= 1) and HL points at the byte *following* the matching byte; otherwise the zero flag is reset (= 0).

A good illustration of the use of CPIR is the enhanced FAST BASIC version of the FIND command of VIEW/MOD presented in Chapter 12.

OTHER USEFUL INSTRUCTIONS

Many other Z-80 instructions can aid us in writing compact machine language subroutines for FAST BASIC.

Shift

To split an 8-bit number into two 4-bit numbers we can use the "shift" group of instructions. For any 8-bit register, r, the instruction SLA r will shift the bits of register r: Bit 7 goes to the carry flag, bits 6 to 0 go to bits 7 to 1, and bit 0 is reset (= 0). For instance, if register B contains 0101 0101, then after SLA B the carry flag is reset, and B contains 1010 1010.

SRL r shifts bit 0 to C, shifts bits 7 to 1 to bits 6 to 0, and resets bit 7 (= 0). Thus if A contains 0101 1100, then after executing SLA A four times A will contain 1100 0000. If, instead, we execute SRL A four times, then A will contain 0000 0101.

BIT and SET

We check the readiness of a device (see Chapter 5) by testing whether a particular bit of a byte is 0 or 1. We can do this by masking (see Chapter 1) and checking the zero flag. Better yet, we can use the luxury of the instruction

```
BIT n,r
```

This instruction puts in the zero flag the complement of bit n of an 8-bit register r. For instance, if register A contains 0101 0101, then BIT 0,A resets the zero flag, while BIT 1,A sets the zero flag. There are also instructions (SET) that set a particular bit of a register or memory location.

Although none of these bit manipulation instructions—and the many more discussed in Appendix 2—are needed for FAST BASIC, they do make life easier if you choose to use them.

Graphics

The bit manipulation instructions are especially useful in doing graphics. Let us recall that, in TRS-80 BASIC, there are two ways to do graphics. The video screen displays 64 × 16 = 1024 locations; these locations are numbered 0 to 1023 (0 to 63 in the first line, 64 to 123 in the second, etc.). The instruction PRINT @X, CHR$(Y) prints at location X the character of code Y. Codes 128 to 191 are the graphics codes (see Appendix C of the TRS-80 Manual).

Each location is divided into six graphics blocks as shown in Figure 11.1.

The code of a graphics character is an 8-bit integer. Bit 7 (the high-order bit) is 1, indicating that this is a graphics code; bit 6 is not used; bits 5, 4, 3, 2, 1, and 0 are set if block 5, 4, 3, 2, 1, and 0 are to be turned on. Thus 1000 0000 = 128_D is the blank and 1011 1111 = 191_D turns all blocks on, forming a rectangle.

An alternative way of turning graphics blocks on and off is provided by the SET and RESET instructions of BASIC. These consider the video display as a 128 × 48 grid of graphics blocks, numbered horizontally 0 to 127 and vertically 0 to 47. SET(12,3) turns on [and RESET(12,3) turn off] block 3 in row 12. On checking the video display worksheet in Appendix C of the TRS-80 Manual, we find that this is block 1 of location 257. Thus SET(12,3) and PRINT @257, CHR$(130) accomplish the same, provided that all the other blocks at location 257 were turned off. [Note that SET(12,3) and RESET(12,3) affect only one graphics block whereas PRINT @257, CHR$(130) affects six blocks.]

PRINT @257, CHR$(130) turns readily into two Z-80 instructions:

```
LD      HL,VIDEO + 257D
LD      (HL),130D
```

This explains why graphics can be so fast in enhanced FAST BASIC. Let us write a number of versions of the program that draws 16 thin horizontal lines on the video display.

Block 0	Block 1
Block 2	Block 3
Block 4	Block 5

FIGURE 11.1. Graphics Blocks

Program 11.4.

```
100 FOR X% = 2 TO 47 STEP 3
110 FOR Y% = 0 TO 127
120 SET(Y%,X%)
130 NEXT
140 NEXT
```

Program 11.5.

```
100 FOR X% = 0 TO 1023
110 PRINT @X%, CHR$(176);
120 NEXT
```

Program 11.6.

```
90 CLEAR 200
100 FOR X% = 0 TO 960 STEP 64
110 PRINT @X%, STRING$(64,CHR$(176));
120 NEXT
```

Program 11.7.

```
100 FOR X% = 15360 TO 16383
110 POKE X%, 176
120 NEXT
```

Program 11.8.

(Disk BASIC)

```
100 POKE 16526, 0 : POKE 16527, 126  (DEFUSR = &H7E00)
110 X = USR(0)
```

Program 11.9 is the USR called by Program 11.8.

Program 11.9.

```
100    VIDEO    EQU    3C00H
120    BSCPAR   EQU    0A9AH
130             ORG    7E00H
140             LD     BC,1024D   ;BC IS THE COUNTER
150             LD     HL,VIDEO
160    LOOP:    LD     (HL),176D  ;WRITING THE GRAPHICS CHARACTER
170             INC    HL         ;UPDATE POINTER
180             DEC    BC         ;DECREMENTING COUNTER
190             LD     A,C        ;TESTING IF
200             OR     B          ;COUNTER IS ZERO
210             JR     NZ,LOOP    ;IF NOT, CONTINUE
220             JP     BSCPAR     ;ELSE WE ARE FINISHED
230             END
```

Here are some timing comparisons.

BASIC Program 11.4	12 seconds
BASIC Program 11.5	8 seconds
BASIC Program 11.6	0.8 second
BASIC Program 11.7	6 seconds
Enhanced FAST BASIC (Programs 11.8 and 11.9)	0.2 second

The conclusion is obvious: By using LD (HL),n-type instructions, graphics become exceedingly fast on the TRS-80. However, for drawing lines of the same graphics character code, STRING$ is only four times slower.

Graphics in BASIC

The foregoing discussion may also help us understand why SET(X,Y) and RESET(X,Y) are so slow. The *only* way the TRS-80 computer can do graphics is with the LD instruction. Thus if we use the BASIC instruction SET(X,Y), then it has to be converted into a load instruction. How is it done?

Say, we want to do SET(63,16).

1. Since vertically there are three graphics blocks in a location, our graphics block is in line INT(16/3) = 5 (the first line is line 0).
2. The remainder in the division 16/3 is 1, so our graphics block is in "line 1" (the second from above) in the location. (Note also that dividing by 3 is more time consuming than dividing by 2.)
3. In line 5 we are in position INT(63/2) = 31, so our location is 31 + 5*64 = 351.
4. The remainder 1 in the division 63/2 means that our graphics block is to the right of the location.
5. Second from above and to the right is block 3. Thus SET(63,16) sets bit 3 of memory location $15360_D + 351_D = 15711_D = 3D5F_H$.

Thus SET(63,16) is

```
LD      HL,3D5FH
SET     3,(HL)
```

The time needed to execute these two machine language instructions (see Appendix 2) is about 12.4 microseconds (1 microsecond is one millionth of a second). Therefore, we can carry out in a second 80,645 such instruction pairs. In contrast, TRS-80 BASIC can only do the SET(X,Y) instructions about 120 times per second!

A Machine Language Trick

One minor technical problem arises: Having figured out that we want to execute a SET n,(HL) and the value of n is in register A, how do we instruct the computer? The easy but cumbersome way is to have all SET 0,(HL) to SET 7,(HL) instructions handy and choose the one we need by comparing A with 0 to 7.

It is much faster to utilize the fact that the code for SET n,(HL) is 2 bytes: The first byte is CB; the second, in binary, is 11ppp110, where ppp is the binary form of n (see Appendix 3). Perform RLC A three times (to get n into bits 3 to 5), OR the result with 11000110 = $C6_H$, and load this number into the second byte of the instruction.

To sum up, use POKEs, PRINT @, and STRING$ to do graphics in TRS-80 BASIC. If these will not do the job, then do your graphics in enhanced FAST BASIC in machine language subroutines with LD (HL),n or with SET n,(HL), RESET n,(HL). In FAST BASIC try to rewrite the program, avoiding the use of the BASIC functions SET(X,Y) and RESET(X,Y). If this cannot be done, rewrite the BASIC program into machine language line by line using the procedure given in Chapter 10. (See Appendix 1 for the ROM routine GRAPH.)

EXTENDING TRS-80 BASIC

In BASIC, when we want to clear the screen, we simply invoke the command CLS; there is no need for POKEs and a USR call. Would it not be nice to have our own BASIC keywords for our machine language subroutines?

The Keyword Jump Table

To understand how to do this, first we should take a look at Table 11.1. When the Interpreter comes across a keyword that is not a TRS-80 BASIC keyword, execution is transferred to a RAM address as shown in Table 11.1. In TRS-80 BASIC, each 3-byte area contains the same instruction: Jump to a ROM address ($012D_H$) that will write "L3 ERROR" on the screen. In Disk BASIC these are replaced by jumps to where the subroutines executing these instructions are located.

For a cassette system these jump addresses provide the ideal way of extending TRS-80 BASIC to include Level III, as well as new, commands.

Unfortunately, only NAME is unused in Disk BASIC, and in the newest version even NAME was given a function (to renumber). Thus we have to look somewhere else for customized BASIC keywords for a disk system.

TABLE 11.1. BASIC Keyword Jump Table

Hex	Decimal	Instruction
4152–4154	16722–16724	CVI
4155–4157	16725–16727	FN
4158–415A	16728–16730	CVS
415B–415D	16731–16733	DEF
415E–4160	16734–16736	CVD
4161–4163	16737–16739	EOF
4164–4166	16740–16742	LOC
4167–4169	16743–16745	LOF
416A–416C	16746–16748	MKI
416D–416F	16749–16751	MKS
4170–4172	16752–16754	MKD
4173–4175	16755–16757	CMD
4176–4178	16758–16760	TIME
4179–417B	16761–16763	OPEN
417C–417E	16764–16766	FIELD
417F–4181	16767–16769	GET
4182–4184	16770–16772	PUT
4185–4187	16773–16775	CLOSE
4188–418A	16776–16778	LOAD
418B–418D	16779–16781	MERGE
418E–4190	16782–16784	NAME
4191–4193	16785–16787	KILL
4197–419A	16791–16793	LSET
419A–419C	16794–16796	RSET
419D–419F	16797–16799	INSTR
41A0–41A2	16800–16802	SAVE
41A3–41A5	16803–16805	LINE

ERTRAP

The implementation we give is modeled after the plan advocated by J. Commander [in issue 7 (1980) of *80Microcomputing*].

The key is provided by the way the Interpreter handles a syntax error. By way of an example, let us assume that we want to introduce the BASIC keywords SHOW and STASH. When STASH is encountered in a BASIC line Program 11.2 should be invoked, to save in memory what is shown on the video display, whereas SHOW should invoke Program 11.1 to display what was previously saved.

Table 11.2 shows the memory locations that help us in implementing this plan.

When the Interpreter encounters SHOW or STASH it will decide that there is a syntax error. There are two kinds of error messages: short ones in TRS-80 BASIC and long ones in Disk BASIC. To decide which error message is available the Interpreter executes a CALL ERTRAP.

As mentioned earlier, the location ERTRAP contains a return in TRS-80 BASIC, whereas in Disk BASIC there is a jump (via a RST instruction) to the long message. We intercept the Interpreter at this point with Program 11.10.

TABLE 11.2.

Label	Value	Type	Explanation
ERTRAP	41A6	EQU	Error processing jumps here; this contains RET in TRS-80 BASIC and a jump (through a RST) to the long error message routine in Disk BASIC
ERCODE	409A	EQU	The error code is stored here; if this location is not 00_H, the line number in which the error occurred will be printed after the BASIC READY prompt and BASIC goes into editing mode
BSCSTM	40E6	EQU	Pointer to the terminator (the end of line 00_H byte or a ":") of the last executed BASIC statement is at this address
RUNSTM	1D1E	JP	HL points at a ":" terminating a BASIC statement or at a byte 00_H terminating a line; execution will proceed from the next statement

Here is the plan.

1. *Initialize*. We save all registers. They will be needed when we exit.
2. *Check for syntax error*. Register E contains the error code. We check to see if it is 2. If it is not, the error is not a syntax error, so it was not caused by SHOW or STASH. (The error codes and messages are listed in Appendix B of the TRS-80 Manual and on pages 6-12 and 6-13 in the TRS-DOS Manual.) In this case we ABORT our program. We restore all registers and then we execute the 3 bytes copied from locations $41A6_H$ to $41A8_H$ by the BASIC Program 11.11. The BASIC processing continues as if there were no interruption.
3. *Syntax error*. If E contains 2, there was a syntax error after the last executed BASIC statement. So we load into HL the pointer to the terminator of that BASIC statement. If HL points at a 00_H byte in the text, then the terminator is at the end of a line and we have to skip 4 bytes to get to the text of the next line. To find the next character we invoke RST 10H, which moves HL to the next character. This is an important pointer, and so we save it in the stack.
4. *Stash*. Now we use string compare to see whether the next five characters spell STASH. If they do, we execute the routine of Program 11.2. Then we exit.
5. *Show*. If they do not spell STASH, we recover the pointer, and see whether the next five characters spell SHOW. If they do, we execute Program 11.1. Then we exit.
6. *Exit*. We exit by pointing HL to the terminator of this statement and jump to RUNSTM.

Program 11.10 implements this plan.

Program 11.10. SHOW and STASH

```
                EQUATES: ERTRAP,ERCODE,BSCSTM,RUNSTM,CPSTR,VIDEO
        SAVE    EQU     0BC00H      ;START OF STORAGE AREA
                ORG     0B000H      ;PROGRAM IS RELOCATABLE
        INIT:   PUSH    AF          ;SAVE ALL REGISTERS
                PUSH    BC
                PUSH    DE
                PUSH    HL
        SYERR:  LD      A,E         ;SYNTAX ERROR? E CONTAINS ERROR
                CP      2           ;IT IS 2 FOR SYNTAX ERROR
                JR      NZ,ABORT    ;IF NOT 2, THEN ABORT
        GETCHR: LD      HL,(BSCSTM);GET NEXT CHAR. IN BASIC
                LD      A,(HL)      ;PROGRAM
                OR      A           ;SEE IF IT IS 00H
                JR      NZ,NXTCHR   ;IF NOT, CHARACTER FOUND
        SKIP:   INC     HL          ;IF IT IS 00H, BSCSTM POINTS AT
                INC     HL          ;END OF LINE TERMINATOR, SO
                INC     HL          ;WE HAVE TO SKIP FOUR BYTES
                INC     HL          ;THE NEXT LINE POINTER AND THE LINE
        NXTCHR: RST     10H         ;NUMBER; SKIP ALL BLANKS
                PUSH    HL          ;SAVE POINTER
        COMP:   LD      BC,COM1     ;WE SET UP HERE THE STRING
                LD      D,5         ;COMPARE ROUTINE
                LD      E,D
                CALL    CPSTR
                JR      Z,STASH     ;IF COMPARE SUCCESSFUL, DO STASH
                LD      BC,COM2     ;COMPARE WITH SECOND COMMAND
                POP     HL
                PUSH    HL
                LD      D,4
                LD      E,D
                CALL    CPSTR
                JR      Z,SHOW      ;IF SUCCESSFUL, DO SHOW
        ABORT:  POP     HL          ;RESTORE REGISTERS
                POP     DE
                POP     BC
                POP     AF
                DEFM    'FIL'       ;PROG. 11.11 POKES HERE
        STASH:  PUSH    HL          ;PROGRAM 11.2
                LD      HL,VIDEO
                LD      DE,SAVE
                LD      BC,1024D
                LDIR
                JR      EXIT
        SHOW:   PUSH    HL          ;PROGRAM 11.1
```

```
                LD      HL,SAVE
                LD      DE,VIDEO
                LD      BC,1024D
                LDIR
        EXIT:   POP     HL          ;RECOVER POINTER TO TEXT
                XOR     A           ;ZERO A
                LD      (ERCODE),A;STORE 00H FOR ERROR CODE
                DEC     HL          ;POINT AT LAST LETTER OF COMMAND
                RST     10H         ;MOVE POINTER TO NEXT NON BLANK
                JP      RUNSTM      ;RUN BASIC FROM POINTER
        COM1:   DEFM    'STASH'
        COM2:   DEFM    'SHOW'
                END
```

We set up Program 11.10 with Program 11.11.

Program 11.11.

```
100 DEFINT A - Z
110 FOR I = 0 TO 2 : P(I) = PEEK(16806 + I) : NEXT
120 POKE 16806, 195 : POKE 16807, 0 : POKE 16808, 176
130 POKE -20431, P(0)  : POKE -20430, P(1) : POKE -20429, P(2)
```

Line 110 of this program records the 3 bytes at ERTRAP; they are stored in P(0) to P(2). Then line 120 rewrites the same three locations: The 3 bytes POKEd in is the assembled form of JP 0B00H, the start of Program 11.10. Finally, we POKE the values recorded in line 110 into the area reserved by Program 11.10 by DEFM 'FIL'. As a result, if the ABORT exit is used, Program 11.10 will exit by encountering the 3 bytes that were originally at ERTRAP. In other words, processing will continue as if Program 11.10 had not intervened.

These programs can be adjusted easily to your particular needs. Program 11.10 is relocatable. You can change Program 11.11 to load Program 11.10 anywhere in memory. Moreover, by POKEing we can change the values of SAVE, so from BASIC we can control the memory block into which we save the video display.

Let us digress for a minute to emphasize again a very important point. In Chapter 3 we learned some POKEs to disable the BREAK key. We warned there of the danger of POKEing into a machine language program. Program 11.10 illustrates how we can POKE into a program even though we do not know what is in the bytes we are replacing. We strongly recommend that you always follow this procedure.

Editor

Many worthwhile enhancements can also be made to the BASIC editor. Two examples are the screen print function and keyboard macros.

The easiest way to implement such an enhancement is by intercepting the keyboard driver. Let the simultaneous pressing of the three keys J, K, and L signify that we want the screen to be printed. Write a BASIC program patterned after Program 11.11. First we check what the keyboard driver address is in the keyboard control block. (NEWDOS/80, KBFIX, and a lot of other programs replace it.) Then we replace it with the address of our machine language routine.

The machine language part starts out by comparing location $341A_H$ with 28 (as we learned in Chapter 5) to determine whether JKL have been pressed. If not, we jump to the address we replaced in the keyboard control block, and we are finished. If location $341A_H$ is 28, then we load VIDEO (= $3C00_H$) into HL, and in a loop of 1024_D steps we do the following. We load into A what (HL) is pointing at and check whether it is in the ASCII range of a printable character. If it is, we print it; otherwise we print a blank (for printing we use the printer driver in the printer control block). We increment HL and continue the loop. To make the printout readable, after every 64th character we print a line feed.

Keyboard macros are more work to implement. Their invocation can be triggered by an unusual keystroke, say 123. Once invoked, special keystrokes can take on new meanings. For instance, shifted characters may represent BASIC keywords. In typing SHIFT G you may actually type GOTO and SHIFT R may become RETURN.

If you do not feel like working out your own keyboard macro, buy one (look for advertisements in the magazines listed in Appendix 7); or you may decide to type in an excellent implementation by P. Pilgrim from Volume III (1980), issue 1, of *80-U.S.*

Review and Programming Practice

1. Use LDIR to move a block of 2,000 bytes starting at location 7000_H to the location starting at 9000_H.
2. "Reverse scrolling" moves lines 1 to 15 of the video display to lines 2 to 16 and writes in line 1 the previous line of text.

   The following BASIC program illustrates reverse scrolling. RUN the program; it will fill 15 lines with the letters K to Y. Pressing the up arrow changes the display to letters J to X, then I to W, and so on.

```
10 CLEAR 2000 : DEFINT A - Z : K = 0
20 FOR I = 0 TO 14
30 PRINT @I*64, STRING$(64,75 + I + K);
40 NEXT
50 X$ = INKEY$
60 IF X$ = CHR$(91) THEN K = K - 1 : GOTO 20
70 GOTO 50
```

   Write an enhanced FAST BASIC version.

3. Describe CPIR.
4. Using the CPIR instruction, count the number of $C9_H$ bytes (CALL) in ROM. Compare this with the number of occurrences of the byte $C3_H$ (JP).
5. Lines 30 to 50 of the following BASIC program put a lot of A's and B's on the screen. Then it says NOW WATCH, and in lines 60 to 100 replaces all the A's with B's.

```
10 CLS
20 PRINT @0, ""
30 FOR I = 1 TO 14
40 PRINT STRING$(32,65); STRING$(32,66);
50 NEXT
60 FOR I = 1 TO 1000 : NEXT
70 PRINT @0, "NOW WATCH";
80 FOR I = 0 TO 896
90 IF PEEK(15424 + I) = 65 THEN POKE 15424 + I, 66
100 NEXT
110 GOTO 110
```

Write an enhanced FAST BASIC version of the program, replacing lines 60 to 100 with a USR.

6. Look up SLA and SRL in Appendix 2. What other instructions are similar?
7. Write an assembly language routine that loads into register B the high-order 4 bits of (16428_D) and into register C the low-order 4 bits of (16428_D).
8. Write the assembly language code to check whether the printer is busy.
9. Convert the following BASIC instructions into machine language.
   (a) PRINT @10, CHR$(65)
   (b) SET(10,15)
10. The following BASIC program displays some characters on the video.

```
10 DEFINT I, Y : CLS
20 FOR I = 1 TO 49
30 READ X : READ Y
40 PRINT @X, CHR$(Y)
50 NEXT
60 GOTO 60
```

```
70 DATA 71, 70, 72, 65, 73, 83, 74, 84, 77, 66, 78, 65, 79, 83,
   80, 73, 81, 67, 147, 82, 148, 65, 149, 78, 150, 68, 151, 79,
   152, 77
80 DATA 155, 71, 156, 82, 157, 65, 158, 80, 159, 72, 160, 73,
   161, 67, 162, 83, 165, 80, 166, 65, 167, 84, 168, 84, 169, 69,
   170, 82, 171, 78
110 DATA 199, 137, 203, 76, 208, 149, 240, 156, 269, 78, 470,
    191, 471, 191, 472, 191, 730, 179, 731, 179, 732, 179, 733,
    179
120 DATA 840, 129, 841, 130, 842, 148, 850, 155, 860, 80, 865,
    91, 880, 191
```

Rewrite this program in enhanced FAST BASIC.

11. Rename STASH; call it STORE. Rewrite Program 11.10 with STORE. (*Hint:* Changes are needed in lines 370 and 700.)

Answers

There are many correct answers to the programming questions. The answers provided here are only guidelines by which to judge your own answers.

1.

```
100    BYTES    EQU    2000
110    SOURCE   EQU    7000H
120    DESTIN   EQU    9000H
130             ORG    7E00H
140             LD     HL,SOURCE
150             LD     DE,DESTIN
160             LD     BC,BYTES
170             LDIR
180             END
```

2. We use the following BASIC program.

(Disk BASIC)

```
10 CLEAR 2000 : DEFINT A - Z : K = 0
20 POKE 16526, 0 : POKE 16527, 126      (DEFUSR = &H7E00)
30 A = USR(0)
45 PRINT @0, STRING$(64,75 + K)
50 X$ = INKEY$
60 IF X$ = CHR$(91) THEN K = K - 1 : GOTO 20
70 GOTO 50
```

The USR is the program given as the answer to the previous programming practice, with BYTES = 896, SOURCE = 3000_H, DESTIN = 3040_H. Of course, line 180 should be JP BSCPAR.

3. CPIR is block search. We place in register A the byte for which we are searching. We load into HL the starting address of the search and into BC the number of bytes to be searched. If the search is successful, the zero flag is set and HL points at the byte *following* the matching byte. If no match is found, the zero flag is reset.

4. We use DE as a counter:

```
100     BSCPAR   EQU      0A9AH
110              ORG      7E00H
120              LD       A,0C9H
130              LD       HL,0
140              LD       BC,2FFFH
150              LD       DE,0
160     LOOP:    CPIR
170              JR       NZ,INCR
180              EX       DE,HL
190              JP       BSCPAR
200     INCR:    INC      DE
210              JR       LOOP
220              END
```

We call this USR with the following BASIC program.

(Disk BASIC)

```
10 X = 0
20 POKE 16526, 0 : POKE 16527, 126     (DEFUSR = &H7E00)
30 X = USR(0)
40 PRINT X
```

The number of $C9_H$ bytes in the ROM of the authors' TRS-80 is 169. Now change 0C9H to 0C3H in line 120. The answer is 135. Caution: These numbers change from ROM to ROM.

5. We call the USR with the following BASIC program.

(Disk BASIC)

```
10 CLS
20 PRINT @0, ""
30 FOR I = 1 TO 14
40 PRINT STRING$(32,65); STRING$(32,66);
50 NEXT
60 FOR I = 1 TO 1000 : NEXT
70 PRINT @0, "NOW WATCH";
80 POKE 16526,0 : 16527, 126                    (DEFUSR = &H7E00)
90 A = USR(0)
100 GOTO 100
```

The machine language subroutine is almost the same as the previous one. There, on a match, we incremented the counter. In this program, on a match, we first *decrement HL to point at the matching byte.* Then we replace A with B, increment HL to restore its value, and continue searching.

```
100    BSCPAR   EQU    0A9AH
110             ORG    7E00H
120             LD     A,65D
130             LD     HL,3C40H
140             LD     BC,896D
150    LOOP:    CPIR
160             JR     Z,REPLAC
170             JP     BSCPAR
180    REPLAC:  DEC    HL
190             LD     (HL),66D
200             INC    HL
210             JR     LOOP
220             END
```

Question: What happens if line 200 is deleted?

6. The shift instructions are in the Bit Manipulation group of instructions in Appendix 2. There are seven headings for shift operations, each containing ten instructions. In addition, there are two 4-bit shifts.

7. We use the instruction SRL to shift right and reset bit 7:

```
        LD     A,(16428D)
        SRL
        SRL
        SRL
        SRL
        LD     A,(16428D)
        AND    0FH
```

8.

```
100             LD      HL,(14312D)
110     BACK:   BIT     7,(HL)
120             JR      Z,BACK
```

9. (a)

```
200             LD      HL,VIDEO + 10
210             LD      (HL),65D
```

(b)

```
200             LD      HL,VIDEO + 199D
210             SET     3,(HL)
```

10. IX points at the data and HL points at the video display. A contains the character to be displayed.

```
100     VIDEO   EQU     3C00H
110     BSCPAR  EQU     0A9AH
120             ORG     7E00H
130             LD      IX,DATA
140             LD      B,49
150     LOOP:   LD      E,(IX+0)
160             LD      D,(IX+1)
170             LD      HL,VIDEO
180             ADD     HL,DE
190             LD      A,(IX+2)
200             LD      (HL),A
210             INC     IX
220             INC     IX
230             INC     IX
240             DJNZ    LOOP
250             JP      BSCPAR
260     DATA:   DEFW    71
270             DEFB    70
280             DEFW    72
290             DEFB    65
300             DEFW    73
310             DEFB    83
320             DEFW    74
330             DEFB    84
340             DEFW    77
350             DEFB    66
360             DEFW    78
370             DEFB    65
380             DEFW    79
390             DEFB    83
400             DEFW    80
410             DEFB    73
420             DEFW    81
430             DEFB    67
440             DEFW    147
450             DEFB    82
460             DEFW    148
470             DEFB    65
480             DEFW    149
490             DEFB    73
500             DEFW    150
510             DEFB    68
520             DEFW    151
530             DEFB    79
```

```
540    DEFW   152
550    DEFB   77
560    DEFW   151
570    DEFB   79
580    DEFW   155
590    DEFB   71
600    DEFW   156
610    DEFB   82
620    DEFW   157
630    DEFB   65
640    DEFW   158
650    DEFB   801
660    DEFW   159
670    DEFB   72
680    DEFW   160
690    DEFB   73
700    DEFW   161
710    DEFB   67
720    DEFW   162
730    DEFB   83
740    DEFW   165
750    DEFB   80
760    DEFW   166
770    DEFB   65
780    DEFW   167
790    DEFB   84
800    DEFW   168
810    DEFB   84
820    DEFW   169
830    DEFB   69
840    DEFW   170
850    DEFB   82
860    DEFW   171
870    DEFB   78
880    DEFW   199
890    DEFB   137
900    DEFW   203
910    DEFB   76
920    DEFW   208
930    DEFB   149
940    DEFW   240
950    DEFB   156
960    DEFW   269
970    DEFB   78
980    DEFW   470
990    DEFB   191
1000   DEFW   471
1010   DEFB   191
1020   DEFW   472
1030   DEFB   191
1040   DEFW   730
1050   DEFB   179
1060   DEFW   731
1070   DEFB   179
1080   DEFW   732
1090   DEFB   179
1100   DEFW   733
1110   DEFB   179
1120   DEFW   840
1130   DEFB   129
1140   DEFW   841
1150   DEFB   130
1160   DEFW   842
1170   DEFB   148
1180   DEFW   850
1190   DEFB   155
1200   DEFW   860
1210   DEFB   80
1220   DEFW   865
1230   DEFB   91
1240   DEFW   880
1250   DEFB   191
1260   END
```

Observe that by doing the program a bit more cleverly we could cut its size by about 30 percent. Instead of defining the new display position with DEFW (which always is added to VIDEO) we could have used DEFB X, where X is the difference between the present display position and the next. This is a 1-byte entry that should be added to HL. This also eliminates the need for line 180.

11. The problem is the following. In a BASIC program when we type STORE it will be recorded as follows: ASCII for S, the

BASIC keyword code for TO (189_D), and the ASCIIs for R and E. Hence in line 370 we need LD D,4 and line 700 has to be replaced by three lines:

```
700    COM1:    DEFM    'S'
702             DEFB    189D
704             DEFM    'RE'
```

CHAPTER TWELVE

A Case Study

This is not the end. It is not even the beginning of the end.
But it is, perhaps, the end of the beginning.
—W. Churchill in *Speech at the Mansion House*

We have finished our discussion of the principles behind FAST BASIC. Now we show in a case study how enhanced FAST BASIC can be applied in practice.

Rather than presenting an artificial example, we decided to convert the program VIEW/MOD (for a listing see Appendix 8), which we wrote as a teaching aid for Part II.

ANALYZING THE PROGRAM

Why Convert?

The BASIC program VIEW/MOD is indispensable for searching the ROM. It is also useful in writing short machine language programs into memory. VIEW/MOD has two great drawbacks:

1. It takes 45 seconds to display 12 lines on the screen, too slow for practical use.
2. It takes 20 to 22 minutes to search 1000_H bytes of memory, about 1 hour to search the whole ROM, about 5 hours and 20 minutes to search all 64K of memory.

VIEW/MOD alleviates the first drawback by displaying only a few lines after the FIND and CHANGE commands. Nevertheless, for the DISPLAY command VIEW/MOD is very slow.

The FIND command is so slow that it is impractical to use.

Analyzing VIEW/MOD

Before we can discuss the enhanced FAST BASIC conversion of the program VIEW/MOD we need to outline its structure. The program has two main subroutines:

1. Convert A (a single-precision variable) into a hex string A$ of length LE: lines 90 to 150.
2. Convert the hex number A$ (an ASCII string) into decimal A; if A$ has a nonhex character, then the error flag FL is set.

Command input and verification are in lines 530 to 600.

As each command is processed, the value of AD (address) is set and a jump is made to line 280 or 290. These are the two entry points into the display module. On entering at 280 we get a 12-line display, whereas in entering at 290 we get an S2 line display; S2 is set before we enter the display module.

The display module is in lines 280 to 520. The FOR NEXT loop in lines 310 to 520 produces the display one line at a time. Each line displays 16 memory locations in hex and as ASCII characters. (See Figure 12.1.) A memory location is processed in lines 350 to 440. Line 350 computes the address of the next location; line 390 PEEKs at the location, and uses the first subroutine to convert the decimal result in A to a 2-byte hex number. The output of the subroutine, S$, is printed on the screen. In line 400 AC$ stores the ASCII for display. It adds CHR$(A) to AC$ if CHR$(A) is a printable character; otherwise it adds a period. AC$ is printed (line 460) after the line in hex has been displayed.

A typical display of VIEW/MOD is shown in Figure 12.1. The last line of the display is the prompt line; it shows the five available commands. Command A shows the next page of display, and command B shows the previous page. C is the change command; it asks the user to input the address where the memory contents are to be changed and then asks for the new contents. Command F needs two addresses, the start and end of the search, and then asks for the string to search for.

After the screen display is completed, AD is updated, and we continue with the command input at line 530. AHEAD and BACK are simple commands. AHEAD goes to line 280 for a new display. BACK adjusts AD and then goes to 280. The command CHANGE is implemented in lines 770 to 1060. Because it is fast enough, we do not convert it into FAST BASIC. However, note line 830: This sets the number of lines in the display.

The command FIND is implemented in lines 1070 to 1640. Lines 1070 to 1130 check the input. They strip the string SS$ of leading and trailing blanks. Line 1140 sets the number of lines of display. Lines 1140 to 1260 compute (using the second subroutine) AD and AF; we search from AD to AF. In lines 1270 to 1470 the string we are searching for, SS$, is examined and each pair of hex numbers is converted to a decimal number C(1) to

```
VIEW/MOD
00C0-->D7B7 2012 214C 4323 7CB5 281B 7E47 2F77 .. .!LC#..(..G/.
00D0-->BE70 28F3 1811 CD5A 1EB7 C297 19EB 2B3E ..(...........+>
00E0-->8F46 77BE 7020 CE2B 1114 44DF DA7A 1911 .F... .+..D.....
00F0-->CEFF 22B1 4019 22A0 40CD 4D1B 2111 01CD ..".@.".@.M.!...
0100-->A728 C319 1A4D 454D 4F52 5920 5349 5A45 .(...MEMORY SIZE
0110-->0052 4144 494F 2053 4841 434B 204C 4556 .RADIO SHACK LEV
0120-->454C 2049 4920 4241 5349 430D 001E 2CC3 EL II BASIC...,.
0130-->A219 D7AF 013E 8001 3E01 F5CF 28CD 1C2B .....>..>...(..+
0140-->FE80 D24A 1EF5 CF2C CD1C 2BFE 30D2 4A1E ...J...,..+.0.J.
0150-->16FF 14D6 0330 FBC6 034F F187 5F06 027A .....0...0......
0160-->1F57 7B1F 5F10 F879 8F3C 47AF 378F 10FD .W.......<G.7...
0170-->4F7A F63C 571A B7FA 7C01 3E80 47F1 B778 0..<W.....>.G...

TYPE A(HEAD), B(ACK), C(HANGE), D(ISPLAY), F(IND)
```

FIGURE 12.1. VIEW/MOD Display

C(N1). The search itself is the loop in lines 1480 to 1620. After the search is complete line 1640 transfers execution to the display module.

Obviously the program is slowed down by the two FOR NEXT loops in lines 340 to 450 and in lines 1480 to 1620 (both require too many conversions). So we convert VIEW/MOD to enhanced FAST BASIC by tackling these two loops.

THE MACHINE LANGUAGE PROGRAMS

The Display Routine

Let us start with the display program for VIEW/MOD. To minimize the amount of work we have to do in machine language, we convert only the hex and ASCII displays of the 16 characters. In looking at Figure 12.1 we see that, accordingly, the BASIC program will produce the initial address of a line and the arrow, while the machine language routine will complete the line. Then BASIC takes over again.

We need two pieces of information to start the machine language routine: the address of the memory location first to be displayed, and the cursor location (the screen location following the arrow).

We obtain the first by calling the machine language routine from the BASIC program with an A% = USR(AD%), where AD% is the address of the memory location from which we want to display the memory. The current cursor position is in the video control block (see Table 3.3).

When we get a byte from memory we have to (1) convert it to hex and display the result and (2) show it as an ASCII character. We need three pointers:

1. HL picks out the byte to be displayed.
2. IX points to the screen (video memory) at the next location where the hex numbers go.
3. IY points to the screen (video memory) at the next location where the ASCII is to go.

Our plan involves the following steps.

1. Initialize the three pointers, HL, IX, and IY.
2. Get the next byte from memory. If it is a printable character, then print it on the right side of the display (pointed out by IY); otherwise print a period.
3. Get the byte from memory again into register A and do the conversion. The subroutine GETHEX converts the low-order 4 bits of register A into the ASCII of the hex character representing that 4-bit binary number. For instance, if the low-order 4 bits of register A are 1011, then GETHEX will convert it to the ASCII of B, that is, 42_H. This then is displayed on the left side of the screen (IX shows where). This is done twice, first with the high-order 4 bits, then with the low-order 4 bits of A.
4. Update the three pointers.

The subroutine SKIP inserts blanks after each group of 4 hex digits. Program 12.1 realizes this plan.

Program 12.1. The Display Routine

```
CURSOR  EQU     4020H       ;ADDRESS OF CURSOR
GETPAR  EQU     0A7FH       ;PLACES IN HL PARAM. TO USR
        ORG     7E00H       ;PROGRAM RELOCATABLE
INIT:   CALL    GETPAR      ;GET ADDRESS, HL POINTS AT MEMORY
        LD      IX,(CURSOR);IX POINTS AT SCREEN FOR HEX
        PUSH    IX          ;COPY INTO IY
        POP     IY
        LD      DE,40D      ;IX + 40 IS THE PLACE FOR ASCII
        ADD     IY,DE
        LD      B,10H       ;B IS THE COUNTER
ASCII:  LD      A,(HL)      ;GET BYTE FROM MEMORY
        CP      20H         ;IF LESS THAN 32, NOT PRINTABLE
        JR      C,NOTPR     ;OR
        CP      7FH         ;IF NOT MORE THAN 127
        JR      C,PRINT     ;DISPLAY IT
NOTPR:  LD      A,'.'       ;OTHERWISE DISPLAY '.'
PRINT:  LD      (IY+0),A
HEX:    INC     IY          ;INCREMENT ASCII POINTER
        LD      A,(HL)      ;GET BYTE FROM MEMORY
```

```
         RRA                   ;ROTATE FOUR TIMES
         RRA                   ;TO GET HIGH ORDER FOUR
         RRA                   ;BITS TO THE LOWER ORDER
         RRA                   ;POSITION
         CALL     GETHEX       ;GET FIRST HEX DIGIT AND PRINT IT
         LD       A,(HL)       ;GET AGAIN BYTE FROM MEMORY
         CALL     GETHEX       ;GET SECOND DIGIT AND PRINT IT
         BIT      0,B          ;IF B IS EVEN
         JR       Z,SKIP       ;THEN ADD A BLANK
         INC      IX
SKIP:    INC      HL           ;INCREMENT MEMORY POINTER
         DJNZ     ASCII        ;CHECK IF DONE
         RET
GETHEX:  AND      0FH          ;MASK THE HIGH ORDER FOUR BITS
         ADD      A,'0'        ;ADD ASCII OF 0
         CP       '9'+1        ;IF LESS THAN 10 DONE
         JR       C,SHOW       ;SO DISPLAY IT
         ADD      A,7H         ;OTHERWISE ADD 7, TO GET ASCII
SHOW:    LD       (IX+0),A     ;DISPLAY IT
         INC      IX           ;INCREMENT HEX POINTER
         RET
         END
```

Now the display takes about 3 seconds. We could speed up the display further by converting one more FOR NEXT loop, that is, by displaying the whole page in machine language (not only a single line). However, now the screen fills up faster than we can read it, so further speed-up does not seem necessary.

The Search Routine

In converting the search routine of VIEW/MOD we again try to minimize the task of the assembly language routine. Thus, still in BASIC, we convert the string we are searching for into binary form.

We have to pass four parameters to the search routine: PK%, the start of the binary string for which we are searching; LE%, the length of the binary string less 1; BC%, the number of bytes we wish to search for; and AD%, the starting address for the search. We pass these parameters by placing them at the start of the simple variable table. Using VTS, the address of the simple variable table, we read these parameters and store them in the stack—with the exception of PK%, which is stored in IX.

We first set up CPIR: HL contains AD%, BC contains BC%, and we load into the register A the first byte we are searching for. Then we rewrite the first byte of the string to make sure that the string found *is not* the string we POKEd into memory. Next comes the block search CPIR. If CPIR terminates with NZ, then we put a 00_H in the first character of BR% to signify an unsuccessful search and we return to BASIC.

If CPIR returns Z, the first byte was found. Then we store in the stack all the registers and we set up the string compare routine. If the compare is successful, we place a 01_H in BR$, clean up the stack, and JP BSCPAR to pass HL (where the string was found) back to BASIC.

Program 12.2 implements this plan.

Program 12.2. The Search Routine

```
CPSTR    EQU     25A1H      ;COMPARE STRING ROUTINE
BSCPAR   EQU     0A9AH      ;RETURN TO BASIC WITH PARAMETER
VTS      EQU     40F9H      ;START OF SIMPLE VARIABLE TABLE
GETINT   MACRO   R1,R2      ;MACRO INCREMENTS HL FOUR TIMES
         INC     HL         ;AND LOADS THE INTEGER HL
         INC     HL         ;IS POINTING AT
         INC     HL         ;INTO THE REGISTER PAIR R1,R2
         INC     HL
         LD      R2,(HL)
         INC     HL
         LD      R1,(HL)
         ENDM
         ORG     7E00H      ;PROGRAM IS RELOCATABLE
INIT:    LD      HL,(VTS)   ;HL POINTS AT SIMPLE VAR. TABLE
         DEC     HL         ;AT FIRST APPLICATION ONE LESS
         GETINT  D,E        ;INC IS NEEDED
         PUSH    DE
         POP     IX         ;PK% IS IN IX
         GETINT  B,C        ;BC% IN BC
         GETINT  D,E        ;LE% IN E
         LD      D,E        ;AND IN D
         PUSH    DE         ;DE SAVED IN STACK
         GETINT  D,E        ;AD% IN DE
         EX      DE,HL      ;AD% IN HL
         POP     DE         ;D = E = LENGTH OF STRING
         LD      A,(IX+0)   ;FIRST CHAR. OF STRING IN A
         INC     A          ;REWRITE STRING IN MEMORY
         LD      (IX+0),A
         DEC     A
         INC     IX         ;IX POINTS AT SECOND CHARACTER
BYTECP:  CPIR               ;BLOCK COMPARE
         JR      Z,STRCP    ;IF SUCCESSFUL, COMPARE STRING
NOTFD:   LD      (IX-1),0   ;STORE 00H IN BR$: NOT FOUND
         RET
STRCP:   PUSH    DE         ;SAVE ALL REGISTERS
         PUSH    HL
         PUSH    BC
```

```
            PUSH    AF
            PUSH    IX
            POP     BC          ;SETTING UP STRING COMPARE
            CALL    CPSTR
            JR      Z,FOUND     ;IF SUCCESSFUL, EXIT
            POP     AF          ;IF NOT, RESTORE REGISTERS
            POP     BC
            POP     HL
            POP     DE
            JR      BYTECP      ;CONTINUE THE BLOCK COMPARE
    FOUND:  LD      (IX-1),1    ;STORE 01H IN BR$: FOUND
            POP     BC          ;CLEARING UP
            POP     BC          ;BASIC STACK
            POP     BC
            POP     BC
            JP      BSCPAR      ;PASSING BACK HL
            END
```

Now the 64K search is accomplished in about 1 second.

THE CONVERTED PROGRAM

We have treated the display and search modules for VIEW/MOD as independent machine language programs. We now have to integrate these subroutines into VIEW/MOD.

The machine language subroutines are POKEd in (from the data statements) during the initialization. The time-consuming FOR NEXT loop in the display module becomes a subroutine call, line 340. The last lines of the search module, lines 1350 to 1640, are replaced. In lines 1330 to 1380 the string being searched for, SS$, is converted from hex to decimal in BASIC and POKEd into memory starting at location 32448_D; these bytes become the binary representation of SS$ and form the basis for the string comparison in machine language.

To convert VIEW/MOD (as listed in Appendix 8) into enhanced FAST BASIC delete lines 40, 50, 60, 280, 300, 310, 320, 330, 340, 350 to 470, 610, 830, 840, 1140, 1150, and 1290 to 1640 from the listing in Appendix 8 and add the following lines.

```
15 DATA 205,127,10,221,42,32,64,221,229,253,225,17,40,0,253,
   25,6,16,126,254,32,56,4,254,127,56,2,62,46,253,119,0,
   253,35,126,31,31,31,31,205,56,126,126,205,56,126,203,
   64,40,2,221,35,35,16,219,201,230,15,198,48,254,58,56,
   2,198,7,221,119,0,221,35,35,201
18 DATA 42,249,64,43,35,35,35,35,94,35,86,213,221,225,35,35,
   35,35,78,35,70,35,35,35,35,94,35,86,83,213,35,35,35,35,
   94,35,86,235,209,221,126,0,60,221,119,0,61,221,35,237,
   177,40,5,221,54,255,0,201,213,229,197,245,221,229,193,
   205,161,37,40,6,241
20 DATA 193,225,209,24,229,221,54,255,1,209,209,209,209,195,
   154,10
40 CLEAR : PK% = 0 : BC% = 0 : LE% = 0 : AD% = 0
50 FOR I = 0 TO 71 : READ A : POKE 32256 + I, A : NEXT
55 FOR I = 0 TO 86 : READ A : POKE 32352 + I, A : NEXT
60 REM    (in Disk BASIC: DEFUSR0 = &H7E00 : DEFUSR1 = &H7E60)
280 REM
300 REM
310 FOR S1 = 1 TO 12
320 PRINT @S1*64, AD$ "-->";
330 AD% = AD + (AD > 32767)*65536
335 POKE 16526, 0 : POKE 16527, 126   (in Disk BASIC: REM)
340 A = USR(AD%)                      (in Disk BASIC: A = USR0(AD%))
470 AD = AD + 16 : IF AD >= 65536 THEN AD = -1*(65536 - AD)
610 AD = AD - 384
1140 LS = LEN(SS$)
1150 LE% = (LS + 1)/3 - 1
1290 AD% =AD + (AD >32767)*65536
1300 BC = AF - AD
1310 BC% = BC + 65536*(BC > 32767)
1320 PK% = 32448
1330 FOR CO = 0 TO LE%
1340 A$ = LEFT$(SS$,2)
1350 GOSUB 160
1360 POKE PK%+CO, A
1370 SS$ = MID$(SS$,4)
1380 NEXT
1385 POKE 16526, 192 : POKE 16527, 126  (in Disk BASIC: REM)
1390 AD = USR(AD%)                   (in Disk BASIC: AD = USR1(AD%))
1400 AD = AD - LE% - 1
1410 PRINT@64, CHR$(31);
1420 IF PEEK(PK%) = 0 THEN PRINT@192, "NOT FOUND" : GOTO 530
1430 A = AD
1440 LE = 4
1450 GOSUB 90
1460 AD$ = S$
1470 GOTO 300
```

Remember to set the MEMORY SIZE? to 32255 before RUNning this program.

Line 15 is the decimal conversion of Program 12.1 and line 18 contains Program 12.2. Lines 50 and 55 POKE these programs into protected memory.

Conclusion

This case study illustrates the use of enhanced FAST BASIC.

First, FAST BASIC provides no help in the difficult task of writing your BASIC program. However, it does provide guidelines as to how your BASIC program should be reorganized for faster execution.

Second, if your BASIC program runs too slowly, carry out an analysis—as we did in this chapter—to determine which parts slow it down. This is usually an easy task. In some instances, if there are a large number of subroutines, it may be necessary to run the program with subroutine counters. Any time a subroutine is used increase its counter by 1. At the completion of the program print out these counters. This will help in finding the most heavily used subroutines.

Third, take the one or two subroutines that are the most time consuming and rewrite them in FAST BASIC. Do not try to do too many conversions at the same time. If the program runs sufficiently fast after one or two conversions, you are finished. If not, convert a few more subroutines.

Last, if even FAST BASIC is not fast enough in doing some graphics or in transferring data, enhance it!

But always keep in mind the basic principle: let TRS-80 BASIC do what it can do well. Use machine language only for the small parts where TRS-80 BASIC needs your help.

Appendixes

APPENDIX ONE

Assorted ROM Routines

The TRS-80 ROM is a very complex net of some 800 routines. Luckily, we do not have to know them all. In this appendix we discuss some useful routines not covered in Part IV.

MATH FUNCTIONS

Thirteen mathematical functions are built into TRS-80 BASIC. Table A1.1 provides the information on how to use these functions in FAST BASIC.

Obviously, neglecting to set the typeflag before a type 1 call is fatal; for instance, INT does not know how to interpret the data in SA without the typeflag. On the other hand, type 2 calls do expect single-precision numbers. Nevertheless, it is good practice to set the typeflag before any of these calls.

TABLE A1.1. Math Functions

Label	Value	Type	Explanation
ABS	0977	CALL	Type 1
ATN	15BD	CALL	Type 2
COS	1541	CALL	Type 2
EXP	1439	CALL	Type 2
FIX	0B26	CALL	Type 2
FLAGDP	0AEC	CALL	Set typeflag of SA to double precision
FLAGIN	0A9D	CALL	Set typeflag of SA to integer
FLAGSP	0AEF	CALL	Set typeflag of SA to single precision
INT	0B37	CALL	Type 1
LOG	0809	CALL	Type 2
RND	14C9	CALL	Type 1
RANDOM	01D3	CALL	Randomize
RSETSA	0778	CALL	Reset SA (SA = 0)*
SGN	098A	CALL	Type 1
SIN	1547	CALL	Type 2
SQR	13E7	CALL	Type 2
TAN	15A8	CALL	Type 2

*If SA contains 0, then RND generates random numbers between 0 and 1. To place 0 in SA use the call RSETSA.

Type 1: Number in SA may be integer, single precision, or double precision; set typeflag to indicate which. Result is put in SA, and typeflag is set.

Type 2: Number in SA is single precision; result is in SA.

Type Conversions

TRS-80 BASIC has three number conversion functions: CINT, CSNG, and CDBL. VAL converts strings representing numbers to numbers. These and one more conversion subroutine are given in Table A1.2.

INPUT/OUTPUT

Input/Output

As a rule, in a FAST BASIC program input and output are done in BASIC. However, there may be cases when this is not practical. For instance, a FAST BASIC disassembler would have to output a large amount of data. It may be impractical to return to BASIC after each line of disassembly. Or we may have to provide a program interrupt through the keyboard (e.g., typing * terminates the program); for this we need a keyboard scan routine. Table A1.3 describes eight of the many subroutines that handle input and output.

TABLE A1.2. Type Conversions

Label	Value	Type	Explanation
CSAASC	0FBD	CALL	Convert SA (set typeflag) to ASCII; result (in decimal) is placed in a buffer starting at 4130_H; result is terminated by a 00_H byte, (HL) = 4130_H
CSAINT	0A7F	CALL	Convert SA to integer*
CSASP	0AB1	CALL	Convert SA to single precision*
CSADP	0ADB	CALL	Convert SA to double precision*
VAL	1E5A	CALL	Convert a string (terminated by a byte 00_H) representing a decimal number to a binary number; HL points at first character, DE contains the result

*Typeflag must be set; result in SA.

TABLE A1.3. Input/Output Routines

Label	Value	Type	Explanation
CLS	01C9	CALL	Clear screen
KBDSCN	002B	CALL	Scan keyboard with A containing the result
OUTSEL	409C	EQU	Output select: contains –1 for cassette, 0 for video, 1 for printer
OUTSTR	28A7	CALL	Output string terminated by byte 00_H or 22_H (ASCII for "); HL points at first character, OUTSEL selects device
OUTCHR	032A	CALL	Output character in register A; OUTSEL selects device
RDSECT	46DD	CALL	For RDSECT and WTSECT: register C contains the drive selected (0 – 3), register D contains the track selected, register E contains the sector selected, HL points at the data buffer; on return Z is set on successful execution, otherwise register A will contain the error code
WTSECT	46E6	CALL	

Note that OUTCHR can output character or control character whose ASCII is A. The complete list of the 256 codes can be found in Appendix C of the TRS-80 BASIC Manual. Thus we can also do CLS by loading $1C_H$ into A and calling OUTCHR (this homes the cursor), then loading $1F_H$ into A and calling OUTCHR again. Observe that the output from CSAASC is in the form required by OUTSTR.

Disk

Two subroutines for disk input/output are quite enough to write some interesting programs. With RDSECT we can read a sector into memory, with the CHANGE command of VIEW/MOD we can change it in memory, and with WTSECT we can write it back onto the disk. (Exercise: Add a disk sector read and a disk sector write command to VIEW/MOD. Use it to change the name of a disk and the names of programs on the disk. The name of a disk is in sector 1 of track 17 in TRS-DOS version 2.3.)

GRAPHICS

Producing graphics is very slow in BASIC. Doing it in FAST BASIC is three to five times faster. This is still, however, a far cry from the speed achieved in enhanced FAST BASIC.

In FAST BASIC the three graphics functions (SET, RESET, POINT) can be used as follows: Load HL with the return address and PUSH HL; load register A with 00_H for POINT, 01_H for RESET, and 80_H for SET and PUSH AF; load A with the X coordinate and PUSH AF; LOAD A with the Y coordinate and JP GRAPH:

Label	Value	Type	Explanation
GRAPH	0150	JP	Call the graphic function selected by value in stack

RESTARTS

RST

The Z-80 instruction set provides us with a few subroutine calls that require a shorter code (1 byte versus the 3 bytes of a regular subroutine call) and which are faster to execute. These are called "restarts": RST 00H, RST 08H, RST 18H, RST 20H, RST 28H, RST 30H, RST 38H. For instance, RST 10H is a subroutine call to the subroutine starting at 10_H.

All RSTs are in ROM. They all contain a jump instruction to RAM: These line up nicely from 4000_H to 4012_H. At this point we find a jump back to ROM. This gives us a chance to intercept these routines.

RST 10H

The most important of these restarts is RST 10H (RST 16D). This is called when HL points at a character in a string and we want to proceed to the next character (not considering the one HL is pointing at) ignoring spaces, horizontal tabs, and linefeeds. After the call register A contains the character found. The carry flag is set if this character is a digit; otherwise it is reset. The zero flag is set if the character is a colon; otherwise it is reset.

For instance, RST 10H is used by the BASIC Interpreter to read a BASIC line. Thus to interrupt the Interpreter, intercept RST 10H at 4003_H (16387_D).

EXPRESSION EVALUATION

Finally, we mention the EVALUation subroutine at $1F21_H$. Let us assume that we have a BASIC line:

```
X = (X - 2 + Y/3) * (Z1 + LOG(U/4))
```

In FAST BASIC we would normally break this up into a number of steps, each one a single operation. However, if this line appeared outside a loop, it would be nice to evaluate it in one step. To accomplish this include in the program this line as seen by the BASIC Interpreter (this means that we use the BASIC keyword codes wherever applicable):

```
EVALU   EQU     1F21H
        LD      HL,LINE
        CALL    EVALU
LINE:   DEFM    'X'
        DEFB    0D5H            ;CODE FOR =
        DEFM    '(X'
        DEFB    0CEH            ;CODE FOR -
        DEFM    '2'
        DEFB    0CDH            ;CODE FOR +
        DEFM    'Y'
        DEFB    0D0H            ;CODE FOR /
        DEFM    '3)'
        DEFB    0CFH            ;CODE FOR *
        DEFM    '(Z1'
        DEFB    0CDH            ;CODE FOR +
        DEFB    00DFH           ;CODE FOR LOG
        DEFM    '(U'
        DEFB    0D0H            ;CODE FOR /
        DEFM    '4))'
        DEFB    0               ;STRING TERMINATOR
```

The appropriate appendix of the TRS-80 BASIC Manual contains the BASIC keyword codes.

APPENDIX TWO

The Z-80 Instruction Set

This appendix gives a brief description of the Z-80 instruction set. For more details see the Z-80 books listed in Appendix 7.

FLAGS

The flags are the bits of register F. In Chapter 1 we introduced "set" and "reset" for bits. We use them in the same sense for flags: To set a flag is to give it value 1, whereas to reset it is to give it value 0.

C: *carry flag* (bit 0 of register F). It is set (= 1) by add and subtract operations that generate a carry (borrow); otherwise these operations reset (= 0) it. Logical operations (AND, OR, XOR) always reset it. (Used also by the rotate instructions, and by DAA, SCF, CCF.)

N: *add/subtract flag* (bit 1 of register F). For add instructions it is set, and for subtracts it is reset.

P/O: *parity/overflow flag* (bit 2 of register F). This is also called the P/V flag in some publications. We explain in Appendix 4 how this flag is used as an overflow flag (O) for arithmetic operations. For logical operations and rotate instructions, this flag is used as the parity flag (P): It is set if the result has an even number of 1 bits; otherwise it is reset. (Used also by block compare instructions, block search instructions, LD A,I and LD A,R, and port input instructions.)

H: *half carry flag* (bit 4 of register F). Reflects the carry and borrow from bit 3 in arithmetic operations.

Z: *zero flag* (bit 6 of register F). For 8-bit arithmetic and logical operations this flag is set if the result is zero; otherwise it is reset. The BIT instruction places the complement of the selected bit in Z. Compare instructions set this flag if the two numbers compared are equal, and reset it otherwise. (Used also by port instructions.)

S: *sign flag* (bit 7 of register F). The 8-bit arithmetic operations place the result in register A and copy bit 7 of register A into this flag. (Used also by port input instructions.)

Note: Some of the following material will refer to "flags affected." These flags are set and reset as described here, unless described otherwise. We refer to P/O either as P or as O, depending on the role it is playing.

EIGHT-BIT DATA TRANSFER

In the description of these instructions let r (and r') denote an 8-bit register (A, B, C, D, E, H, L); let n denote an 8-bit integer, nm a 16-bit integer, and d an 8-bit signed integer. The 8-bit data transfer instruction are all load instructions. They are of the form

LD into, from

where "into" is one of r, (BC), (DE), (HL), (IX+d), (IY+d), (nm) and "from" is any one of these or n. (For examples see Chapter 7.) The architecture of the Z-80 microprocessor succeeded in implementing about 60 percent of the possible combinations. These are shown in Figure A2.1 (excluding registers I and R).

In Figure A2.1 an arrow indicates that a load instruction is available. Thus LD r,(HL) is available for any register r, but LD r,(DE) is legitimate only for register A.

This illustration helps us to visualize whether a load is available to us. However, it does more: It also helps find a way to do a two-step load if a single load is not available. For instance, there is no LD (HL),(nm) instruction. Following the arrows, we find that LD A,(nm) and LD (HL),A will do the job.

In addition, there are the load instructions LD A,I, LD A,R, LD I,A, and LD R,A, where R is the refresh register and I the interrupt register.

Here is a complete list of 8-bit loads.

LD r,r'	(2.25)	LD r,n	(3.95)	LD r,(HL)	(3.95)
LD r,(IX+d)	(10.71)	LD r,(IY+d)	(10.71)	LD (HL),r	(3.95)
LD (IX+d),r	(10.71)	LD (IY+d),r	(10.71)	LD (HL),n	(5.64)
LD (IX+d),n	(10.71)	LD (IY+d),n	(10.71)	LD A,(BC)	(3.95)
LD A,(DE)	(3.95)	LD A,(nm)	(7.33)	LD (BC),A	(3.95)
LD (DE),A	(3.95)	LD (nm),A	(7.33)	LD I,A	(5.07)
LD R,A	(5.07)	LD A,I	(5.07)	LD A,R	(5.07)

The number in parentheses following an instruction is the estimated execution time in microseconds (that is, one millionth of a second). The flags affected are S, Z, H, P, and N, with the exception of the last two instructions, which do not affect the flags.

SIXTEEN-BIT DATA TRANSFER

The 16-bit load instructions are shown in Figure A2.2. As you can see, about 30 percent of the possible instructions have been implemented. The double-headed arrow, for instance, between BC and (nm) means that both LD BC,(nm) and LD (nm),BC are legal. The only double arrow represents an exchange instruction: EX DE,HL, which interchanges DE and HL.

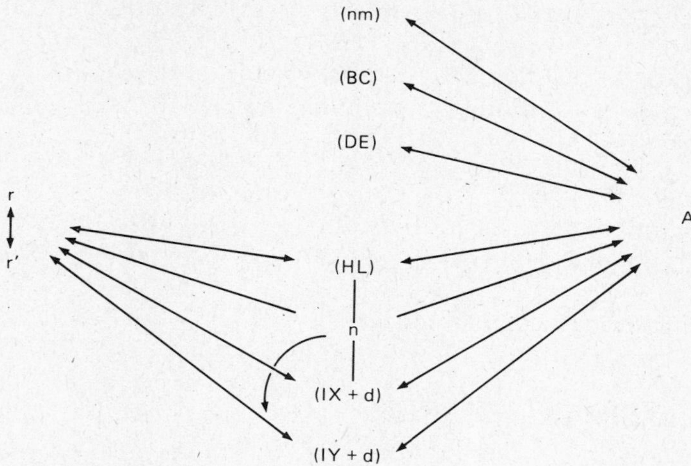

FIGURE A2.1. Eight-Bit Loads

Three exchange instructions are not shown on the diagram, namely, EX (SP),HL, EX (SP),IX, and EX (SP),IY.

Additional 16-bit transfer instructions are:

1. PUSH and POP, applicable to all register pairs (AF, BC, DE, HL) and to the 16-bit registers IX and IY; see Chapter 7 for an explanation how these work.
2. The exchange instructions: EX AF,AF', which exchanges AF and AF' and EXX which exchanges BC, DE, and HL with BC', DE', and HL', respectively.

Here is a complete list of 16-bit loads and exchange instructions (rp is one of the register pairs BC, DE, or HL or the 16-bit register SP; rp' is one of AF, BC, DE, HL; and nm is a 16-bit integer).

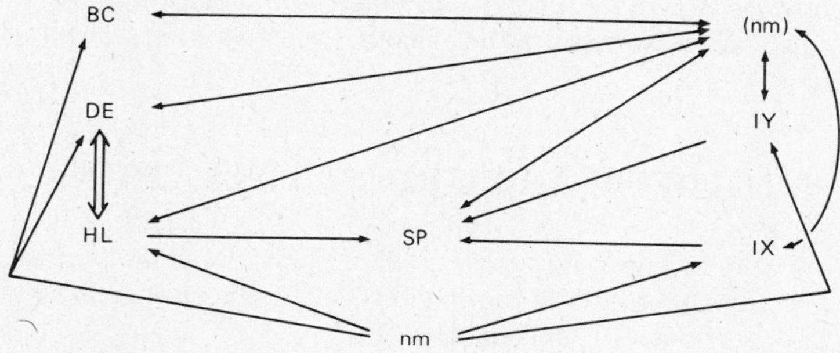

FIGURE A2.2. Sixteen-Bit Load Instructions

LD rp,nm	(5.64)	LD IX,nm	(7.89)	LD IY,nm	(7.89)
LD HL,(nm)	(9.02)	LD rp,(nm)	(11.27)	LD IX,(nm)	(11.27)
LD IY,(nm)	(11.27)	LD (nm),HL	(9.02)	LD (nm),rp	(11.27)
LD (nm),IX	(11.27)	LD (nm),IY	(11.27)	LD SP,HL	(3.38)
LD SP,IX	(5.64)	LD SP,IY	(5.64)	PUSH rp'	(6.2)
PUSH IX	(8.46)	PUSH IY	(8.46)	POP rp'	(5.64)
POP IX	(7.89)	POP IY	(7.89)	EX DE,HL	(2.25)
EX AF,AF'	(2.25)	EXX	(2.25)	EX (SP),HL	(10.71)
EX (SP),IX	(12.97)	EX (SP),IY	(12.97)		

None of these instructions affect the flags.

BLOCK TRANSFER AND SEARCH

LDIR and CPIR are described in Chapter 11. LDDR and CPDR do the same except that the final addresses of the source and destination blocks are used so HL and DE are decremented in each step. LDI, LDD, CPI, and CPD are the one-step versions of LDIR, LDDR, CPIR, CPDR. For example, LDI transfers the byte (HL) to (DE), increments DE and HL, and decrements BC (the flag O shall be reset when BC becomes 0).

Here is a complete list of these instructions.

LDI	(9.02)	LDIR	(11.84 if BC not 0; 9.02 if BC = 0)
LDD	(9.02)	LDDR	(11.84 if BC not 0; 9.02 if BC = 0)
CPI	(9.02)	CPIR	(11.84 if BC not 0 and A not (HL); 9.02 if BC is 0 or A is (HL))
CPD	(9.02)	CPDR	(11.84 if BC not 0 and A not (HL); 9.02 if BC is 0 or A is (HL))

All the block transfers reset H and N. LDI and LDD set O if BC is not 1, and reset it otherwise. LDIR and LDDR reset O. CPI, CPD, CPIR and CPDR affect H and S; if A = (HL), then Z is set; otherwise it is reset. O is set if BC is not 1; otherwise it is reset.

The execution times shown for the block transfers and block compares is for one cycle, and so the execution time can be obtained by multiplying this by the value of BC.

EIGHT-BIT ARITHMETIC AND LOGICAL OPERATIONS

These operations add to, subtract from, AND, OR, XOR, and compare register A (the "accumulator") with another register, memory location, or number; the result is always in register A.

We can add register A to all 8-bit registers, to (HL), (IX+d), (IY+d), or to an 8-bit integer n. So we have (r is an 8-bit register, n is an 8-bit integer, and d is an 8-bit signed integer) the following.

Arithmetic operations:

ADD A,r	(2.25)	ADD A,n	(3.95)	ADD A,(HL)	(3.95)
ADD A,(IX+d)	(10.71)	ADD A,(IY+d)	(10.71)		
ADC A,r	(2.25)	ADC A,n	(3.95)	ADC A,(HL)	(3.95)
ADC A,(IX+d)	(10.71)	ADC A,(IY+d)	(10.71)		
CP r	(2.25)	CP n	(3.95)	CP (HL)	(3.95)
CP (IX+d)	(10.71)	CP (IY+d)	(10.71)		
SUB r	(2.25)	SUB n	(3.95)	SUB (HL)	(3.95)
SUB (IX+d)	(10.71)	SUB (IY+d)	(10.71)		
SBC A,r	(2.25)	SBC A,n	(2.25)	SBC A,(HL)	(3.95)
SBC A,(IX+d)	(10.71)	SBC A,(IY+d)	(10.71)		

All flags are affected.

Examples: Let A contain $F1_H$. Then after ADD A,2H, A contains $F3_H$ and the carry flag is reset since there is no carry. However, after ADD A,0EH, register A is 00_H and the carry flag is set.

ADC is add with carry; it works similarly, except that if before the operation the carry flag is set, then we add 1 to the result of the addition. SUB is subtract and SBC is subtract with carry. The latter means that the carry flag acts as borrow for the subtraction. CP is compare. The flags are set by CP as by the compare ROM routines (see Table 8.2).

Logical operations:

AND r	(2.25)	AND n	(3.95)	AND (HL)	(3.95)
AND (IX+d)	(10.71)	AND (IY+d)	(10.71)		
OR r	(2.25)	OR n	(3.95)	OR (HL)	(3.95)
OR (IX+d)	(10.71)	OR (IY+d)	(10.71)		
XOR r	(2.25)	XOR n	(3.95)	XOR (HL)	(3.95)
XOR (IX+d)	(10.71)	XOR (IY+d)	(10.71)		

All flags are affected.

The same registers and locations can be decremented and incremented.

Decrements and increments:

DEC r	(2.25)	DEC (HL)	(6.2)	DEC (IX+d)	(12.97)
DEC (IY+d)	(12.97)				
INC r	(2.25)	INC (HL)	(6.2)	INC (IX+d)	(12.97)
INC (IY+d)	(12.97)				

Flags affected are S, Z, H, O, and N.

SIXTEEN-BIT ARITHMETIC OPERATIONS

Although the result of an 8-bit arithmetic operations is always in register A, in the 16-bit case, HL, IX, and IY all can play this role.

ADD HL,BC, ADD HL,DE, ADD HL,HL, ADD HL,SP store the result in HL. Only the carry flag works as in the 8-bit case; it contains the overflow.

ADD IX,BC, . . . , ADD IX,SP, ADD IY,BC, . . . , ADD IY,SP store the result in IX and IY respectively. ADC HL and SBC HL are the add with carry and subtract with carry (borrow); they apply to HL and one of BC, DE, HL, SP, with the result in HL. The carry flag works for both.

Here is the complete list of available instructions (rp is one of the register pairs BC, DE, or HL, or the 16-bit register SP, rp_1 is one of BC, DE, IX, SP; rp_2 is one of BC, DE, IY, SP).

ADD HL,rp (6.2) ADD IX,rp_1 (8.46) ADD IY,rp_2 (8.46)

Flags affected: H is set if there is a carry from bit 11, and reset otherwise; N is reset; C contains the carry from bit 15.

ADC HL,rp (8.46) SBC HL,rp (8.46)

Flags affected: S, Z, O, C, N; H has the carry (borrow) from bit 12.

We can decrement and increment any register pair:

DEC rp	(3.38)	DEC IX	(5.64)	DEC IY	(5.64)
INC rp	(3.38)	INC IX	(5.64)	INC IY	(5.64)

These instructions do not affect the flags!

BIT MANIPULATION

These instructions rotate, shift, set, reset, and test bits. If you need almost any type of bit manipulation, a careful search will reveal that it can be done with the instructions of this section. Some examples are given in Chapters 11 and 12.

The rotate instructions move around the 8 bits of a register or a memory location and the carry flag. The shift instructions, as a rule, introduce a 0.

Rotate left through C.
Pattern—cyclic rotation to the left with C:

C ← bit 7 ← . . . ← bit 0 ← C

Instructions:

RL r	(4.51)	RL (HL)	(8.46)
RL (IX+d)	(12.97)	RLA (IY+d)	(12.97)

All flags are affected.

RLA (2.25) performs the same function as RL A except that it affects only H, N, and C.

Example: If the register A contains 0101 0101 and the flag C is set, then after performing RL A (or RLA) the register A will contain 1010 1011 and C is reset.

Rotate right through C.

Pattern—cyclic rotation to the right with C:

C → bit 7 → . . . → bit 0 → C

Instructions:

RL r	(4.51)	RL (HL)	(8.46)
RL (IX+d)	(12.97)	RLA (IY+d)	(12.97)

All flags are affected.

RLA (2.25) performs the same function as RR A; it affects only H, N, and C.

Rotate left.

Pattern—cyclic rotation of the 8 bits to the left; bit 7 is also copied into C:

bit 0 ← bit 7 ← bit 6 ← . . . ← bit 1 ← bit 0

and bit 7 → C.

Instructions:

RLC r	(4.51)	RLC (HL)	(8.46)
RLC (IX+d)	(11.27)	RLC (IY+d)	(11.27)

Flags affected: S, Z, P; H, N reset, C as indicated.

RLCA (2.25) carried out the same function as RLC A; flags affected are H, N, C.

Rotate right.

Pattern—cyclic rotation of the 8 bits to the right; bit 0 is also copied into C:

bit 0 → bit 7 → bit 6 → . . . → bit 1 → bit 0

and also bit 0 → C.

Instructions:

RRC r	(4.51)	RRC (HL)	(8.46)
RRC (IX+d)	(12.97)	RRC (IY+d)	(12.97)

Flags affected: P; H, N reset, C as indicated.

RRCA (2.25) carries out the same function as RRC A (except that P is not affected).

Shift left arithmetic.

Pattern—all bits are shifted left one and 0 into bit 0:

C ← bit 7 ← bit 6 ← . . . ← bit 1 ← bit 0 ← 0

Instructions:

SLA r	(4.51)	SLA (HL)	(8.46)
SLA (IX+d)	(12.97)	SLA (IY+d)	(12.97)

All flags are affected.

Shift right arithmetic.

Pattern—bit 7 is not changed; everything is shifted right one:

bit 7 → bit 7 → bit 6 → . . . → bit 1 → bit 0 → C

Instructions:

SRA r	(4.51)	SRA (HL)	(8.46)
SRA (IX+d)	(12.97)	SRA (IY+d)	(12.97)

Shift right logical.

Pattern—all bits are shifted right one and 0 into bit 7:

0 → bit 7 → bit 6 → . . . → bit 1 → bit 0 → C

Instructions:

SRL r	(4.51)	SRL (HL)	(8.46)
SRL (IX+d)	(12.97)	SRL (IY+d)	(12.97)

All flags are affected.

Four-bit shifts.

RLD (10.14) is a cyclic rotation (high-order 4 bits refer to bits 4 to 7 and low-order 4 bits to bit 0 to 3): the low-order 4 bits of (HL) → high-order 4 bits of (HL) → low-order 4 bits of A → low-order 4 bits of (HL).

RRD (10.14) does the same, interchanging the role of the high-order 4 bits and the low-order 4 bits of the target byte.

Flags affected: S, Z, P; H, N reset.

Bit testing.

Places the complement of the selected bit in flag Z. Instructions (b is 0 to 7 and r is an 8-bit register):

BIT b,r	(4.51)	BIT b,(HL)	(6.76)
BIT b,(IX+d)	(11.27)	BIT b,(IY+d)	(11.27)

Flags affected: H set, N reset, Z as specified.

Bit setting and resetting.

Sets or resets a bit.

Instructions (b is 0 to 7 and r is an 8-bit register):

SET b,r and RES b,r (4.51)
SET b,(HL) and RES b,(HL) (6.76)
SET b,(IX+d) and RES b,(IX+d) (9.02)
SET b,(IY+d) and RES b,(IY+d) (9.02)

No flags are affected.

JUMPS, CALLS, AND RETURNS

We have become familiar with a number of jump instruction in Parts III and IV (nm is a 16-bit integer):

JP nm (5.64)
JR label (or JR $ + d, where d is the displacement) (6.76)
JP cond,nm, where cond is NZ (nonzero), Z (zero), NC (no carry), C (carry), PO (parity odd), PE (parity even), P (sign positive), M (sign negative) (5.64)
JR cond,label, where cond is Z, NZ, C, NC (6.76 if condition met, 3.95 if condition not met)
DJNZ label (7.89 if B not 0, 4.51 if B is 0)

There are three more jump instructions:

JP (HL) (2.25) place HL in PC and continues program execution from there
JP (IX) and JP (IY) (4.51) perform the same with IX and IY, respectively

We have also come across most CALLs and RETurns:

CALL nm (9.58)
CALL cond, nm (all eight conditions) (9.58 if condition met, 5.64 if condition not met)
RET (5.64)
RET cond (all eight conditions) (5.64 if condition met, 2.82 if not met)
RST 0H, 8H, 10H, . . . , 30H, 38H (6.2)

There are two more RET instructions, RETI and RETN (7.89), used in interrupt programming.

None of these affect any flags.

MISCELLANEOUS INSTRUCTIONS

IN A,(n) (6.2) (flags not affected) and IN r,(C) (6.76) (flags check input data) place a byte of data in register A from a port selected by n or register C respectively.

OUT (n),A (6.2) and OUT (C),r outputs a byte from register A to the selected port (flags not affected).

INIR (11.84 if B not 0, 9.02 if B is 0) is the block input instruction; register C selects the port, B is the byte counter, and HL is the buffer address (only N and H are affected), INDR is the same with HL pointing at the top of the buffer (Z and N are set). INI and IND are the one step versions of these (Z is set if B = 1, N is set).

DAA is used for BCD (binary coded arithmetic).

CPL (2.25) complements register A (flags H and N are set).

NEG (4.51) takes the two's complement of register A. (All flags affected.)

CCF (2.25) inverts the flag C (C is copied into H, N is reset), while SCF (2.25) sets flag C. (H and N are reset.)

NOP (2.25) is no operation, causes a pause, while HALT (2.25) suspends the operation of the CPU until an interrupt or reset.

DI (2.25) disables interrupts (for the TRS-80 this means the clock interrupt and the disk interrupt); EI (2.25) enables the interrupts. IM 0, IM 1, and IM 2 (4.51) set the interrupt mode; IM 0 and IM 2 are unavailable on the TRS-80 computer.

APPENDIX THREE

Two Listings of the Z-80 Instruction Set

In this appendix we give two listings of the Z-80 instruction set: first an alphabetic listing and then a numeric listing.

The alphabetic listing can be utilized to do hand assembly of short assembly language programs. Hand assembly is a useful exercise; it develops familiarity with the instruction set. Here are a few examples:

1. CALL 901H: CALL is DC, so CALL 901H is DC0109 (note that 0901 is inverted)
2. LD B,A: 47
3. LD H,5 (IX+5): DD6605

The numeric listing is very useful in small disassemblies of machine language programs. Here is an example:

CA 7E 19 23 5E

Upon looking up CA in the numeric listing we find that it is the first byte of 3-byte instruction JP Z,nm; thus CA 7E 19 is JP Z,2319H; the next byte is 23, which is INC HL; the last byte is 5E, which is LD E,(HL).

In this book we use the convention that n denotes an 8-bit integer, nm denotes a 16-bit integer, and d denotes a signed 8-bit integer. In the tables of this appendix, in the assembled form, these will be denoted by no, mono (notice the reversed order), and do, respectively, to make clear how many hex digits are needed to write them.

Alphabetic Listing

Hex	Mnemonic		Hex	Mnemonic	
8E	ADC	A,(HL)	CB4B	BIT	1,E
DD8Edo	ADC	A,(IX+d)	CB4C	BIT	1,H
FD8Edo	ADC	A,(IY+d)	CB4D	BIT	1,L
8F	ADC	A,A	CB56	BIT	2,(HL)
88	ADC	A,B	DDCBdo56	BIT	2,(IX+d)
89	ADC	A,C	FDCBdo56	BIT	2,(IY+d)
8A	ADC	A,D	CB57	BIT	2,A
8B	ADC	A,E	CB50	BIT	2,B
8C	ADC	A,H	CB51	BIT	2,C
8D	ADC	A,L	CB52	BIT	2,D
CEno	ADC	A,n	CB53	BIT	2,E
ED4A	ADC	HL,BC	CB54	BIT	2,H
ED5A	ADC	HL,DE	CB55	BIT	2,L
ED6A	ADC	HL,HL	CB5E	BIT	3,(HL)
ED7A	ADC	HL,SP	DDCBdo5E	BIT	3,(IX+d)
86	ADD	A,(HL)	FDCBdo5E	BIT	3,(IY+d)
DD86do	ADD	A,(IX+d)	CB5F	BIT	3,A
FD86do	ADD	A,(IY+d)	CB58	BIT	3,B
87	ADD	A,A	CB59	BIT	3,C
80	ADD	A,B	CB5A	BIT	3,D
81	ADD	A,C	CB5B	BIT	3,E
82	ADD	A,D	CB5C	BIT	3,H
83	ADD	A,E	CB5D	BIT	3,L
84	ADD	A,H	CB66	BIT	4,(HL)
85	ADD	A,L	DDCBdo66	BIT	4,(IX+d)
C6no	ADD	A,n	FDCBdo66	BIT	4,(IY+d)
09	ADD	HL,BC	CB67	BIT	4,A
19	ADD	HL,DE	CB60	BIT	4,B
29	ADD	HL,HL	CB61	BIT	4,C
39	ADD	HL,SP	CB62	BIT	4,D
DD09	ADD	IX,BC	CB63	BIT	4,E
DD19	ADD	IX,DE	CB64	BIT	4,H
DD29	ADD	IX,IX	CB65	BIT	4,L
DD39	ADD	IX,SP	CB6E	BIT	5,(HL)
FD09	ADD	IY,BC	DDCBdo6E	BIT	5,(IX+d)
FD19	ADD	IY,DE	FDCBdo6E	BIT	5,(IY+d)
FD29	ADD	IY,IY	CB6F	BIT	5,A
FD39	ADD	IY,SP	CB68	BIT	5,B
A6	AND	(HL)	CB69	BIT	5,C
DDA6do	AND	(IX+d)	CB6A	BIT	5,D
FDA6do	AND	(IY+d)	CB6B	BIT	5,E
A7	AND	A	CB6C	BIT	5,H
A0	AND	B	CB6D	BIT	5,L
A1	AND	C	CB76	BIT	6,(HL)
A2	AND	D	DDCBdo76	BIT	6,(IX+d)
A3	AND	E	FDCBdo76	BIT	6,(IY+d)
A4	AND	H	CB77	BIT	6,A
A5	AND	L	CB70	BIT	6,B
E6no	AND	n	CB71	BIT	6,C
CB46	BIT	0,(HL)	CB72	BIT	6,D
DDCBdo46	BIT	0,(IX+d)	CB73	BIT	6,E
FDCBdo46	BIT	0,(IY+d)	CB74	BIT	6,H
CB47	BIT	0,A	CB75	BIT	6,L
CB40	BIT	0,B	CB7E	BIT	7,(HL)
CB41	BIT	0,C	DDCBdo7E	BIT	7,(IX+d)
CB42	BIT	0,D	FDCBdo7E	BIT	7,(IY+d)
CB43	BIT	0,E	CB7F	BIT	7,A
CB44	BIT	0,H	CB78	BIT	7,B
CB45	BIT	0,L	CB79	BIT	7,C
CB4E	BIT	1,(HL)	CB7A	BIT	7,D
DDCBdo4E	BIT	1,(IX+d)	CB7B	BIT	7,E
FDCBdo4E	BIT	1,(IY+d)	CB7C	BIT	7,H
CB4F	BIT	1,A	CB7D	BIT	7,L
CB48	BIT	1,B	DCmono	CALL	C,nm
CB49	BIT	1,C	FCmono	CALL	M,nm
CB4A	BIT	1,D	D4mono	CALL	NC,nm

Hex	Mnemonic	
CDmono	CALL	nm
C4mono	CALL	NZ,nm
F4mono	CALL	P,nm
ECmono	CALL	PE,nm
E4mono	CALL	PO,nm
CCmono	CALL	Z,nm
3F	CCF	
BE	CP	(HL)
DDBEdo	CP	(IX+d)
FDBEdo	CP	(IY+d)
BF	CP	A
B8	CP	B
B9	CP	C
BA	CP	D
BB	CP	E
BC	CP	H
BD	CP	L
FEno	CP	n
EDA9	CPD	
EDB9	CPDR	
EdA1	CPI	
EDB1	CPIR	
2F	CPL	
27	DAA	
35	DEC	(HL)
DD35do	DEC	(IX+d)
FD35do	DEC	(IY+d)
3D	DEC	A
05	DEC	B
0B	DEC	BC
0D	DEC	C
15	DEC	D
1B	DEC	DE
1D	DEC	E
25	DEC	H
2B	DEC	HL
DD2B	DEC	IX
FD2B	DEC	IY
2D	DEC	L
3B	DEC	SP
F3	DI	
10do	DJNZ	,d
FB	EI	
E3	EX	(SP),HL
DDE3	EX	(SP),IX
FDE3	EX	(SP),IY
08	EX	AF,AF'
EB	EX	DE,HL
D9	EXX	
76	HALT	
ED46	IM	0
ED56	IM	1
ED5E	IM	2
ED78	IN	A,(C)
DBno	IN	A,(n)
ED40	IN	B,(C)
ED48	IN	C,(C)
ED50	IN	D,(C)
ED58	IN	E,(C)
ED60	IN	H,(C)
ED68	IN	L,(C)
34	INC	(HL)
DD34do	INC	(IX+d)
FD34do	INC	(IY+d)
3C	INC	A
04	INC	B
03	INC	BC
0C	INC	C
14	INC	D

Hex	Mnemonic	
13	INC	DE
1C	INC	E
24	INC	H
23	INC	HL
DD23	INC	IX
FD23	INC	IY
2C	INC	L
33	INC	SP
EDAA	IND	
EDBA	INDR	
EDA2	INI	
EDB2	INIR	
E9	JP	(HL)
DDE9	JP	(IX)
FDE9	JP	(IY)
DAmono	JP	C,nm
FAmono	JP	M,nm
D2mono	JP	NC,nm
C3mono	JP	nm
C2mono	JP	NZ,nm
F2mono	JP	P,nm
EAmono	JP	PE,nm
E2mono	JP	PO,nm
CAmono	JP	Z,nm
38do	JR	C,d
18do	JR	d
30do	JR	NC,d
20do	JR	NZ,d
28do	JR	Z,d
02	LD	(BC),A
12	LD	(DE),A
77	LD	(HL),A
70	LD	(HL),B
71	LD	(HL),C
72	LD	(HL),D
73	LD	(HL),E
74	LD	(HL),H
75	LD	(HL),L
36no	LD	(HL),n
DD77do	LD	(IX+d),A
DD70do	LD	(IX+d),B
DD71do	LD	(IX+d),C
DD72do	LD	(IX+d),D
DD73do	LD	(IX+d),E
DD74do	LD	(IX+d),H
DD75do	LD	(IX+d),L
DD36dono	LD	(IX+d),n
FD77do	LD	(IY+d),A
FD70do	LD	(IY+d),B
FD71do	LD	(IY+d),C
FD72do	LD	(IY+d),D
FD73do	LD	(IY+d),E
FD74do	LD	(IY+d),H
FD75do	LD	(IY+d),L
FD36dono	LD	(IY+d),n
32mono	LD	(nm),A
ED43mono	LD	(nm),BC
ED53mono	LD	(nm),DE
22mono	LD	(nm),HL
DD22mono	LD	(nm),IX
FD22mono	LD	(nm),IY
ED73mono	LD	(nm),SP
0A	LD	A,(BC)
1A	LD	A,(DE)
7E	LD	A,(HL)
DD7Edo	LD	A,(IX+d)
FD7Edo	LD	A,(IY+d)
3Amono	LD	A,(nm)
7F	LD	A,A

Hex	Mnemonic		Hex	Mnemonic	
78	LD	A,B	2Amono	LD	HL,(nm)
79	LD	A,C	21mono	LD	HL,nm
7A	LD	A,D	ED47	LD	I,A
7B	LD	A,E	DD2Amono	LD	IX,(nm)
7C	LD	A,H	DD21mono	LD	IX,nm
ED57	LD	A,I	FD2Amono	LD	IY,(nm)
7D	LD	A,L	FD21mono	LD	IY,nm
3Eno	LD	A,n	6E	LD	L,(HL)
ED5F	LD	A,R	DD6Edo	LD	L,(IX+d)
46	LD	B,(HL)	FD6Edo	LD	L,(IY+d)
DD46do	LD	B,(IX+d)	6F	LD	L,A
FD46do	LD	B,(IY+d)	68	LD	L,B
47	LD	B,A	69	LD	L,C
40	LD	B,B	6A	LD	L,D
41	LD	B,C	6B	LD	L,E
42	LD	B,D	6C	LD	L,H
43	LD	B,E	6D	LD	L,L
44	LD	B,H	2Eno	LD	L,n
45	LD	B,L	ED4F	LD	R,A
06no	LD	B,n	ED7Bmono	LD	SP,(nm)
ED4Bmono	LD	BC,(nm)	F9	LD	SP,HL
01mono	LD	BC,nm	DDF9	LD	SP,IX
4E	LD	C,(HL)	FDF9	LD	SP,IY
DD4Edo	LD	C,(IX+d)	31mono	LD	SP,nm
FD4Edo	LD	C,(IY+d)	EDA8	LDD	
4F	LD	C,A	EDB8	LDDR	
48	LD	C,B	EDA0	LDI	
49	LD	C,C	EDB0	LDIR	
4A	LD	C,D	ED44	NEG	
4B	LD	C,E	00	NOP	
4C	LD	C,H	B6	OR	(HL)
4D	LD	C,L	DDB6do	OR	(IX+d)
0Eno	LD	C,n	FDB6do	OR	(IY+d)
56	LD	D,(HL)	B7	OR	A
DD56do	LD	D,(IX+d)	B0	OR	B
FD56do	LD	D,(IY+d)	B1	OR	C
57	LD	D,A	B2	OR	D
50	LD	D,B	B3	OR	E
51	LD	D,C	B4	OR	H
52	LD	D,D	B5	OR	L
53	LD	D,E	F6no	OR	n
54	LD	D,H	EDBB	OTDR	
55	LD	D,L	EDB3	OTIR	
16no	LD	D,n	ED79	OUT	(C),A
ED5Bmono	LD	DE,(nm)	ED41	OUT	(C),B
11mono	LD	DE,nm	ED49	OUT	(C),C
5E	LD	E,(HL)	ED51	OUT	(C),D
DD5Edo	LD	E,(IX+d)	ED59	OUT	(C),E
FD5Edo	LD	E,(IY+d)	ED61	OUT	(C),H
5F	LD	E,A	ED69	OUT	(C),L
58	LD	E,B	D3no	OUT	(n),A
59	LD	E,C	EDAB	OUTD	
5A	LD	E,D	EDA3	OUTI	
5B	LD	E,E	F1	POP	AF
5C	LD	E,H	C1	POP	BC
5D	LD	E,L	D1	POP	DE
1Eno	LD	E,n	E1	POP	HL
66	LD	H,(HL)	DDE1	POP	IX
DD66do	LD	H,(IX+d)	FDE1	POP	IY
FD66do	LD	H,(IY+d)	F5	PUSH	AF
67	LD	H,A	C5	PUSH	BC
60	LD	H,B	D5	PUSH	DE
61	LD	H,C	E5	PUSH	HL
62	LD	H,D	DDE5	PUSH	IX
63	LD	H,E	FDE5	PUSH	IY
64	LD	H,H	CB86	RES	0,(HL)
65	LD	H,L	DDCBdo86	RES	0,(IX+d)
26no	LD	H,n	FDCBdo86	RES	0,(IY+d)

Hex	Mnemonic	
CB87	RES	0,A
CB80	RES	0,B
CB81	RES	0,C
CB82	RES	0,D
CB83	RES	0,E
CB84	RES	0,H
CB85	RES	0,L
CB8E	RES	1,(HL)
DDCBdo8E	RES	1,(IX+d)
FDCBdo8E	RES	1,(IY+d)
CB8F	RES	1,A
CB88	RES	1,B
CB89	RES	1,C
CB8A	RES	1,D
CB8B	RES	1,E
CB8C	RES	1,H
CB8D	RES	1,L
CB96	RES	2,(HL)
DDCBdo96	RES	2,(IX+d)
FDCBdo96	RES	2,(IY+d)
CB97	RES	2,A
CB90	RES	2,B
CB91	RES	2,C
CB92	RES	2,D
CB93	RES	2,E
CB94	RES	2,H
CB95	RES	2,L
CB9E	RES	3,(HL)
DDCBdo9E	RES	3,(IX+d)
FDCBdo9E	RES	3,(IY+d)
CB9F	RES	3,A
CB98	RES	3,B
CB99	RES	3,C
CB9A	RES	3,D
CB9B	RES	3,E
CB9C	RES	3,H
CB9D	RES	3,L
CBA6	RES	4,(HL)
DDCBdoA6	RES	4,(IX+d)
FDCBdoA6	RES	4,(IY+d)
CBA7	RES	4,A
CBA0	RES	4,B
CBA1	RES	4,C
CBA2	RES	4,D
CBA3	RES	4,E
CBA4	RES	4,H
CBA5	RES	4,L
CBAE	RES	5,(HL)
DDCBdoAE	RES	5,(IX+d)
FDCBdoAE	RES	5,(IY+d)
CBAF	RES	5,A
CBA8	RES	5,B
CBA9	RES	5,C
CBAA	RES	5,D
CBAB	RES	5,E
CBAC	RES	5,H
CBAD	RES	5,L
CBB6	RES	6,(HL)
DDCBdoB6	RES	6,(IX+d)
FDCBdoB6	RES	6,(IY+d)
CBB7	RES	6,A
CBB0	RES	6,B
CBB1	RES	6,C
CBB2	RES	6,D
CBB3	RES	6,E
CBB4	RES	6,H
CBB5	RES	6,L
CBBE	RES	7,(HL)

Hex	Mnemonic	
DDCBdoBE	RES	7,(IX+d)
FDCBdoBE	RES	7,(IY+d)
CBBF	RES	7,A
CBB8	RES	7,B
CBB9	RES	7,C
CBBA	RES	7,D
CBBB	RES	7,E
CBBC	RES	7,H
CBBD	RES	7,L
C9	RET	
D8	RET	C
F8	RET	M
D0	RET	NC
C0	RET	NZ
F0	RET	P
E8	RET	PE
E0	RET	PO
C8	RET	Z
ED4D	RETI	
ED45	RETN	
CB16	RL	(HL)
DDCBdo16	RL	(IX+d)
FDCBdo16	RL	(IY+d)
CB17	RL	A
CB10	RL	B
CB11	RL	C
CB12	RL	D
CB13	RL	E
CB14	RL	H
CB15	RL	L
17	RLA	
CB06	RLC	(HL)
DDCBdo06	RLC	(IX+d)
FDCBdo06	RLC	(IY+d)
CB07	RLC	A
CB00	RLC	B
CB01	RLC	C
CB02	RLC	D
CB03	RLC	E
CB04	RLC	H
CB05	RLC	L
07	RLCA	
ED6F	RLD	
CB1E	RR	(HL)
DDCBdo1E	RR	(IX+d)
FDCBdo1E	RR	(IY+d)
CB1F	RR	A
CB18	RR	B
CB19	RR	C
CB1A	RR	D
CB1B	RR	E
CB1C	RR	H
CB1D	RR	L
1F	RRA	
CB0E	RRC	(HL)
DDCBdo0E	RRC	(IX+d)
FDCBdo0E	RRC	(IY+d)
CB0F	RRC	A
CB08	RRC	B
CB09	RRC	C
CB0A	RRC	D
CB0B	RRC	E
CB0C	RRC	H
CB0D	RRC	L
0F	RRCA	
ED67	RRD	
C7	RST	00H
CF	RST	08H

Hex	Mnemonic	Hex	Mnemonic
D7	RST 10H	CBE2	SET 4,D
DF	RST 18H	CBE3	SET 4,E
E7	RST 20H	CBE4	SET 4,H
EF	RST 28H	CBE5	SET 4,L
F7	RST 30H	CBEE	SET 5,(HL)
FF	RST 38H	DDCBdoEE	SET 5,(IX+d)
9E	SBC A,(HL)	FDCBdoEE	SET 5,(IY+d)
DD9Edo	SBC A,(IX+d)	CBEF	SET 5,A
FD9Edo	SBC A,(IY+d)	CBE8	SET 5,B
9F	SBC A,A	CBE9	SET 5,C
98	SBC A,B	CBEA	SET 5,D
99	SBC A,C	CBEB	SET 5,E
9A	SBC A,D	CBEC	SET 5,H
9B	SBC A,E	CBED	SET 5,L
9C	SBC A,H	CBF6	SET 6,(HL)
9D	SBC A,L	DDCBdoF6	SET 6,(IX+d)
DEno	SBC A,n	FDCBdoF6	SET 6,(IY+d)
ED42	SBC HL,BC	CBF7	SET 6,A
ED52	SBC HL,DE	CBF0	SET 6,B
ED62	SBC HL,HL	CBF1	SET 6,C
ED72	SBC HL,SP	CBF2	SET 6,D
37	SCF	CBF3	SET 6,E
CBC6	SET 0,(HL)	CBF4	SET 6,H
DDCBdoC6	SET 0,(IX+d)	CBF5	SET 6,L
FDCBdoC6	SET 0,(IY+d)	CBFE	SET 7,(HL)
CBC7	SET 0,A	DDCBdoFE	SET 7,(IX+d)
CBC0	SET 0,B	FDCBdoFE	SET 7,(IY+d)
CBC1	SET 0,C	CBFF	SET 7,A
CBC2	SET 0,D	CBF8	SET 7,B
CBC3	SET 0,E	CBF9	SET 7,C
CBC4	SET 0,H	CBFA	SET 7,D
CBC5	SET 0,L	CBFB	SET 7,E
CBCE	SET 1,(HL)	CBFC	SET 7,H
DDCBdoCE	SET 1,(IX+d)	CBFD	SET 7,L
FDCBdoCE	SET 1,(IY+d)	CB26	SLA (HL)
CBCF	SET 1,A	DDCBdo26	SLA (IX+d)
CBC8	SET 1,B	FDCBdo26	SLA (IY+d)
CBC9	SET 1,C	CB27	SLA A
CBCA	SET 1,D	CB20	SLA B
CBCB	SET 1,E	CB21	SLA C
CBCC	SET 1,H	CB22	SLA D
CBCD	SET 1,L	CB23	SLA E
CBD6	SET 2,(HL)	CB24	SLA H
DDCBdoD6	SET 2,(IX+d)	CB25	SLA L
FDCBdoD6	SET 2,(IY+d)	CB2E	SRA (HL)
CBD7	SET 2,A	DDCBdo2E	SRA (IX+d)
CBD0	SET 2,B	FDCBdo2E	SRA (IY+d)
CBD1	SET 2,C	CB2F	SRA A
CBD2	SET 2,D	CB28	SRA B
CBD3	SET 2,E	CB29	SRA C
CBD4	SET 2,H	CB2A	SRA D
CBD5	SET 2,L	CB2B	SRA E
CBDE	SET 3,(HL)	CB2C	SRA H
DDCBdoDE	SET 3,(IX+d)	CB2D	SRA L
FDCBdoDE	SET 3,(IY+d)	CB3E	SRL (HL)
CBDF	SET 3,A	DDCBdo3E	SRL (IX+d)
CBD8	SET 3,B	FDCBdo3E	SRL (IY+d)
CBD9	SET 3,C	CB3F	SRL A
CBDA	SET 3,D	CB38	SRL B
CBDB	SET 3,E	CB39	SRL C
CBDC	SET 3,H	CB3A	SRL D
CBDD	SET 3,L	CB3B	SRL E
CBE6	SET 4,(HL)	CB3C	SRL H
DDCBdoE6	SET 4,(IX+d)	CB3D	SRL L
FDCBdoE6	SET 4,(IY+d)	96	SUB (HL)
CBE7	SET 4,A	DD96do	SUB (IX+d)
CBE0	SET 4,B	FD96do	SUB (IY+d)
CBE1	SET 4,C	97	SUB A

Hex	Mnemonic		Hex	Mnemonic	
90	SUB	B	FDAEdo	XOR	(IY+d)
91	SUB	C	AF	XOR	A
92	SUB	D	A8	XOR	B
93	SUB	E	A9	XOR	C
94	SUB	H	AA	XOR	D
95	SUB	L	AB	XOR	E
D6no	SUB	n	AC	XOR	H
AE	XOR	(HL)	AD	XOR	L
DDAEdo	XOR	(IX+d)	EEno	XOR	n

Numeric Listing

Hex	Mnemonic		Hex	Mnemonic	
00	NOP		34	INC	(HL)
01mono	LD	BC,nm	35	DEC	(HL)
02	LD	(BC),A	36no	LD	(HL),n
03	INC	BC	37	SCF	
04	INC	B	38do	JR	C,d
05	DEC	B	39	ADD	HL,SP
06no	LD	B,n	3Amono	LD	A,(nm)
07	RLCA		3B	DEC	SP
08	EX	AF,AF'	3C	INC	A
09	ADD	HL,BC	3D	DEC	A
0A	LD	A,(BC)	3Eno	LD	A,n
0B	DEC	BC	3F	CCF	
0C	INC	C	40	LD	B,B
0D	DEC	C	41	LD	B,C
0Eno	LD	C,n	42	LD	B,D
0F	RRCA		43	LD	B,E
10do	DJNZ	,d	44	LD	B,H
11mono	LD	DE,nm	45	LD	B,L
12	LD	(DE),A	46	LD	B,(HL)
13	INC	DE	47	LD	B,A
14	INC	D	48	LD	C,B
15	DEC	D	49	LD	C,C
16no	LD	D,n	4A	LD	C,D
17	RLA		4B	LD	C,E
18do	JR	d	4C	LD	C,H
19	ADD	HL,DE	4D	LD	C,L
1A	LD	A,(DE)	4E	LD	C,(HL)
1B	DEC	DE	4F	LD	C,A
1C	INC	E	50	LD	D,B
1D	DEC	E	51	LD	D,C
1Eno	LD	E,n	52	LD	D,D
1F	RRA		53	LD	D,E
20do	JR	NZ,d	54	LD	D,H
21mono	LD	HL,nm	55	LD	D,L
22mono	LD	(nm),HL	56	LD	D,(HL)
23	INC	HL	57	LD	D,A
24	INC	H	58	LD	E,B
25	DEC	H	59	LD	E,C
26no	LD	H,n	5A	LD	E,D
27	DAA		5B	LD	E,E
28do	JR	Z,d	5C	LD	E,H
29	ADD	HL,HL	5D	LD	E,L
2Amono	LD	HL,(nm)	5E	LD	E,(HL)
2B	DEC	HL	5F	LD	E,A
2C	INC	L	60	LD	H,B
2D	DEC	L	61	LD	H,C
2Eno	LD	L,n	62	LD	H,D
2F	CPL		63	LD	H,E
30do	JR	NC,d	64	LD	H,H
31mono	LD	SP,nm	65	LD	H,L
32mono	LD	(nm),A	66	LD	H,(HL)
33	INC	SP	67	LD	H,A

Hex	Mnemonic
68	LD L,B
69	LD L,C
6A	LD L,D
6B	LD L,E
6C	LD L,H
6D	LD L,L
6E	LD L,(HL)
6F	LD L,A
70	LD (HL),B
71	LD (HL),C
72	LD (HL),D
73	LD (HL),E
74	LD (HL),H
75	LD (HL),L
76	HALT
77	LD (HL),A
78	LD A,B
79	LD A,C
7A	LD A,D
7B	LD A,E
7C	LD A,H
7D	LD A,L
7E	LD A,(HL)
7F	LD A,A
80	ADD A,B
81	ADD A,C
82	ADD A,D
83	ADD A,E
84	ADD A,H
85	ADD A,L
86	ADD A,(HL)
87	ADD A,A
88	ADC A,B
89	ADC A,C
8A	ADC A,D
8B	ADC A,E
8C	ADC A,H
8D	ADC A,L
8E	ADC A,(HL)
8F	ADC A,A
90	SUB B
91	SUB C
92	SUB D
93	SUB E
94	SUB H
95	SUB L
96	SUB (HL)
97	SUB A
98	SBC A,B
99	SBC A,C
9A	SBC A,D
9B	SBC A,E
9C	SBC A,H
9D	SBC A,L
9E	SBC A,(HL)
9F	SBC A,A
A0	AND B
A1	AND C
A2	AND D
A3	AND E
A4	AND H
A5	AND L
A6	AND (HL)
A7	AND A
A8	XOR B
A9	XOR C
AA	XOR D
AB	XOR E

Hex	Mnemonic
AC	XOR H
AD	XOR L
AE	XOR (HL)
AF	XOR A
B0	OR B
B1	OR C
B2	OR D
B3	OR E
B4	OR H
B5	OR L
B6	OR (HL)
B7	OR A
B8	CP B
B9	CP C
BA	CP D
BB	CP E
BC	CP H
BD	CP L
BE	CP (HL)
BF	CP A
C0	RET NZ
C1	POP BC
C2mono	JP NZ,nm
C3mono	JP nm
C4mono	CALL NZ,nm
C5	PUSH BC
C6no	ADD A,n
C7	RST 00H
C8	RET Z
C9	RET
CAmono	JP Z,nm
CB00	RLC B
CB01	RLC C
CB02	RLC D
CB03	RLC E
CB04	RLC H
CB05	RLC L
CB06	RLC (HL)
CB07	RLC A
CB08	RRC B
CB09	RRC C
CB0A	RRC D
CB0B	RRC E
CB0C	RRC H
CB0D	RRC L
CB0E	RRC (HL)
CB0F	RRC A
CB10	RL B
CB11	RL C
CB12	RL D
CB13	RL E
CB14	RL H
CB15	RL L
CB16	RL (HL)
CB17	RL A
CB18	RR B
CB19	RR C
CB1A	RR D
CB1B	RR E
CB1C	RR H
CB1D	RR L
CB1E	RR (HL)
CB1F	RR A
CB20	SLA B
CB21	SLA C
CB22	SLA D
CB23	SLA E
CB24	SLA H

Hex	Mnemonic
CB25	SLA L
CB26	SLA (HL)
CB27	SLA A
CB28	SRA B
CB29	SRA C
CB2A	SRA D
CB2B	SRA E
CB2C	SRA H
CB2D	SRA L
CB2E	SRA (HL)
CB2F	SRA A
CB38	SRL B
CB39	SRL C
CB3A	SRL D
CB3B	SRL E
CB3C	SRL H
CB3D	SRL L
CB3E	SRL (HL)
CB3F	SRL A
CB40	BIT 0,B
CB41	BIT 0,C
CB42	BIT 0,D
CB43	BIT 0,E
CB44	BIT 0,H
CB45	BIT 0,L
CB46	BIT 0,(HL)
CB47	BIT 0,A
CB48	BIT 1,B
CB49	BIT 1,C
CB4A	BIT 1,D
CB4B	BIT 1,E
CB4C	BIT 1,H
CB4D	BIT 1,L
CB4E	BIT 1,(HL)
CB4F	BIT 1,A
CB50	BIT 2,B
CB51	BIT 2,C
CB52	BIT 2,D
CB53	BIT 2,E
CB54	BIT 2,H
CB55	BIT 2,L
CB56	BIT 2,(HL)
CB57	BIT 2,A
CB58	BIT 3,B
CB59	BIT 3,C
CB5A	BIT 3,D
CB5B	BIT 3,E
CB5C	BIT 3,H
CB5D	BIT 3,L
CB5E	BIT 3,(HL)
CB5F	BIT 3,A
CB60	BIT 4,B
CB61	BIT 4,C
CB62	BIT 4,D
CB63	BIT 4,E
CB64	BIT 4,H
CB65	BIT 4,L
CB66	BIT 4,(HL)
CB67	BIT 4,A
CB68	BIT 5,B
CB69	BIT 5,C
CB6A	BIT 5,D
CB6B	BIT 5,E
CB6C	BIT 5,H
CB6D	BIT 5,L
CB6E	BIT 5,(HL)
CB6F	BIT 5,A
CB70	BIT 6,B

Hex	Mnemonic
CB71	BIT 6,C
CB72	BIT 6,D
CB73	BIT 6,E
CB74	BIT 6,H
CB75	BIT 6,L
CB76	BIT 6,(HL)
CB77	BIT 6,A
CB78	BIT 7,B
CB79	BIT 7,C
CB7A	BIT 7,D
CB7B	BIT 7,E
CB7C	BIT 7,H
CB7D	BIT 7,L
CB7E	BIT 7,(HL)
CB7F	BIT 7,A
CB80	RES 0,B
CB81	RES 0,C
CB82	RES 0,D
CB83	RES 0,E
CB84	RES 0,H
CB85	RES 0,L
CB86	RES 0,(HL)
CB87	RES 0,A
CB88	RES 1,B
CB89	RES 1,C
CB8A	RES 1,D
CB8B	RES 1,E
CB8C	RES 1,H
CB8D	RES 1,L
CB8E	RES 1,(HL)
CB8F	RES 1,A
CB90	RES 2,B
CB91	RES 2,C
CB92	RES 2,D
CB93	RES 2,E
CB94	RES 2,H
CB95	RES 2,L
CB96	RES 2,(HL)
CB97	RES 2,A
CB98	RES 3,B
CB99	RES 3,C
CB9A	RES 3,D
CB9B	RES 3,E
CB9C	RES 3,H
CB9D	RES 3,L
CB9E	RES 3,(HL)
CB9F	RES 3,A
CBA0	RES 4,B
CBA1	RES 4,C
CBA2	RES 4,D
CBA3	RES 4,E
CBA4	RES 4,H
CBA5	RES 4,L
CBA6	RES 4,(HL)
CBA7	RES 4,A
CBA8	RES 5,B
CBA9	RES 5,C
CBAA	RES 5,D
CBAB	RES 5,E
CBAC	RES 5,H
CBAD	RES 5,L
CBAE	RES 5,(HL)
CBAF	RES 5,A
CBB0	RES 6,B
CBB1	RES 6,C
CBB2	RES 6,D
CBB3	RES 6,E
CBB4	RES 6,H

Hex	Mnemonic	
CBB5	RES	6,L
CBB6	RES	6,(HL)
CBB7	RES	6,A
CBB8	RES	7,B
CBB9	RES	7,C
CBBA	RES	7,D
CBBB	RES	7,E
CBBC	RES	7,H
CBBD	RES	7,L
CBBE	RES	7,(HL)
CBBF	RES	7,A
CBC0	SET	0,B
CBC1	SET	0,C
CBC2	SET	0,D
CBC3	SET	0,E
CBC4	SET	0,H
CBC5	SET	0,L
CBC6	SET	0,(HL)
CBC7	SET	0,A
CBC8	SET	1,B
CBC9	SET	1,C
CBCA	SET	1,D
CBCB	SET	1,E
CBCC	SET	1,H
CBCD	SET	1,L
CBCE	SET	1,(HL)
CBCF	SET	1,A
CBD0	SET	2,B
CBD1	SET	2,C
CBD2	SET	2,D
CBD3	SET	2,E
CBD4	SET	2,H
CBD5	SET	2,L
CBD6	SET	2,(HL)
CBD7	SET	2,A
CBD8	SET	3,B
CBD9	SET	3,C
CBDA	SET	3,D
CBDB	SET	3,E
CBDC	SET	3,H
CBDD	SET	3,L
CBDE	SET	3,(HL)
CBDF	SET	3,A
CBE0	SET	4,B
CBE1	SET	4,C
CBE2	SET	4,D
CBE3	SET	4,E
CBE4	SET	4,H
CBE5	SET	4,L
CBE6	SET	4,(HL)
CBE7	SET	4,A
CBE8	SET	5,B
CBE9	SET	5,C
CBEA	SET	5,D
CBEB	SET	5,E
CBEC	SET	5,H
CBED	SET	5,L
CBEE	SET	5,(HL)
CBEF	SET	5,A
CBF0	SET	6,B
CBF1	SET	6,C
CBF2	SET	6,D
CBF3	SET	6,E
CBF4	SET	6,H
CBF5	SET	6,L
CBF6	SET	6,(HL)
CBF7	SET	6,A
CBF8	SET	7,B

Hex	Mnemonic	
CBF9	SET	7,C
CBFA	SET	7,D
CBFB	SET	7,E
CBFC	SET	7,H
CBFD	SET	7,L
CBFE	SET	7,(HL)
CBFF	SET	7,A
CCmono	CALL	Z,nm
CDmono	CALL	nm
CEno	ADC	A,n
CF	RST	08H
D0	RET	NC
D1	POP	DE
D2mono	JP	NC,nm
D3no	OUT	(n),A
D4mono	CALL	NC,nm
D5	PUSH	DE
D6no	SUB	n
D7	RST	10H
D8	RET	C
D9	EXX	
DAmono	JP	C,nm
DBno	IN	A,(n)
DCmono	CALL	C,nm
DD09	ADD	IX,BC
DD19	ADD	IX,DE
DD21mono	LD	IX,nm
DD22mono	LD	(nm),IX
DD23	INC	IX
DD29	ADD	IX,IX
DD2Amono	LD	IX,(nm)
DD2B	DEC	IX
DD34do	INC	(IX+d)
DD35do	DEC	(IX+d)
DD36dono	LD	(IX+d),n
DD39	ADD	IX,SP
DD46do	LD	B,(IX+d)
DD4Edo	LD	C,(IX+d)
DD56do	LD	D,(IX+d)
DD5Edo	LD	E,(IX+d)
DD66do	LD	H,(IX+d)
DD6Edo	LD	L,(IX+d)
DD70do	LD	(IX+d),B
DD71do	LD	(IX+d),C
DD72do	LD	(IX+d),D
DD73do	LD	(IX+d),E
DD74do	LD	(IX+d),H
DD75do	LD	(IX+d),L
DD77do	LD	(IX+d),A
DD7Edo	LD	A,(IX+d)
DD86do	ADD	A,(IX+d)
DD8Edo	ADC	A,(IX+d)
DD96do	SUB	(IX+d)
DD9Edo	SBC	A,(IX+d)
DDA6do	AND	(IX+d)
DDAEdo	XOR	(IX+d)
DDB6do	OR	(IX+d)
DDBEdo	CP	(IX+d)
DDCBdo06	RLC	(IX+d)
DDCBdo0E	RRC	(IX+d)
DDCBdo16	RL	(IX+d)
DDCBdo1E	RR	(IX+d)
DDCBdo26	SLA	(IX+d)
DDCBdo2E	SRA	(IX+d)
DDCBdo3E	SRL	(IX+d)
DDCBdo46	BIT	0,(IX+d)
DDCBdo4E	BIT	1,(IX+d)
DDCBdo56	BIT	2,(IX+d)

Hex	Mnemonic	
DDCBdo5E	BIT	3,(IX+d)
DDCBdo66	BIT	4,(IX+d)
DDCBdo6E	BIT	5,(IX+d)
DDCBdo76	BIT	6,(IX+d)
DDCBdo7E	BIT	7,(IX+d)
DDCBdo86	RES	0,(IX+d)
DDCBdo8E	RES	1,(IX+d)
DDCBdo96	RES	2,(IX+d)
DDCBdo9E	RES	3,(IX+d)
DDCBdoA6	RES	4,(IX+d)
DDCBdoAE	RES	5,(IX+d)
DDCBdoB6	RES	6,(IX+d)
DDCBdoBE	RES	7,(IX+d)
DDCBdoC6	SET	0,(IX+d)
DDCBdoCE	SET	1,(IX+d)
DDCBdoD6	SET	2,(IX+d)
DDCBdoDE	SET	3,(IX+d)
DDCBdoE6	SET	4,(IX+d)
DDCBdoEE	SET	5,(IX+d)
DDCBdoF6	SET	6,(IX+d)
DDCBdoFE	SET	7,(IX+d)
DDE1	POP	IX
DDE3	EX	(SP),IX
DDE5	PUSH	IX
DDE9	JP	(IX)
DDF9	LD	SP,IX
DEno	SBC	A,n
DF	RST	18H
E0	RET	PO
E1	POP	HL
E2mono	JP	PO,nm
E3	EX	(SP),HL
E4mono	CALL	PO,nm
E5	PUSH	HL
E6no	AND	n
E7	RST	20H
E8	RET	PE
E9	JP	(HL)
EAmono	JP	PE,nm
EB	EX	DE,HL
ECmono	CALL	PE,nm
ED40	IN	B,(C)
ED41	OUT	(C),B
ED42	SBC	HL,BC
ED43mono	LD	(nm),BC
ED44	NEG	
ED45	RETN	
ED46	IM	0
ED47	LD	I,A
ED48	IN	C,(C)
ED49	OUT	(C),C
ED4A	ADC	HL,BC
ED4Bmono	LD	BC,(nm)
ED4D	RETI	
ED4F	LD	R,A
ED50	IN	D,(C)
ED51	OUT	(C),D
ED52	SBC	HL,DE
ED53mono	LD	(nm),DE
ED56	IM	1
ED57	LD	A,I
ED58	IN	E,(C)
ED59	OUT	(C),E
ED5A	ADC	HL,DE
ED5Bmono	LD	DE,(nm)
ED5E	IM	2
ED5F	LD	A,R
ED60	IN	H,(C)

Hex	Mnemonic	
ED61	OUT	(C),H
ED62	SBC	HL,HL
ED67	RRD	
ED68	IN	L,(C)
ED69	OUT	(C),L
ED6A	ADC	HL,HL
ED6F	RLD	
ED72	SBC	HL,SP
ED73mono	LD	(nm),SP
ED78	IN	A,(C)
ED79	OUT	(C),A
ED7A	ADC	HL,SP
ED7Bmono	LD	SP,(nm)
EDA0	LDI	
EDA1	CPI	
EDA2	INI	
EDA3	OUTI	
EDA8	LDD	
EDA9	CPD	
EDAA	IND	
EDAB	OUTD	
EDB0	LDIR	
EDB1	CPIR	
EDB2	INIR	
EDB3	OTIR	
EDB8	LDDR	
EDB9	CPDR	
EDBA	INDR	
EDBB	OTDR	
EEno	XOR	n
EF	RST	28H
F0	RET	P
F1	POP	AF
F2mono	JP	P,nm
F3	DI	
F4mono	CALL	P,nm
F5	PUSH	AF
F6no	OR	n
F7	RST	30H
F8	RET	M
F9	LD	SP,HL
FAmono	JP	M,nm
FB	EI	
FCmono	CALL	M,nm
FD09	ADD	IY,BC
FD19	ADD	IY,DE
FD21mono	LD	IY,nm
FD22mono	LD	(nm),IY
FD23	INC	IY
FD29	ADD	IY,IY
FD2Amono	LD	IY,(nm)
FD2B	DEC	IY
FD34do	INC	(IY+d)
FD35do	DEC	(IY+d)
FD36dono	LD	(IY+d),n
FD39	ADD	IY,SP
FD46do	LD	B,(IY+d)
FD4Edo	LD	C,(IY+d)
FD56do	LD	D,(IY+d)
FD5Edo	LD	E,(IY+d)
FD66do	LD	H,(IY+d)
FD6Edo	LD	L,(IY+d)
FD70do	LD	(IY+d),B
FD71do	LD	(IY+d),C
FD72do	LD	(IY+d),D
FD73do	LD	(IY+d),E
FD74do	LD	(IY+d),H
FD75do	LD	(IY+d),L

Hex	Mnemonic	
FD77do	LD	(IY+d),A
FD7Edo	LD	A,(IY+d)
FD86do	ADD	A,(IY+d)
FD8Edo	ADC	A,(IY+d)
FD96do	SUB	(IY+d)
FD9Edo	SBC	A,(IY+d)
FDA6do	AND	(IY+d)
FDAEdo	XOR	(IY+d)
FDB6do	OR	(IY+d)
FDBEdo	CP	(IY+d)
FDCBdo06	RLC	(IY+d)
FDCBdo0E	RRC	(IY+d)
FDCBdo16	RL	(IY+d)
FDCBdo1E	RR	(IY+d)
FDCBdo26	SLA	(IY+d)
FDCBdo2E	SRA	(IY+d)
FDCBdo3E	SRL	(IY+d)
FDCBdo46	BIT	0,(IY+d)
FDCBdo4E	BIT	1,(IY+d)
FDCBdo56	BIT	2,(IY+d)
FDCBdo5E	BIT	3,(IY+d)
FDCBdo66	BIT	4,(IY+d)
FDCBdo6E	BIT	5,(IY+d)
FDCBdo76	BIT	6,(IY+d)
FDCBdo7E	BIT	7,(IY+d)
FDCBdo86	RES	0,(IY+d)
FDCBdo8E	RES	1,(IY+d)
FDCBdo96	RES	2,(IY+d)
FDCBdo9E	RES	3,(IY+d)
FDCBdoA6	RES	4,(IY+d)
FDCBdoAE	RES	5,(IY+d)
FDCBdoB6	RES	6,(IY+d)
FDCBdoBE	RES	7,(IY+d)
FDCBdoC6	SET	0,(IY+d)
FDCBdoCE	SET	1,(IY+d)
FDCBdoD6	SET	2,(IY+d)
FDCBdoDE	SET	3,(IY+d)
FDCBdoE6	SET	4,(IY+d)
FDCBdoEE	SET	5,(IY+d)
FDCBdoF6	SET	6,(IY+d)
FDCBdoFE	SET	7,(IY+d)
FDE1	POP	IY
FDE3	EX	(SP),IY
FDE5	PUSH	IY
FDE9	JP	(IY)
FDF9	LD	SP,IY
FEno	CP	n
FF	RST	38H

APPENDIX FOUR

Binary Arithmetic

In this appendix we learn some more advanced features of binary arithmetic. It is not necessary to know these to program in FAST BASIC. Nevertheless, they are useful for a deeper understanding of FAST BASIC programming.

ADDING AND SUBTRACTING BINARY NUMBERS

Binary Subtraction

Here is an example of a subtraction, 101001 – 1011:

		Borrow line	0 1 1 1 1 0
Number subtracted	1 0 1 1	Number subtracted	1 0 1 1
		Result line	1 1 1 1 0
Number	1 0 1 0 0 1	Number	1 0 1 0 0 1

Note that the fourth line is the number 101001 and the second line is the number subtracted, 1011. If you examine the right side, it looks like an addition: The first line is the carry line and 1011 + 11110 = 101001.

Since 1011 + 11110 = 101001, we obtain 101001 – 1011 = 11110. We do our subtraction as follows: We set the subtraction up as on the left-hand side and we try to complete it to make it into an addition.

We start the subtraction in the first column from the right. We ask: What number when added to 1 (in the number subtracted line) makes 1 (in the number line)? The answer is 0, so we put 0 in the result line and 0 (since we did not have to borrow) in the next position left in the borrow line.

Now we move to the second column from the right. What number when added to 1 (in the number subtracted line) makes 0 (in the number line)? 0 is too small, so we have to borrow 1. We put 1 in the borrow line, one column to the left, and repeat the question: What number when added to 1 (in the number subtracted line) makes 10 (in the number line)? Now the answer is 1, so we put 1 in the result line.

Keep in mind that we have to add the number from the borrow line to the number from the number-subtracted line before we pose the question.

Two's Complement Arithmetic

We learned in Chapter 2 how to find the 8-bit two's complement representation of a number in the range −128 to 127. If we add as unsigned binary numbers the 8-bit two's complement representations of two numbers, when is the result correct?

Let us look at a few examples. We start with $44_D + (-3_D)$ (C is the carry from bit 7):

8-bit two's complement representation of 44_D		0010 1100
8-bit two's complement representation of -3_D		+ 1111 1101
	C = 1	0010 1001

and (ignoring C) the result is 0010 1001 $= 41_D$, which is correct.

For a second example, let us compute 3 − 44:

8-bit two's complement representation of 3_D		0000 0011
8-bit two's complement representation of -44_D		+ 1101 0100
	C = 0	1101 0111

Again (ignoring C), the result is correct: $3_D - 44_D = -41_D$ and the 8-bit two's complement representation of -41_D is 1101 0111.

Next, let us try $-3_D + (-10_D)$:

8-bit two's complement representation of -3_D		1111 1101
8-bit two's complement representation of -10_D		+ 1111 0110
	C = 1	1111 0011

The result is, indeed, -13_D.

Sometimes we get incorrect results:

8-bit two's complement representation of -115_D		1000 1101
8-bit two's complement representation of -15_D		+ 1111 0001
	C = 1	0111 1110

0111 1110 is the 8-bit two's complement representation of 126_D and not of -130_D. (Remember, -130_D is too small to have an 8-bit two's complement representation.)

Here is a final example:

8-bit two's complement representation of 65_D		0100 0001
8-bit two's complement representation of 64_D	+	0100 0000
	$C = 0$	1000 0001

We have obtained $65_D + 64_D = -127_D$, which is incorrect.

As we see, adding 8-bit two's complement representations of numbers does not always give correct result. To determine when the result is correct, in addition to the carry flag, C, we need another flag to signify the carry from bit 6; let us call this flag C_6. This rule is very important: The 8-bit two's complement arithmetic is always correct, unless $C = 0$ and $C_6 = 1$ or $C = 1$ and $C_6 = 0$.

Overflow Flag

Just as for unsigned 8-bit arithmetic we need the carry flag, C, to keep track of what is happening when the result exceeds 255_D, for 8-bit two's complement arithmetic we need a flag that tells us when the result is incorrect. This flag is called the "overflow flag," and is denoted by O or P/O (P here stands for parity, see Appendix 2).

This flag works as follows: P/O = 0 if C and C_6 are the same (both are 0 or both are 1); otherwise P/O = 1. If P/O = 0, then the result of an 8-bit two's complement arithmetic is correct, and if P/O = 1, then it is incorrect. (Reading carefully—in Chapter 1—the definition of XOR, we realize that P/O = C XOR C_6.)

For 16-bit integers the carry flag, C, is the carry from bit 15 (the high-order bit) and the result of 16-bit two's complement addition is correct exactly if C XOR, the carry from bit 14, is 0.

BINARY FRACTIONS

Binary Fractions

What is the binary fraction 101.001? In decimal, 25.371 stands for

$$2 \times 10^1 + 5 \times 10^0 + 3 \times 10^{-1} + 7 \times 10^{-2} + 1 \times 10^{-3}$$

where

$$10^{-1} = 1/10^1 = 0.1 \quad 10^{-2} = 1/10^2 = 0.01 \quad 10^{-3} = 1/10^3 = 0.001$$

Similarly, we shall use negative exponents of 2:

$2^{-1} = 1/2^1 = 0.5$ (decimal)
$2^{-2} = 1/2^2 = 0.25$ (decimal)
$2^{-3} = 1/2^3 = 0.125$ (decimal)
$2^{-4} = 1/2^4 = 0.0625$ (decimal)

Thus the binary fraction 101.101 is $4 + 1 + 0.5 + 0.125 = 5.625$ in decimal.

Single Precision

All single-precision variables are stored as binary fractions. To illustrate this, let the value of the single-precision variable SP be 123456. This variable is displayed in Table 4.2. By using the BASE CONVERSION UTILITY in the program TUTOR we get the binary value:

11110001001000000

Let us bring this number into "normal form" (* is multiplication):

$2^{exp} * 0.11110001001000000$

where exp counts how many times we had to move the decimal point. In our example the decimal point was moved $17_D = 11_H$ times. In normal form the decimal point is always followed by 1 (unless the number is 0). We store this number in single-precision form as follows: We break up (.)11110001001000000 into groups of 8 bits (adding 0's to get 24 digits):

11110001 00100000 00000000

and store these as MSB, byte 2, and LSB (note that in Table 4.2 the order is reversed).

The MSB always has to start with a 1; we use this feature to make it the "sign bit." For positive numbers we make it a 0 and for negative numbers we leave it a 1. The exponent (in binary, 00010001) is stored in the last byte with bit 7 the "sign bit": If the exponent is positive, bit 7 is 1; otherwise it is 0.

We have just learned two new ways of storing signs, as promised in Chapter 2.

The number 0 is stored with exp = 0; the other 3 bytes are junk. By the foregoing analysis, SP = 123456 is stored as

00000000 00100000 01110001 10010001

or in hex:

00 20 71 91

which agrees with Table 4.2.

Double Precision

Double precision works in the same way, except that now we have 7 bytes rather than 3 bytes in which to store the binary fraction. As an example let us take a very large number:

2000111222333

Convert it to binary:

11101000 11010111 11110101 10011111 00011110 1

We bring this into normal form by moving the decimal point $41_D = 29_H$ places; setting bit 7 (for a positive exponent) we get $A9_H$ for the exponent byte. Finally, in the binary fraction the first 1 has to be reset (since the number is positive), giving us

01101000 11010111 11110101 10011111 00011110 10000000 00000000

or in hex:

68 D7 F5 9F 1E 80 00

This agrees with the printout in Table 4.2.

Use the VARPTR program to gain some experience in figuring out the double-precision storage format of a number: Redefine DB# in the program, look for its display in the simple variable table, and see if it agrees with your computations.

Having this much information about single- and double-precision numbers is very useful. This may help you to understand their accuracy: It is 24 bits for single precision and 56 bits for double precision. We retain complete accuracy when multiplying with a power of 2, as this will change only the exponent.

APPENDIX FIVE

Hex Tables

It is very important that a FAST BASIC programmer be able to handle hex. The two tables in this appendix should make this task much easier.

HEX ADDITION TABLE

Use this table as you would the binary addition table in Chapter 1. For instance, to figure out A + F go to the intersection of line A and column F; there you find 19, so A + F = 19. In multidigit additions the result is 9 and the carry is 1.

	0	1	2	3	4	5	6	7	8	9	A	B	C	D	E	F	
0	0	1	2	3	4	5	6	7	8	9	A	B	C	D	E	F	0
1	1	2	3	4	5	6	7	8	9	A	B	C	D	E	F	10	1
2	2	3	4	5	6	7	8	9	A	B	C	D	E	F	10	11	2
3	3	4	5	6	7	8	9	A	B	C	D	E	F	10	11	12	3
4	4	5	6	7	8	9	A	B	C	D	E	F	10	11	12	13	4
5	5	6	7	8	9	A	B	C	D	E	F	10	11	12	13	14	5
6	6	7	8	9	A	B	C	D	E	F	10	11	12	13	14	15	6
7	7	8	9	A	B	C	D	E	F	10	11	12	13	14	15	16	7
8	8	9	A	B	C	D	E	F	10	11	12	13	14	15	16	17	8
9	9	A	B	C	D	E	F	10	11	12	13	14	15	16	17	18	9
A	A	B	C	D	E	F	10	11	12	13	14	15	16	17	18	19	A
B	B	C	D	E	F	10	11	12	13	14	15	16	17	18	19	1A	B
C	C	D	E	F	10	11	12	13	14	15	16	17	18	19	1A	1B	C
D	D	E	F	10	11	12	13	14	15	16	17	18	19	1A	1B	1C	D
E	E	F	10	11	12	13	14	15	16	17	18	19	1A	1B	1C	1D	E
F	F	10	11	12	13	14	15	16	17	18	19	1A	1B	1C	1D	1E	F
	0	1	2	3	4	5	6	7	8	9	A	B	C	D	E	F	

HEX CONVERSION TABLE

We convert a 1- or 2-digit hex number to decimal by looking it up under hex (the first column) and reading the decimal number in the third column. Thus D_H ($0D_H$) is 013_D, that is, 13_D, and $F6_H$ is 246_D. We convert a 3- or

4-digit hex number such as $C1A2_H$ as follows: We look up C1 under hex, and read the next column, 49408_D; this is the decimal value of $C100_H$. Then we look up A2 under decimal: 162_D and add it to the previous value; $C1A2_H$ in decimal is 49408 + 162 = 49570_D. For another example, let us convert 789_H: In the second column 07_H gives 1792_D; 89_H is 137_D, so 789_H is 1792 + 137 = 1929_D.

Now we convert from decimal to hex. If the number is less than 256_D, we look it up in the third column, and read the first column. Thus 245_D is $F5_H$ and 19_D is 13_H. Between 256_D and 65535_D proceed as follows: Say we want to convert 46703_D. We look up in the second column the largest number *not to exceed* 46703_D; this is 46592_D, giving $B6_H$ in the first column. Then 46703 – 46592 = 111_D. Looking up 111_D we get $6F_H$, so 46703_D is $B66F_H$. For a second example, take 56832_D. This number occurs in the second column. Reading the first column we get DE_H, hence 56832_D is $DE00_H$. Finally, we convert 3172_D to hex. The largest number in the second column not to exceed 3172_D is 3072_D, giving us $0C_H$. Then, 3172 – 3072 = 100_D. Looking up 100 in the third column gives 64_H, so 3172_D is $C64_H$.

Hex	Decimal × 256	Decimal	Hex	Decimal × 256	Decimal
00	00000	000	22	08704	034
01	00256	001	23	08960	035
02	00512	002	24	09216	036
03	00768	003	25	09472	037
04	01024	004	26	09728	038
05	01280	005	27	09984	039
06	01536	006	28	10240	040
07	01792	007	29	10496	041
08	02048	008	2A	10752	042
09	02304	009	2B	11008	043
0A	02560	010	2C	11264	044
0B	02816	011	2D	11520	045
0C	03072	012	2E	11776	046
0D	03328	013	2F	12032	047
0E	03584	014	30	12288	048
0F	03840	015	31	12544	049
10	04096	016	32	12800	050
11	04352	017	33	13056	051
12	04608	018	34	13312	052
13	04864	019	35	13568	053
14	05120	020	36	13824	054
15	05376	021	37	14080	055
16	05632	022	38	14336	056
17	05888	023	39	14592	057
18	06144	024	3A	14848	058
19	06400	025	3B	15104	059
1A	06656	026	3C	15360	060
1B	06912	027	3D	15616	061
1C	07168	028	3E	15872	062
1D	07424	029	3F	16128	063
1E	07680	030	40	16384	064
1F	07936	031	41	16640	065
20	08192	032	42	16896	066
21	08448	033	43	17152	067

Hex	Decimal × 256	Decimal	Hex	Decimal × 256	Decimal
44	17408	068	7F	32512	127
45	17664	069	80	32768	128
46	17920	070	81	33024	129
47	18176	071	82	33280	130
48	18432	072	83	33536	131
49	18688	073	84	33792	132
4A	18944	074	85	34048	133
4B	19200	075	86	34304	134
4C	19456	076	87	34560	135
4D	19712	077	88	34816	136
4E	19968	078	89	35072	137
4F	20224	079	8A	35328	138
50	20480	080	8B	35584	139
51	20736	081	8C	35840	140
52	20992	082	8D	36096	141
53	21248	083	8E	36352	142
54	21504	084	8F	36608	143
55	21760	085	90	36864	144
56	22016	086	91	37120	145
57	22272	087	92	37376	146
58	22528	088	93	37632	147
59	22784	089	94	37888	148
5A	23040	090	95	38144	149
5B	23296	091	96	38400	150
5C	23552	092	97	38656	151
5D	23808	093	98	38912	152
5E	24064	094	99	39168	153
5F	24320	095	9A	39424	154
60	24576	096	9B	39680	155
61	24832	097	9C	39936	156
62	25088	098	9D	40192	157
63	25344	099	9E	40448	158
64	25600	100	9F	40704	159
65	25856	101	A0	40960	160
66	26112	102	A1	41216	161
67	26368	103	A2	41472	162
68	26624	104	A3	41728	163
69	26880	105	A4	41984	164
6A	27136	106	A5	42240	165
6B	27392	107	A6	42496	166
6C	27648	108	A7	42752	167
6D	27904	109	A8	43008	168
6E	28160	110	A9	43264	169
6F	28416	111	AA	43520	170
70	28672	112	AB	43776	171
71	28928	113	AC	44032	172
72	29184	114	AD	44288	173
73	29440	115	AE	44544	174
74	29696	116	AF	44800	175
75	29952	117	B0	45056	176
76	30208	118	B1	45312	177
77	30464	119	B2	45568	178
78	30720	120	B3	45824	179
79	30976	121	B4	46080	180
7A	31232	122	B5	46336	181
7B	31488	123	B6	46592	182
7C	31744	124	B7	46848	183
7D	32000	125	B8	47104	184
7E	32256	126	B9	47360	185

Hex	Decimal × 256	Decimal	Hex	Decimal × 256	Decimal
BA	47616	186	DD	56576	221
BB	47872	187	DE	56832	222
BC	48128	188	DF	57088	223
BD	48384	189	E0	57344	224
BE	48640	190	E1	57600	225
BF	48896	191	E2	57856	226
C0	49152	192	E3	58112	227
C1	49408	193	E4	58368	228
C2	49664	194	E5	58624	229
C3	49920	195	E6	58880	230
C4	50176	196	E7	59136	231
C5	50432	197	E8	59392	232
C6	50688	198	E9	59648	233
C7	50944	199	EA	59904	234
C8	51200	200	EB	60160	235
C9	51456	201	EC	60416	236
CA	51712	202	ED	60672	237
CB	51968	203	EE	60928	238
CC	52224	204	EF	61184	239
CD	52480	205	F0	61440	240
CE	52736	206	F1	61696	241
CF	52992	207	F2	61952	242
D0	53248	208	F3	62208	243
D1	53504	209	F4	62464	244
D2	53760	210	F5	62720	245
D3	54016	211	F6	62976	246
D4	54272	212	F7	63232	247
D5	54528	213	F8	63488	248
D6	54784	214	F9	63744	249
D7	55040	215	FA	64000	250
D8	55296	216	FB	64256	251
D9	55552	217	FC	64512	252
DA	55808	218	FD	64768	253
DB	56064	219	FE	65024	254
DC	56320	220	FF	65280	255

APPENDIX SIX

Label Listing

In this book we recommend the use of labels in assembly language programs to designate memory locations and ROM routines. This appendix lists these labels in alphabetic order.

ROM subroutines and jumps are followed by the first few bytes of machine code to help the user check whether the routine is in place. The hex numbers in quotation marks are addresses. If a ROM (or RAM loaded from cassette or disk) contains all these codes but in different locations, these addresses may also be different. Search for these sections of code (with the FIND command of the program VIEW/MOD listed in Appendix 8—preferably in the FAST BASIC version described in Chapter 12) using hex numbers not in quotes. Once a section of machine code is identified, the user should note the value of the label in this appendix. If the verification is completed, FAST BASIC can be used.

Label	Value	Type	Explanation
ABS	0977	CALL	Table A1.1: Type 1[2] (CD "94 09" F0 E7 FA "5B 0C" CA "F6 0A" 21 "23 41" 7E EE 80 77 C9)
ADDDP	0C77	CALL	Table 8.3: Add SA and SA_1; result in SA (21 "2E 41" 7E B7 C8 47 2B 4E)
ADDINT	0BD2	CALL	Table 8.3: Add DE and HL; result in HL and in SA if no overflow; result in SA if overflow (flag = 4) (7C 17 9F 47 E5 7A 17)
ADDSP	0716	CALL	Table 8.3: Add RA and SA; result in SA (78 B7 C8 3A "24 41" B7 CA "B4 09" 90 30 0C)
ATN	15BD	CALL	Table A1.1: Type 2[3] (CD "55 09" FC "E2 13" FC "82 09" 3A "24 41" FE 81 38 0C)
BASIC	1A19	JP	Table 8.1: Return to BASIC and display the BASIC READY prompt (if you have difficulty with $1A19_H$, try $06CC_H$ or 0072_H instead) (CD "8B 03" CD "AC 41" CD "F8 01" CD "F9 20" 21 "29 19" CD "A7 28" 3A "9A 40" D6 02)
BSCPAR	0A9A	JP	Table 8.1: Return to BASIC program with parameter (22 "21 41" 3E 02 32 "AF 40" C9)
BSCSTM	40E6	EQU	Table 11.2: Pointer to the terminator (the end of line 00_H byte or a ":") of the last executed BASIC statement is at this address
BSCTXT	40A4	EQU	Table 3.2 and Table 9.3: The start of the BASIC program (text) is at this address

Label	Value	Type	Explanation
CLS	01C9	CALL	Table A1.3: Clear screen (3E 1C CD "3A 03" 3E 1F C3)
COS	1541	CALL	Table A1.1: Type 2[3] (21 "8B 15" CD "0B 07" and continue with the SIN code)
CPDP	0A78	CALL	Table 8.3: Compare SA and SA_1[1] (CD "4F 0A" C2 "5E 09" C9)
CPINT	0A39	CALL	Table 8.3: Compare DE and HL[1] (7A AC 7C FA "5F 09" BA C2 "60 09" 7D 93)
CP16	0018	RST	Table 8.3: Compare DE and HL as 16-bit integers[1] (C3 "06 40")
CPSP	0A0C	CALL	Table 8.3: Compare RA and SA[1] (78 B7 CA "55 09" 21 "5E 09" E5 CD "55 09")
CPSTR	25A1	CALL	Table 9.3: Compare two strings; HL and BC point at the strings, D and E contain the lengths[1] (7B B2 C8 7A D6 01 D8)
CSAASC	0FBD	CALL	Table A1.2: Convert SA (set typeflag) to ASCII; result (in decimal) is placed in a buffer starting at 4130_H; the result is terminated by a 00_H byte, (HL) = 4130_H (AF CD "34 10" E6 08 28 02 36 2B)
CSADP	0ADB	CALL	Table A1.2: Convert SA to double precision[5] (E7 D0 CA "F6 06" FC "CC 0A" 21 00 00 22)
CSAINT	0A7F	CALL	Table A1.2: Convert SA to integer[5] (E7 2A "21 41" F8 CA "F6 06" D4 "B9 06" 21 "B2 07" E5 3A "24 41" FE 90 30 0E CD)
CSASP	0AB1	CALL	Table A1.2: Convert SA to single precision[5] (E7 E0 FA "CC 0A" CA "F6 06" CD "BF 09")
CURSOR	4020	EQU	Table 3.3: The current cursor is at this address
DELAY	0060	CALL	Table 8.3: Load BC with n; loop n times (0B 78 B1 20 FB C9)
DIVDP	0DE5	CALL	Table 8.3: Divide SA by SA_1; result in SA (3A "2E 41" B7 CA "9A 19" CD "07 09" 34 34 CD "39 0E" 21 "51 41" 71 41 11)
DIVINT	2490	CALL	Table 8.3: Divide DE by HL; result in SA in single-precision format (E5 EB CD "CF 06" E1 CD "A4 09" CD "CF 0A")
DIVSP	08A2	CALL	Table 8.3: Divide RA by SA; result in SA (CD "55 09" CA "9A 19" 2E FF CD "14 09" 34 34 2B 7E 32 "89 40" 2B 7E 32)
DOS	402D	JP	Table 8.1: Return to DOS; do not initialize (C3 "00 44")
DOSCLD	0000	JP	Table 8.1: Reinitialize DOS; "cold" entry to DOS
ERCODE	409A	EQU	Table 11.2: The error code is at this address
ERTRAP	41A6	EQU	Table 11.2: Error processing jumps here; this contains RET in TRS-80 BASIC and a jump (through a RST) to the long error message routine in Disk BASIC
EVALU	1F21	CALL	Appendix 1: Evaluate expression (CD "0D 26" CF D5 EB 22)
EXP	1439	CALL	Table A1.1: Type 2[3] (CD "A4 09" 01 "38 81" 11 "3B AA" CD "47 08" 3A "24 41" FE 88 D2 "31 09" CD "40 0B" C6 80 C6 02 DA)
FIX	0B26	CALL	Table A1.1: Type 2[3] (E7 F8 CD "55 09" F2 "37 08" CD "82 09" CD "37 08" C3 "7B 09")
FLAGDP	0AEC	CALL	Table 8.5 and Table A1.1: Set typeflag for SA to double precision (3E 08 01 "3E 04" C3)
FLAGIN	0A9D	CALL	Table A1.1: Set typeflag of SA to integer (3E 02 32 "AF 40" C9)
FLAGSP	0AEF	CALL	Table A1.1: Set typeflag of SA to single precision (3E 04 C3 "9F 0A")
GETPAR	0AF7	CALL	Load the parameter A in USR(A) into HL; this must be the first instruction of the USR

Label	Value	Type	Explanation
GRAPH	0150	JP	Appendix 1: Call a graphics function selected by value in stack (16 FF 14 D6 03 30 FB C6)
INT	0B37	CALL	Table A1.1: Type 1^2 (E7 F8 30 1E 28 B9)
KBDSCN	002B	CALL	Table A1.3: Scan keyboard with A containing the result (11 "15 40" 18 E3)
LDDEHL	09D2	CALL	Table 8.4: Load single-precision number pointed to by HL into area pointed to by DE; needs FLAGSP (EB and continue with LDHLDE)
LDHLDE	09D3	CALL	Table 8.4: Load single-precision number pointed to by DE into area pointed to by HL; needs FLAGSP (3A "AF 40" 47 1A 77 13 23 05)
LDHLSA	09CB	CALL	Table 8.4: Load SA into area pointed to by HL (11 "21 41" 06 04 18 05)
LDRAHL	09C2	CALL	Table 8.4: Load single-precision number pointed to by HL into RA (5E 23 56 23 4E 23 46)
LDRASA	09BF	CALL	Table 8.4: Load SA into RA (21 "21 41" and we continue with the code of LDRAHL)
LDSAHL	09B1	CALL	Table 8.4: Load single-precision number pointed to by HL into SA (CD "C2 09" and continue with LDSARA)
LDSARA	09B4	CALL	Table 8.4: Load RA into SA (EB 22 "21 41" 60 69 22 "23 41" EB C9)
LDSTSA	09A4	CALL	Table 8.4: Load SA into stack (EB 2A "21 41" E3 E5 2A "23 41" E3 E5 EB C9)
LOG	0809	CALL	Table A1.1: Type 2^3 (CD "55 09" B7 EA "4A 1E" 21 "24 41" 7E 01 "35 80" 11 "F3 04" 90 F5 70 D5 C5)
MLTDP	0DA1	CALL	Table 8.3: Multiply SA and SA_1; result in SA (CD "55 09" C8 CD "0A 09" CD "39 0E" 71 13 06 07 1A 13)
MLTINT	0BF2	CALL	Table 8.3: Multiply DE and HL; result in HL and in SA if no overflow (flag = 2); result in SA if overflow (flag = 4) (7C B5 CA "9A 0A" E5 D5 CD "45 0C" C5 44 4D)
MLTSP	0847	CALL	Table 8.2: Multiply RA and SA; result in SA (CD "55 09" C8 2E 00 CD "14 09" 79 32 "4F 41" EB 22 "50 41")
MOVEA	09D6	CALL	Table 9.3: Move data; DE points at source, HL points at destination, A contains the count—how many characters to move (47 and continues with MOVEB)
MOVEB	09D7	CALL	Same as MOVEA but B contains the count (1A 77 13 23 05 20 F9)
MVALT	09FC	CALL	Table 8.5: Move SA into alternate software accumulator (SA_1); needs FLAGDP (21 "27 41" 11 "D3 09" D5 11 "21 41" E7 D8 11)
MVDEHL	09D3	CALL	Table 8.5: Move the number pointed to by HL to the area pointed to by DE; needs FLAGDP (see LDDEHL)
MVHLDE	09D2	CALL	Table 8.5: Move the number pointed to by DE to the area pointed to by HL; needs FLAGDP (see LDHLDE)
MVSAHL	09F7	CALL	Table 8.5: Move the number pointed to by HL into the software accumulator; needs FLAGDP (11 "D2 09" 18 06 and continue with MVALT)
MVSTR	21E3	CALL	Table 9.3: Move string into string space; HL points at the first byte of the buffer and BC points at the variable name (23 7E B7 2B C5 CA)
MVVAR	0982	CALL	Chapter 8: Move the number of bytes shown by the typeflag from the area pointed to by DE to the area pointed to by HL (21 "23 41" 7E EE 80 77)

Label	Value	Type	Explanation
OUTCHR	032A	CALL	Table A1.3: Output character in register A; OUTSEL selects device (C5 4F CD "C1 41" 3A "9C 40" B7 79 C1 FA)
OUTSEL	409C	EQU	Table A1.3: Output select; contains –1 for cassette, 0 for video, 1 for printer
OUTSTR	28A7	CALL	Table A1.3: Output string terminated by byte 00_H or 22_H (ASCII for "); HL points at first character, OUTSEL selects device (CD "65 28" CD "DA 29" CD "C4 09" 14 15 C8)
POWER	13F7	CALL	Table 8.3: Raise RA to the power SA; result in SA (CD "55 09" 78 28 3C F2 "04 14" B7 CA)
RANDOM	01D3	CALL	Table A1.1: Randomize (ED 5F 32 "AB 40" C9)
RDSECT	46DD	CALL	Disk sector read; register C contains the drive selected (0–3); register D contains the track selected; register E contains the sector selected; HL points at the data buffer. On return Z is set on successful execution; otherwise register A will contain the error code (3E 88 CD "71 46")
RND	14C9	CALL	Table A1.1: Type 1[2] (CD "7F 0A" 7C B7 FA "4A 1E" B5 CA "F0 14" E5 CD)
RSETSA	0778	CALL	Table A1.1: Set SA to 0[4] (AF 32 "24 41" C9)
RUNSTM	1D1E	JP	Table 11.2: HL points at a ":" terminating a BASIC statement or at a byte 00_H terminating a line; execution will proceed from the next statement (CD "58 03" B7 C4 "A0 1D" 22 "E6 40" ED 73 "E8 40" 7E FE 3A)
SA	411D	EQU	Table 8.2 and 8.5: The first byte of the software accumulator
SAFLAG	40AF	EQU	Table 8.2 and 8.5: Contains the typeflag of the software accumulator (SA)
SA1	4127	EQU	Table 8.5: The first byte of the alternate software accumulator (SA_1)
SGN	098A	CALL	Table A1.1: Type 1[2] (CD "94 09" 6F 17 9F)
SIN	1547	CALL	Table A1.1: Type 2[3] (CD "A4 09" 01 "49 83" 11 "DB 0F" CD "B4 09" C1 D1 CD)
SQR	13E7	CALL	Table A1.1: Type 2[3] (CD "A4 09" 21 "80 13" CD "B1 09" 18 03)
SUBDP	0C70	CALL	Table 8.3: Subtract SA_1 from SA; result in SA (21 "2D 41" 7E EE 80 77 21 "2E 41" 7E B7)
SUBINT	0BC7	CALL	Table 8.3: Subtract HL from DE; result in HL and in SA if no overflow (flag = 2); result in SA if overflow (flag = 4) (7C 17 9F 47 CD)
SUBSP	0713	CALL	Table 8.3: Subtract SA from RA; result in SA (CD "82 09" 78 B7 C8 3A "24 41" B7)
TAN	15A8	CALL	Table A1.1: Type 2[3] (CD "A4 09" CD "47 15" C1 E1 CD "A4 09" EB CD)
VAL	1E5A	CALL	Table A1.2: Convert a string (terminated by a byte 00_H) representing a decimal number to a binary number; HL points at first character; DE contains the result (2B 11 00 00 D7 D0 E5 F5 21 "98 19" DF)
VARPTR	260D	CALL	Chapter 8: Get variable address in DE; HL points at variable name (AF 32 "AE 40" 46 CD "3D 1E" DA "97 19" AF 4F D7 38 05)
VIDEO	3C00	EQU	Table 3.2 and Chapter 7: First byte of video display
VTA	40FB	EQU	Table 3.2: The starting address of the array variable table is stored here

Label	Value	Type	Explanation
VTS	40F9	EQU	Table 3.2: The starting address of the simple variable table is stored here
WTSECT	46E6	CALL	Disk sector write; same setup as for RDSECT (3E A8 CD "71 46")

Notes:

[1]Result of compares:
If the two are equal, the zero flag is set (= 1).
If the two are unequal, the zero flag is reset (= 0).
If the first is smaller, the carry flag is reset (= 0).
If the second is smaller, the carry flag is set (= 1).

[2]Type 1: Number in SA may be integer, single precision, or double precision; set typeflag to indicate which. Result is put in SA, typeflag is set.

[3]Type 2: Number in SA is single precision; result in SA.

[4]If SA contains 0, then RND generates random numbers between 0 and 1. To place 0 in SA use this call.

[5]Typeflag must be set; result in SA.

APPENDIX SEVEN

Additional Reading and Software

BOOKS

BASIC

Two Radio Shack reference manuals for the TRS-80 Model I contain all the information about Level II BASIC and DOS BASIC:

Level II BASIC Reference Manual
TRSDOS and DISK BASIC Reference Manual
There are a number of books teaching Level II programming:

User's Manual for Level I

also by Radio Shack is an excellent introduction; although it teaches Level I BASIC, the reader should have no difficulty omitting the Level I features.

TRS-80 BASIC
by B. Albrecht, D. Inman, and R. Zamora
John Wiley & Sons, Inc., New York, N.Y.
is an excellent self-teaching guide.

Learning Level II
by D. A. Lien
Compusoft Publ., San Diego, Calif.
is a continuation of the Radio Shack Level I manual by the same author.

These books teach BASIC. Reading any one of these books should make the reader fairly comfortable with Level II BASIC.

Programming Techniques for Level II BASIC
by W. Barden, Jr.
is a Radio Shack book that goes beyond the above books; it is highly recommended.

The passage from TRS-80 BASIC to Disk BASIC is easy with one important exception: One has to learn how to handle disk files. This important topic is taught in

Data File Programming in BASIC
by L. Finkel and J. R. Brown
John Wiley & Sons, Inc., New York, N.Y.

Devices

To understand how the peripheral devices work, one should read some more Radio Shack manuals:

Expansion Interface
TRS-80 RS-232-C Interface
TRS-80 Micro Computer Technical Reference Handbook

They have a lot of information about the cassettes, printers, floppy disks, and the RS-232-C interface. A programmer may tend to ignore these manuals since they are "hardware oriented." This would be a mistake: Some understanding of how the peripherals are connected to the computer is necessary for input/output programming.

None of these manuals give you much information about the floppy-disk controller. It is described in detail in

FD1771A/B-01 Floppy Disk Formatter/Controller Data Sheet
Western Digital Corporation

This can be purchased separately from Western Digital or it can be obtained as part of the Radio Shack manual:

Expansion Interface Service Manual

Machine Language

If you want to go beyond FAST BASIC and immerse yourself in machine language programming, you need a detailed description of the instruction set and a large number of short example programs.

Z80-Assembly Language Programming Manual
Zilog, Inc.

is an excellent description of the instruction set. (Call Zilog at (408) 446-4666.)

Both needs are satisfied by the following four books.

Z80 Assembly Language Programming
by L. R. Leventhal
Osborne and Associates, Inc., Berkeley, Calif.

Programming the Z80
by R. Zaks
Sybex, Berkeley, Calif.

Z80 Software Gourmet Guide and Cookbook
By N. Wadsworth
Scelbi Publications, Elmwood, Conn.

8080/Z80 Assembly Language
by A. R. Miller
John Wiley and Sons, Inc., New York, N.Y.

The last book teaches about the predecessor of Z-80, the 8080 alongside the Z-80.

Less ambitious in scope is the Radio Shack book:
TRS-80 Assembly Language Programming
by W. Barden, Jr.
However, this book examines how the Z-80 is used in the TRS-80; it also teaches the use of some Radio Shack software—the Editor/Assembler and the debugging tool, T-BUG.

ROM

The secrets of the Level II ROM have been revealed by a succession of books, given here in order of appearance.

Supermap
by R. Fuller
Fuller Software
(630 East Springdale, Grand Prairie, Texas 75051) has 41 pages of commented disassembly. This book seems to be the source of most subsequent books. The 1980 edition includes a commented listing of BOOT/SYS (the disk bootstrap) and of SYS0/SYS, SYS1/SYS.

Software Technical Manual
by Houston Micro Computer Technologies

(5313 Bissonett, Bellaire, Texas 77401) presents in 40 pages a number of important ROM calls; examples are given on how these can be utilized in a machine language program by the experienced programmer.

Inside Level II
by J. Blattner and B. Mumford
Mumford Micro Systems
(Box 435, Summerland, Calif. 93067) introduces many important ROM calls and proposes the use of hybrid programs in which the machine language segment is stored under the BASIC program.

The Book Accessing the TRS-80 ROM
by R. E. Daly IV, S. C. Hill, R. Soltoff, T. B. Stibolt, Jr., and R. P. Wilkes
Insiders Software Consultants
(P.O. Box 2441, Springfield, Va. 22152) is a three-volume work. At the time of this writing only the first volume has appeared. This volume lists the math ROM calls and gives a commented listing of each. Examples are presented of how to use these calls in machine language programming.

Microsoft BASIC Decoded and Other Mysteries
by J. Farvour
International Jewelry Guild
(1260 West Foothill Boulevard, Upland, Calif. 91786) has a 60-page description of the internal workings of the Level II editor, BASIC Interpreter, input/output drivers, machine language monitor, etc., including many DOS functions (both TRS-DOS and NEWDOS). Most of the description is detailed enough actually to name the subroutines that perform the required functions. This is followed by a 120-page complete commented disassembly of the Level II ROM, with another 120 pages partly filled with additional comments as needed.

Both this book and

TRS-80 Disk & Other Mysteries
by H. C. Pennington
International Jewelry Guild
have a lot of information about disks.

Finally, we mention the book

Pathways Through the ROM
by G. Blank, R. Fuller, J. Hartford, J. T. Phillip, and R. M. Richardson
Soft Side Publications
(6 South Street, Milford, N.H. 03055) compiles a chapter of *The TRS-80 Disassembled Handbook* by R. M. Richardson and the *Supermap* of R. Fuller, with a BASIC monitor and a BASIC disassembler, and a DOS map of J. Hartford. The Western Digital controller specification sheet mentioned previously is also reproduced.

Algorithms

The best source of information on the use of algorithms in programming is

The Art of Computer Programming
by D. E. Knuth
Addison-Wesley, Reading, Mass.

Of the projected seven volumes, three have appeared at this writing (including combinatorics, lists, trees, random numbers, sorting, and searching).

MAGAZINES

Of the many magazines, we mention three; these are all devoted to the TRS-80.

80 Microcomputing
(Pine Street, Peterborough, N.H. 03458) is the largest, presently publishing about 250 pages per month. It contains articles on BASIC and also on machine language. The readers of this book should find the departments "The Assembly Line" and "80 Applications" of special interest.

80-U.S.
(3838 South Warner Street, Tacoma, Wash. 98409) publishes bimonthly about 130 pages. The department "System/Command" and "View from the Top of the Stack" are of special interest.

The Alternate Source
(1806 Ada, Lansing, Mich. 48910) publishes bimonthly, presently about 75 pages per issue. The previous two magazines appeal to all TRS-80 users, but this is "the magazine of advanced applications and software." The readers of this book should feel well qualified to read this magazine.

All three magazines are very useful. There are, of course, many magazines that deal with microcomputers in general. Many of them carry articles of interest to TRS-80 owners.

SOFTWARE

Editors and Assemblers

First and foremost we need a good Editor/Assembler to work in FAST BASIC. The following features are desirable for efficient work.

1. Macros
2. External definition of constants
3. The ability to add to the assembly language program a file or some lines of a file

4. External macro definitions
5. Global editing features, screen editing, keyboard macros

Feature 1 means that we can use macros. At present only one tape-based assembler has macro capabilities—Microsoft's Editor/Assembler Plus. There are many disk-based macro assemblers. Microsoft's Macro Assembler is also sold by Radio Shack.

Feature 2 is very desirable so we can, once and for all, define the constants in a file. Features 3 and 4 serve the same purpose for machine language segments and macros. With an assembler that has these features we should be able to write FAST BASIC programs almost as fast as we can write BASIC programs.

Feature 5 is desirable for the convenience it provides in editing the programs. For instance, global replace can rename a constant in a whole program in one editing step.

Unfortunately, at present there are no macro assemblers that provide all these features. Measure any assembler against these criteria before you decide to buy. A number of keyboard editors can provide you with feature 5; test them to see whether they can work with your assembler.

Read the magazines listed in the previous section for announcements and reviews of new editors and assemblers.

Debugging Tools

Second in our priority listing are the debugging tools for both BASIC and machine language programs. Although large computers are always supplied with extensive debugging programs, very little is available for the TRS-80 user. There are now some BASIC single steppers that are very helpful. Cross-referencing programs are also available. They provide listings of all occurrences of a variable, a line number, and so on.

Some of the machine language single steppers can single step even in the ROM, which is a most useful feature. They should also show the disassembled form of the instruction being executed. However, most of the debugging in FAST BASIC is done in BASIC, and thus one first should buy a sophisticated BASIC debugger.

APPENDIX EIGHT

BASIC Program Listings

TUTOR

This program helps the reader to understand the concepts introduced in Chapter 1. The program can perform five tasks:

```
1 DISPLAY CONTENTS OF MEMORY LOCATION

2 BASE CONVERSION (EXERCISE AND UTILITY)

3 BINARY AND HEX ADDITION EXERCISES

4 ARITHMETIC UTILITY

5 DISPLAY AN ADDRESS
```

The first option is discussed in Chapter 1; it displays in binary the contents of a memory location.

The second option converts numbers from one base to another. It has two modes: an exercise mode and a utility mode. In the exercise mode the user supplies the answer and the computer checks the accuracy of the response. In the utility mode the answers are supplied by the program.

The third option teaches binary and hex additions. The utility version of this is option 4. In fact, in option 4 we can add numbers in different bases.

The fifth option displays an address stored at X and X + 1, where X is the address typed in by the user.

This is the listing of the disk version. The cassette version is in two parts: TUTOR1 and TUTOR2. TUTOR1 does options 1 to 3 and TUTOR2 does options 4 and 5.

For TUTOR1 type lines 1 to 1400 of the listing below with the following changes: In lines 1 and 310 change TUTOR to TUTOR1; delete lines 360 and 370; in line 410 change 5 to 3; in line 430 delete "1410, 1850".

For TUTOR2 type lines 1 to 430 and 1410 to 2140 with the following changes: In lines 1 and 310 change TUTOR to TUTOR2; change lines 330 to 350 to PRINT; in line 360 change 4 to 1 and in line 370 change 5 to 2; in line 410 change 5 to 2; in line 430 delete "440,660,1010,".

```
1 CLS : PRINT@280,"TUTOR"
2 PRINT @396,"AN EXCERCISE/UTILITY PROGRAM"
3 PRINT @898, "COPYRIGHT (C) 1980 BY FORT RICHMOND SOFTWARE
  COMPANY";
4 FOR I=1 TO 1000 : NEXT
10 GOTO 300
20 FOR I%=1 TO LO%
30 IF X$(I%)="B" THEN X(I%)=2 : X$(I%)="BINARY" : GOTO 80
40 IF X$(I%)="D" THEN X(I%)=10 : X$(I%)="DECIMAL" : GOTO 80
50 IF X$(I%)="H" THEN X(I%)=16 : X$(I%)="HEX" : GOTO 80
60 IF X$(I%)="O" THEN X(I%)=8 : X$(I%)="OCTAL" : GOTO 80
70 LO%=5
80 NEXT
90 RETURN
100 S$=""
110 A1=A-INT(A/X(2))*X(2)
120 IF A1<10 THEN S$=CHR$(48+A1)+S$ ELSE S$=CHR$(55+A1)+S$
130 A=INT(A/X(2))
140 IF A>0 THEN 110
150 IF SN=1 THEN S$="-"+S$
160 IF LEN(S$)>LE THEN 180
170 S$=STRING$(LE-LEN(S$),"0")+S$
180 RETURN
190 EX=1 : ER=0 : Y=LEN(A$)
200 FOR X%=1 TO Y
210 IF X%<>1 THEN EX=EX*X(1)
220 AS=ASC(MID$(A$,Y-X%+1,1))
230 IF AS<48 THEN ER=1 : X%=Y : GOTO 270
240 IF AS>64 THEN S=AS-55 ELSE S=AS-48
250 IF S>X(1)-1 THEN ER=1 : X%=Y : GOTO 270
260 A=A+(S*EX)
270 NEXT
280 RETURN
290 REM
300 CLS
310 PRINT @128,"OPTIONS FOR TUTOR : "
320 PRINT
330 PRINT TAB(21) "1 DISPLAY CONTENTS OF MEMORY LOCATION"
340 PRINT TAB(21) "2 BASE CONVERSION (EXERCISE AND UTILITY)"
350 PRINT TAB(21) "3 BINARY AND HEX ADDITION EXERCISES"
360 PRINT TAB(21) "4 ARITHMETIC UTILITY"
370 PRINT TAB(21) "5 DISPLAY AN ADDRESS"
380 PRINT
390 PRINT "NOTE :  TYPING X IN ANY OF THE
    PROGRAMS RETURNS THIS PAGE"
400 PRINT @896, "TYPE THE NUMBER OF THE DESIRED OPTION";
410 INPUT Q : IF Q>5 OR Q<1 OR Q<>INT(Q) THEN 410
420 CLS
430 ON Q GOTO 440,660,1010,1410,1850
440 CLEAR
450 PRINT : PRINT "THIS PROGRAM RETURNS THE CONTENTS OF THE
    MEMORY LOCATION" : PRINT "TYPE X TO RETURN TO THE MAIN  MENU"
    : PRINT : PRINT
460 S$=""
470 INPUT "TYPE IN ADDRESS (0 - 65535)";A$
480 IF I=2 THEN I=1 : PRINT @285,CHR$(31);A$ELSE I=I+1
490 IF LEN(A$)=0 THEN 460
500 IF (LEFT$(A$,1)="0" AND LEN(A$)>1)  OR LEFT$(A$,1)=" "THEN
    A$=MID$(A$,2) :  GOTO 490
510 IF A$="X" GOTO 290
520 IF VAL(A$)>65535 THEN PRINT : PRINT "NUMBER TOO BIG" : PRINT
    : PRINT : GOTO 460
530 IF VAL(A$)<0 THEN PRINT : PRINT "NUMBER TOO SMALL" : PRINT :
    PRINT : GOTO 460
540 IF " "+A$<>STR$(VAL(A$)) THEN 640
550 A=VAL(A$)+65000*(VAL(A$)>32767)
560 PRINT : PRINT "(";A$;") = ";
570 S=PEEK(A)
580 IF S-FIX(S/2)*2=1 THEN S$="1"+S$ ELSE S$="0"+S$
```

```
590 S=FIX(S/2)
600 IF S>0 THEN 580
610 S$=STRING$(8-LEN(S$),"0")+S$
620 PRINT LEFT$(S$,4);" ";RIGHT$(S$,4)
630 PRINT : PRINT : GOTO 460
640 PRINT : PRINT "TRY AGAIN" : PRINT : PRINT
650 GOTO 460
660 REM
670 CLEAR 400 : CLS
680 PRINT "THIS IS A BASE CONVERSION PROGRAM"
690 DEFDBL A-Z
700 PRINT
710 INPUT "THIS PROGRAM CAN BE USED AS AN EXERCISE OR AS A
    UTILITY.
    TYPE E FOR EXERCISE, U FOR UTILITY";UT$
720 IF UT$="U" THEN UT=1
730 IF UT$="X" THEN 290
740 INPUT "B=BINARY, H=HEX, D=DECIMAL, O=OCTAL
    TO CONVERT FROM BASE X TO BASE Y, TYPE :  X,Y";X$(1),X$(2)
750 IF X$(1)="X" OR X$(2)="X" GOTO 290
760 LO%=2
770 GOSUB 20
780 IF LO%>3 THEN 740
790 PRINT @64,CHR$(31); : PRINT @64,"THIS SECTION CONVERTS FROM
    ";X$(1) " TO "; X$(2)
800 PRINT"(TYPE X TO RETURN TO MENU, T TO CHANGE PARAMETERS)"
810 PRINT
820 A$="0"
830 PRINT@320*(I+1)-64,"NUMBER TO CONVERT"; : INPUT A$
840 IF A$="T" THEN 660
850 IF A$="X" THEN 290
860 IF I=2 THEN I=1 : PRINT @275, CHR$(31); : PRINT A$ ELSE I=I+1
870 RS$=""
880 IF UT=1 THEN PRINT : GOTO 920
890 INPUT "TYPE IN THE RESPONSE";RS$
900 IF RS$="X" THEN 290
910 IF RS$="T" THEN 660
920 GOSUB 190
930 IF ER=1 THEN 990
940 GOSUB 100
950 IF UT=1 THEN PRINT : PRINTA$; " (IN ";X$(1);") IS ";S$;" (IN
    ";X$(2); ")" : GOTO 970
960 IF RS$=S$ THEN PRINT : PRINT "CORRECT ANSWER" ELSE PRINT :
    PRINT "WHOOPS! THE CORRECT ANSWER IS ";S$
970 PRINT
980 GOTO 820
990 PRINT : PRINT "THE NUMBER IS NOT IN BASE";X(1);"FORM" : PRINT
    : GOTO820
1000 PRINT : PRINT  "NUMBER TOO LARGE" : PRINT : RESUME 820
1010 REM
1020 PRINT " BINARY AND HEX ADDITION EXERCISES.
     WHEN A PROBLEM APPEARS THE RESULT SHOULD BE TYPED IN
     FROM RIGHT TO LEFT"
1030 CLEAR 100
1040 PRINT : INPUT " TYPE IN EITHER B FOR BINARY OR H FOR
     HEXADECIMAL";X$(2)
1050 IF X$(2)="X" GOTO 290
1060 IF X$(2)="B" THEN X(2)=2 :  GOTO 1090
1070 IF X$(2)="H" THEN X(2)=16 : GOTO 1090
1080 GOTO 1040
1090 CLS
1100 PRINT CHR$(23)
1110 RANDOM
1120 FOR I=1 TO 4 : PRINT : NEXT
1130 T=0 : FOR R=1 TO 2
1140 IF X(2)=2 THEN A=RND(255) : LE=8 ELSE A=RND(32765) : LE=4
1150 IF B(R)<>0 THEN A=B(R)
1160 T=T+A
1170 B(R)=A
```

```
1180 GOSUB 100
1190 PRINT TAB(5);S$
1200 IF R=1 THENPRINT TAB(3)"+";
1210 NEXT
1220 A=T : GOSUB 100
1230 PRINT TAB(5) STRING$(LE,"-")
1240 PRINT TAB(4+LE) CHR$(138);
1250 PRINT CHR$(24);
1260 FOR A=1 TO LEN(S$)
1270 IN$=INKEY$ : IF IN$="" THEN 1270
1280 AS=ASC(IN$)
1290 IF AS<48 OR (AS>58 AND AS<65) OR AS>70 THEN 1270 ELSE
     J$(A)=IN$ : PRINT J$(A); : J$=J$(A)+J$
1300 IF J$(A)="X" GOTO 290
1310 PRINT CHR$(24); : PRINT CHR$(24);
1320 PRINT CHR$(138);
1330 PRINT CHR$(24);
1340 NEXT
1350 PRINT : PRINT : IF S$<>J$ THEN PRINT "WHOOPS. NOT CORRECT."
     : PRINT "TYPE A TO TRY AGAIN"; ELSE PRINT "CORRECT ANSWER"
1360 PRINT : PRINT "TYPE X TO RETURN TO THE MENU" :  PRINT "PRESS
     ANY OTHER KEY TO CONTINUE"
1370 CO$=INKEY$ : IF CO$="" THEN 1370
1380 T$="" : J$="" : R=0
1390 IF CO$="A" THEN 1090 ELSE B(1)=0 : B(2)=0
1400 IF CO$="X" THEN 290 ELSE 1090
1410 CLEAR
1420 DEFDBL A-Z
1430 CLS : PRINT "THIS IS THE ARITHMETIC PACKAGE"
1440 PRINT
1450 PRINT "IT ADDS NUMBERS IN THE SAME OR IN DIFFERENT BASES AND
     DISPLAYS
     THE RESULT IN THE BASE YOU SPECIFY."
1460 PRINT
1470 PRINT "FOR INSTANCE, YOU SPECIFY :
         HEX FOR THE FIRST NUMBER
         BINARY FOR THE SECOND NUMBER
         DECIMAL FOR THE RESULT.

         NOW IF YOU INPUT 2F3 FOR THE FIRST NUMBER AND -100010 FOR
     THE SECOND NUMBER, THE RESULT 721 IS DISPLAYED."
1480 PRINT
1490 INPUT "TO INITIALIZE THE PROGRAM INPUT THE BASE OF THE FIRST
     NUMBER
     (B=BINARY, H=HEX, O=OCTAL, D=DECIMAL)";X$(1)
1500 INPUT "INPUT THE BASE FOR THE SECOND NUMBER";X$(2)
1510 INPUT "INPUT THE BASE FOR THE RESULT";X$(3)
1520 IF X$(1)="X" OR X$(2)="X" OR X$(3)="X" THEN 290
1530 LO%=3
1540 GOSUB 20
1550 IF LO%>3 THEN 1490
1560 CLS : PRINT "THIS IS THE ARITHMETIC PACKAGE."
1570 CLS : PRINT "THIS SECTION ADDS A NUMBER IN ";X$(1);" WITH A
     NUMBER IN ";X$(2) : PRINT "THE RESULT WILL BE DISPLAYED IN
     "; X$(3) : PRINT "NOTE :  NUMBERS MAY BE SIGNED OR UNSIGNED"
1580 A$(1)="0" : A$(2)="0" : PRINT : PRINT "TYPE IN THE FIRST
     NUMBER"; : INPUT A$(1)
1590 IF A$(1)="" THEN 1580
1600 SI$=LEFT$(A$(1),1) : IF SI$=" " THEN 1590 ELSE IF SI$="-"
     THEN SN(1)=1 : A$(1)=MID$(A$(1),2)
1610 I=I+1 : IF I=2 THEN I=1 : PRINT@282,CHR$(31);A$(1)
1620 PRINT "TYPE IN THE SECOND NUMBER"; : INPUT A$(2)
1630 SI$=LEFT$(A$(2),1) : IF SI$=" " THEN 1600 ELSE IF SI$="-"
     THEN SN(2)=1 : A$(2)=MID$(A$(2),2)
1640 ON ERROR GOTO 1840
1650 T=0
1660 FOR I%=1 TO 2
1670 A$=A$(I%)
1680 A=0
1690 X(1)=X(I%)
```

```
1700 GOSUB 190
1710 IF ER=1 THEN 1830
1720 IF SN(I%)=1 THEN T=T-A ELSE T=T+A
1730 NEXT
1740 IF T<0 THEN SN=1 : T=-T
1750 A=T
1760 X(2)=X(3)
1770 GOSUB 100
1780 PRINT "THE RESULT OF THE ADDITION (IN ";X$(3);") IS ";S$
1790 PRINT : PRINT : PRINT "TYPE T TO RETURN TO THE BEGINNING OF
     THE PROGRAM,
     X TO TO RETURN TO THE MAIN MENU,
     ANY OTHER KEY TO CONTINUE IN THIS SECTION"
1800 W$=INKEY$ : IF W$="" THEN 1800 ELSE IF W$="T" THEN 1420
1810 IF W$="X" THEN 290
1820 GOTO 1580
1830 PRINT " NUMBER IS NOT IN BASE"X(I%)"FORM" : GOTO 1790
1840 PRINT "NUMBER IS TOO LARGE"  : RESUME 1790
1850 CLEAR : DEFDBL A-Z
1860 PRINT : PRINT : PRINT "TYPE IN THE ADDRESS OF A MEMORY
     LOCATION (0 - 65535)."
1870 PRINT "THIS PROGRAM WILL REGARD THE CONTENTS OF THIS MEMORY
     LOCATION
     AND OF THE NEXT AS AN ADDRESS AND DISPLAYS IT IN HEX AND
     DECIMAL"
1880 PRINT @384,CHR$(31)
1890 PRINT@384, "TYPE IN THE BASE OF THE ADDRESS (H=HEX,
     D=DECIMAL)"; : INPUT X$
1900 IF X$="X" THEN 290
1910 X(2)=16 : IF X$="D" THEN X(1)=10 ELSE IF X$="H" THEN X(1)=16
     ELSE GOTO 1880
1920 PRINT @448, "TYPE IN THE ADDRESS"; : INPUT A$
1930 IF LEN(A$)=0 THEN PRINT@448,CHR$(31); : GOTO 1920
1940 IF LEFT$(A$,1)=" " OR (LEFT$(A$,1)="0" AND LEN(A$)>1) THEN
     A$=MID$(A$,2) : GOTO 1930
1945 IF RIGHT$(A$,1)=" " THEN A$=LEFT$(A$,LEN(A$)-1):GOTO 1930
1950 IF LEFT$(A$,1)="-" THEN PRINT@448,CHR$(31); : GOTO 1920
1960 GOSUB 190
1970 IF A>65536 THEN PRINT@448,CHR$(31); : GOTO 1920
1980 IF ER=1 THEN PRINT "NUMBER IS NOT IN BASE";X(I)"FORM" :
     PRINT @448,CHR$(31); : GOTO 1920
1990 A=A+(A>32676)*65536
2000 TO=PEEK(A)
2010 A=A+1
2020 A=A+(A>32676)*65536
2030 TO=TO+PEEK(A)*256
2040 A=TO
2050 GOSUB 100
2060 PRINT : PRINT : PRINT "THE ADDRESS AT ";A$;" IS";TO;"IN
     DECIMAL AND "; S$;" IN HEX"
2070 PRINT : PRINT "TYPE X TO RETURN TO THE MENU,
      T TO CHANGE BASE OF ADDRESS,
      ANY OTHER KEY TO CONTINUE"
2080 W$=INKEY$ : IF W$="" THEN 2080
2090 IF W$="T" THEN 1880
2100 IF W$="X" THEN 290 ELSE PRINT @450,CHR$(31); : GOTO 1920
2110 A=A+(S*EX)
2120 EX=EX*X(1)
2130 NEXT
2140 RETURN
```

VARPTR

This program is used in Chapter 4 to display entries in the variable tables. The program is self-prompting. It does not distinguish between singly and multiply dimensioned arrays.

```
1 CLS : PRINT@280,"VARPTR"
2 PRINT @392,"A UTILITY TO DISPLAY THE VARIABLE TABLES"
3 PRINT @898,"COPYRIGHT (C) 1980 BY FORT RICHMOND SOFTWARE
  COMPANY";
4 FOR I=1 TO 1000 : NEXT
10 CLEAR 300
20 GOTO 130
30 IF Y=10 THEN S$=MID$(STR$(A),2) : GOTO 80 ELSE S$=""
40 A1=A-INT(A/16)*16
50 IF A1<10 THEN S$=CHR$(48+A1)+S$ ELSE S$=CHR$(55+A1)+S$
60 A=INT(A/16)
70 IF A>0 THEN 40
80 L=LEN(S$)
90 IF L>LE THEN 110
100 S$=STRING$(LE-L,"0")+S$
110 IF L>3 THEN S$="("+S$+")"
120 RETURN
130 DIMDB#(4) : DIM S1$(4) : DIMS2$(4)
140 DIM SP(4)
150 DEFDBL A
160 DIM IN%(10)
170 IN%=2
180 SP=123456
190 DB#=2000111222333
200 S1$="HI" : S2$=" GEORGE" : S2$=S1$+S2$
210 S3$=MID$(S2$,1,2)+MID$(S2$,4)
220 S1$(0)=S1$ : S2$(0)=S1$+"HI"+" GEORGE"
230 FOR I=1 TO 3 : IN%(I)=1500*I
240 SP(I)=3000*I
250 DB#(I)=97578981259*I
260 S1$(I)=S1$(I-1)+"HI"
270 S2$(I)=S2$(I-1)+" GEORGE"
280 NEXT I
290 CLS
300 CLS : PRINT "THIS PROGRAM DISPLAYS ITEM BY ITEM THE SIMPLE
    VARIABLE TABLE AND THE ARRAY VARIABLE TABLE.
    YOU HAVE A CHOICE OF HEX OR DECIMAL FORMAT." : PRINT
310 TC=0 : PRINT "H: HEX FORMAT
    D: DECIMAL FORMAT" : INPUT "TYPE H OR D";Y$
320 IF Y$="H" THEN Y$="HEX" : Y=16 ELSE IF Y$="D" THEN
    Y$="DECIMAL" : Y=10 ELSE GOTO 310
330 PRINT : PRINT "SV: SIMPLE VARIABLE TABLE
    AV: ARRAY VARIABLE TABLE" : INPUT "TYPE SV OR AV";TB$
340 IF TB$="SV" THEN S=PEEK(16633)+256*PEEK(16634)+3 : SV=1 :
    GOTO 860 ELSE IF TB$<>"AV" THEN 330
350 A1=0 : A=0 : S#=0 : L=0 : LO=0 : NS$="" : WE$="" : CH=0 :
    LN=0 : AV=0 : W$="" : CO=0 : FL=0 : FR=0 : AS=0 : X9=0 :
    X$="" : S=0 : SV=0 : TC=0 : SS$="" : S$=""
360 S=PEEK(16635)+256*PEEK(16636)+8
370 IF CO>0 THEN 860 ELSE 870
380 CLS
390 PRINT "ARRAY #";TC+1"OF ARRAY VARIABLE TABLE ";
400 PRINT "(";Y$;" FORMAT)"
410 A=S-8 : GOSUB 30 : NS$=S$ : A=PEEK(S-8) : GOSUB 30 : PRINT
    NS$ " = ";S$;TAB(16)"TYPE FLAG FOR ";X$" ARRAY"
420 A=S-7 : GOSUB 30 : NS$=S$ : A=PEEK(S-7) : GOSUB 30 : PRINT
    NS$" = ";S$;TAB(16)"CODE FOR SECOND LETTER IN VARIABLE NAME:
    ";CHR$(PEEK(S-7))
430 A=S-6 : GOSUB 30 : NS$=S$ : A=PEEK(S-6) : GOSUB 30 : PRINT
    NS$" = ";S$;TAB(16);"ASCII OF FIRST LETTER IN VARIABLE NAME:
    ";CHR$(PEEK(S-6))
440 A=S-5 : GOSUB 30 : NS$=S$ : A=PEEK(S-5) : GOSUB 30 : PRINT
    NS$" = ";S$;TAB(16);"LSB OF THE ARRAY STORAGE SIZE"
450 A=S-4 : GOSUB 30 : NS$=S$ : A=PEEK(S-4) : GOSUB 30 : PRINT
    NS$" = ";S$;TAB(16);"MSB OF THE ARRAY STORAGE SIZE"
460 A=S-3 : GOSUB 30 : NS$=S$ : A=PEEK(S-3) : GOSUB 30 : PRINT
    NS$" = ";S$;TAB(16);"NUMBER OF DIMESIONS"
470 A=S-2 : GOSUB 30 : NS$=S$ : A=PEEK(S-2) : GOSUB 30 : PRINT
    NS$" = ";S$;TAB(16)"LSB OF DIMENSION #1";TAB(45)"TYPE ANY
    KEY"
```

```
480 A=S-1 : GOSUB 30 : NS$=S$ : A=PEEK(S-1) : GOSUB 30 : PRINT
    NS$;" = ";S$;TAB(16)"MSB OF DIMENSION #1";TAB(45)"TO
    CONTINUE"
490 W$=INKEY$ : IF W$="" THEN 490
500 AS=PEEK(S-2)+PEEK(S-1)*256
510 CO=CO+1
520 IF AS=CO-1 THEN  S=S+8 : CO=0 : TC=TC+1 : IF
    S>PEEK(16637)+PEEK(16638)*256 THEN CLS : PRINT "END OF THE
    TABLE" : PRINT : GOTO 310 ELSE GOTO 370
530 PRINT"ELEMENT #";CO"OF THE ARRAY"
540 IF FL<>3 THEN 650 ELSE GOTO 940
550 TC=TC+1
560 CLS
570 PRINT : PRINT "ENTRY #";TC"IN THE SIMPLE VARIABLE TABLE ";
580 PRINT "(";Y$;" FORMAT)"
590 PRINT
600 IF FL=3 THEN 910
610 IF FL+S>PEEK(16635)+PEEK(16636)*256 THEN PRINT "THERE ARE NO
    MORE VARIABLES IN THE SIMPLE VARIABLE TABLE" : GOTO 790
620 A=S-3 : GOSUB 30 : PRINT S$" ="PEEK(S-3);TAB(16)"TYPE FLAG
    FOR ";X$
630 A=S-2 : GOSUB 30 : NS$=S$ : A=PEEK(S-2) : GOSUB 30 : PRINT
    NS$" = "S$;TAB(16)"CODE FOR SECOND LETTER IN VARIABLE NAME:
    ";:PRINT CHR$(PEEK(S-2))
640 A=S-1 : GOSUB 30 : NS$=S$ : A=PEEK(S-1) : GOSUB 30 : PRINT
    NS$" = ";S$;TAB(16)"ASCII OF FIRST LETTER IN VARIABLE NAME:
    ";CHR$(PEEK(S-1))
650 FR=(FL<>2)+FL-1
660 A=S : GOSUB 30 : NS$=S$ : A=PEEK(S) : GOSUB 30 : PRINT NS$" =
    ";S$;TAB(16) "LSB OF VALUE   <---- VARPTR"
670 IF FL=2 THEN 740
680 A=S+1 : GOSUB 30 : NS$=S$ : A=PEEK(S+1) : GOSUB 30 : PRINT
    NS$" = ";S$;TAB(16) "BYTE 2 OF VALUE"
690 IF FL=4 THEN 740
700 FOR LO=2 TO 5
710 A=S+LO : GOSUB 30 : NS$=S$ : A=PEEK(S+LO) : GOSUB 30 :  PRINT
    NS$" = "S$;
720 IF INT(LO/2)=LO/2 THEN PRINT TAB(16)"BYTE"LO+1"OF
    VALUE";TAB(34) ELSE PRINT TAB(48)"BYTE"LO+1 "OF VALUE"
730 NEXT
740 A=S+FR : GOSUB 30 : NS$=S$ : A=PEEK(S+FR) : GOSUB 30 : PRINT
    NS$" = ";S$;TAB(16)"MSB OF VALUE"
750 IF FL=2 THEN 790
760 A=S+FR+1 : GOSUB 30 : NS$=S$ : A=PEEK(S+FR+1) : GOSUB 30 :
    PRINT NS$" = "S$;TAB(16) "EXPONENT IS "; : A=PEEK(S+FR+1) :
    IF A<128 THEN SS$="-" ELSE SS$=""
770 IF A<>0 THEN A=A-128 ELSE A=0 : SS$=""
780 GOSUB 30 : PRINT SS$+S$
790 PRINT @960, "T :  TOP OF PROGRAM, ";
800 IF SV=0 THEN PRINT "J :  ABORT ARRAY, ";
810 PRINT "ELSE :  CONTINUE";
820 WE$=INKEY$ : IF WE$="" THEN 820
830 IF WE$="T" THEN 170
840 IFWE$="J" AND SV=0 THEN S=S+FL*(AS-CO+1)+8 : IF
    S>PEEK(16637)+256*PEEK(16638) THEN CLS : PRINT "END OF ARRAY
    TABLE" : PRINT : GOTO 310 ELSE CO=0 : TC=TC+1 : GOTO 370
850 S=(SV=1)*-3+S+FL
860 IF SV=0  THEN PRINT@512+(TC>0)*-64,CHR$(31); : GOTO 510
870 FL=PEEK((SV-1)*5-3+S) : IF FL=2 THEN X$="INTEGER VARIABLE" :
    GOTO 900
880 IF FL=4 THEN X$="SINGLE PRECISION VARIABLE"  : GOTO 900
890 IF FL=8 THEN X$="DOUBLE PRECISION VARIABLE" ELSE X$="STRING
    VARIABLE"
900 IF SV=1 THEN 550 ELSE 380
910 A=S-3 : GOSUB 30 : PRINT S$" =";PEEK(S-3);TAB(16) "VARIABLE
    TYPE FLAG FOR "X$
920 A=S-2 : GOSUB 30 : NS$=S$ : A=PEEK(S-2) : GOSUB 30 : PRINT
    NS$" = ";S$;TAB(16)"CODE FOR SECOND LETTER IN VARIABLE NAME :
    "; : PRINTCHR$(PEEK(S-2))
```

```
930 A=S-1 : GOSUB 30 : NS$=S$ : A=PEEK(S-1) : GOSUB 30 : PRINT
    NS$" = ";S$;TAB(16)"ASCII OF FIRST LETTER IN VARIABLE NAME :
    "; : PRINT CHR$(PEEK(S-1))
940 LN=PEEK(S)
950 A=S : GOSUB 30 : NS$=S$ : A=PEEK(S) : GOSUB 30 : PRINT NS$" =
    ";S$;TAB(16)"LENGTH OF THE STRING     <---- VARPTR"
960 A=S+1 : GOSUB 30 : NS$=S$ : A=PEEK(S+1) : GOSUB 30 : PRINT
    NS$" = ";S$;TAB(16)"LSB OF STARTING ADDRESS"
970 A=S+2 : GOSUB 30 : NS$=S$ : A=PEEK(S+2) : GOSUB 30 : PRINT
    NS$" = ";S$;TAB(16)"MSB OF STARTING ADDRESS"
980 PRINT
990 S#=PEEK(S+1)+256*PEEK(S+2)
1000 IF LN=0 THEN PRINT "STRING NOT DEFINED" : GOTO 790
1010 A#=S# : GOSUB 30 : PRINT " ";
1020 IF LEN(S$)=2THEN PRINT ""; ELSE PRINT MID$(S$,2,LEN(S$)-2);
1030 PRINT "  ---->   ";
1040 FOR LO=0 TO LN-1
1050 IF S#+LO>32767 AND CH=0 THEN S#=S#-65536 : CH=1
1060 X$=CHR$(PEEK(S#+LO))
1070 IF X$="(" OR X$=")" THEN 1080 ELSE PRINT X$;
1080 NEXT
1090 PRINT : CH=0 : GOTO 790
```

VIEW/MOD

This utility *views* any memory location and *mod*ifies any RAM memory location. (Note: Lowercase letters are not shown on the screen; to modify this, change line 400.) The CHANGE command can be utilized to type in short machine language programs. Chapter 12 discusses the enhanced FAST BASIC version of this program. The program is self-prompting.

```
10 CLS : PRINT@280,"VIEW/MOD
20 PRINT : PRINT TAB(5)"A UTILITY TO DISPLAY, MODIFY, AND SEARCH
   THE MEMORY"
30 PRINT @896,"COPYRIGHT (C) 1980 BY FORT RICHMOND SOFTWARE
   COMPANY";
40 FOR I=1 TO 1000 : NEXT
50 CLEAR 300
60 DIM CO(85)
70 DEFINT D-R : DEFINT T-Z
80 GOTO 250
90 S$=""
100 A1=A-INT(A/16)*16
110 IF A1<10 THEN S$=CHR$(48+A1)+S$ ELSE S$=CHR$(55+A1)+S$
120 A=INT(A/16)
130 IF A>0 THEN 100
140 IF LEN(S$)<LE THEN S$=STRING$(LE-LEN(S$),"0")+S$
150 RETURN
160 EX=1 : FL=0 : A=0 : Y=LEN(A$)
170 FOR X=1 TO Y
180 IF X=1 THEN EX=1 ELSE EX=EX*16
190 AS%=ASC(MID$(A$,Y-X+1,1))
200 IF AS%<48 OR (57<AS% AND AS%<65) OR 70<AS% THEN FL=1 : X=Y :
    GOTO 230
210 IF AS%>64 THEN S=AS%-55 ELSE S=AS%-48
220 A=A+(S*EX)
230 NEXT
240 RETURN
250 AD$="0000" : AD=0
260 CLS : PRINT"VIEW/MOD"
270 GOTO 540
280 S2=12 : BA=384
290 CLS :  PRINT "VIEW/MOD"
300 IF AD>65536 THEN BA=192 : GOTO530
```

```
310 FOR S1=1 TO S2
320 AC$=""
330 PRINT AD$"-->";
340 FOR I=0 TO 15
350 C1=AD+I
360 IF C1>65535 THEN 530
370 IF C1>32767 THEN C1=C1-65536
380 IF C1=-1 THEN BA=192+S1*16 : S1=S2 : I=15
390 A=PEEK(C1)
400 IF A<32 OR A>90 THEN AC$=AC$+"." ELSE AC$=AC$+CHR$(A)
410 LE=2
420 GOSUB 90
430 PRINT S$;
440 IF I/2<>INT(I/2) THEN PRINT " ";
450 NEXT
460 PRINT " "+AC$;
470 AD=AD+16
480 LE=4
490 A=AD
500 GOSUB 90
510 AD$=S$
520 NEXT
530 PRINT@832,CHR$(31);
540 PRINT@960,"TYPE A(HEAD), B(ACK), C(HANGE), D(ISPLAY),
    F(IND)";
550 IN$="" : IN$=INKEY$
560 IF IN$="" GOTO 550
570 AZ%=ASC(IN$)-64
580 IF AZ%<1 GOTO 600
590 ON AZ%GOTO 280,610,770,670,540,1070
600 PRINT@832,"COMMAND NOT ACCEPTED
    INPUT NEW COMMAND"; : GOTO 540
610 AD=AD-BA
620 IF AD<0 THEN AD=0
630 A=AD
640 LE=4
650 GOSUB 90 : AD$=S$
660 GOTO 280
670 PRINT@832,CHR$(31); : AD$=""
680 PRINT@832,"FIRST ADDRESS TO BE DISPLAYED (IN HEX)";
    : INPUT AD$
690 LE=LEN(AD$)
700 IF LE=0 OR LE>4 THEN PRINT@836,CHR$(31);
    : GOTO 680
710 A$=AD$
720 GOSUB 160
730 AD$=STRING$(4-LE,"0")+AD$
740 IF FL=1 PRINT@768,CHR$(31);"ADDRESS SHOULD BE IN HEX"; : GOTO
    680
750 AD=A
760 GOTO 280
770 PRINT @832,CHR$(31);
780 AD$="" : CS$=""
790 PRINT@832,"FIRST ADDRESS TO BE CHANGED (IN HEX)"; : INPUT AD$
800 IF LEN(AD$)>4 OR LEN(AD$)=0 THEN PRINT@768,CHR$(31);
    : GOTO790
810 PRINT@896,"INPUT NEW CONTENTS (E.G.,AF 08 9B)"; : INPUT CS$
820 IF CS$="" THEN PRINT@896,CHR$(31); : GOTO 810
830 S2=INT((LEN(CS$)+1)/48+.95)
840 BA=192+S2*16
850 A$=AD$
860 GOSUB 160
870 IF FL=1 THEN PRINT@768,CHR$(31); : PRINT@768,"ADDRESS SHOULD
    BE IN HEX"; : GOTO 790
880 AD=A
890 IF AD<12001 THEN PRINT@704,CHR$(31); : PRINT @768,"CANNOT
    CHANGE ROM"; : GOTO 790
900 IF CS$="" THEN PRINT@896,CHR$(31); : GOTO 810
910 IF LEFT$(CS$,1)=" " THEN CS$=MID$(CS$,2) : GOTO 900
920 IF RIGHT$(CS$,1)=" " THEN CS$=MID$(CS$,1,LEN(CS$)-1) :
    GOTO 900
```

```
930 Y1=LEN(CS$)
940 FOR I=0 TO Y1
950 CO$=LEFT$(CS$,2)
960 A$=CO$
970 GOSUB 160
980 IF FL=1 THEN PRINT@704,"CONTENTS MUST BE IN HEX";
    : PRINT@896,CHR$(31); : GOTO 810
990 CS$=MID$(CS$,4)
1000 AP=AD+I
1010 IF AP>32767 THEN AP=AP-65536
1020 IF AP=-1 THEN I=Y1
1030 POKE AP,A
1040 IF LEN(CS$)=0 THEN I=Y1+1
1050 NEXT
1060 GOTO 290
1070 PRINT@832,CHR$(31);
1080 PRINT@832,"INPUT STARTING AND TERMINATING ADDRESS
     (E.G., DEFD FFFF)"; : INPUT ST$
1090 IF RIGHT$(ST$,1)=" " THEN ST$=LEFT$(ST$,9)
1100 IF LEN(ST$)<>9 THEN PRINT@832,CHR$(31); : GOTO 1080
1110 PRINT@896,"INPUT THE SEQUENCE TO SEARCH FOR (E.G., AF DE
     BC)"; : INPUT SS$
1120 IF LEN(SS$)=0 THEN PRINT@896,CHR$(31); : GOTO 1110
1130 IF RIGHT$(SS$,1)=" " THEN SS$=MID$(SS$,1,LEN(SS$)-1) : GOTO
     1120
1140 S2=INT((LEN(SS$)+1)/48+.95)
1150 BA=192+S2*16
1160 AD$=MID$(ST$,1,4)
1170 AF$=MID$(ST$,6,4)
1180 A$=AD$
1190 GOSUB 160
1200 IF FL=1 THEN 1070
1210 AD=A
1220 A$=AF$
1230 GOSUB 160
1240 IF FL=1 THEN 1070
1250 AF=A
1260 IF AF<AD THEN 1070
1270 IF SS$="" THEN PRINT@896,CHR$(31); : GOTO 1110
1280 IF LEFT$(SS$,1)=" " THEN SS$=MID$(SS$,2) : GOTO 1270
1290 CO$=LEFT$(SS$,2)
1300 A$=CO$
1310 GOSUB 160
1320 IF FL=1 THEN PRINT@896,CHR$(31); : GOTO 1110
1330 CO=A
1340 LS=((LEN(SS$)+1)/3)-1
1350 SS$=MID$(SS$,3)
1360 IF LS=0 THEN 1450
1370 FOR N1=1 TO LS
1380 IF LEFT$(SS$,1)=" " THEN SS$=MID$(SS$,2)
1390 A$=LEFT$(SS$,2)
1400 SS$=MID$(SS$,3)
1410 GOSUB 160
1420 CO(N1)=A
1430 IF FL=1 THEN PRINT@896,CHR$(31); : GOTO 1110
1440 NEXT
1450 IF AD>32767 THEN AD=AD-65536 : AF=AF-65536
1460 BC=AF-AD+1
1470 SB=BC
1480 FOR LO!=1 TO BC
1490 A=AD+(-65536*(AD<0)) : GOSUB 90
1500 PRINT@128,CHR$(31) : PRINT"SEARCHING ";S$
1510 IF CO=PEEK(AD) THEN LO!=BC : NEXT : GOTO 1550
1520 AD=AD+1
1530 NEXT
1540 PRINT@128,CHR$(31); : PRINT "NOT FOUND " : BA=BA-S2*16 :
     AD=AD-SB : AD=AD+(AD<0)*-65536 : GOTO 530
1550 IF AD>32767 THEN AD=AD-65536 : AF=AF-65536
1560 BC=AF-AD
1570 IF LS=0 THEN 1630
```

```
1580 IF AD=-1 THEN AD=AD+1 : GOTO 1540
1590 FOR N1=1 TO LS
1600 IF (AD+N1)>32767 THEN AD=AD-65536
1610 IF CO(N1)<>PEEK(AD+N1) THEN AD=AD+1 : N1=LS : NEXT : GOTO
     1480
1620 NEXT
1630 AD=AD+(-65536*(AD<0)) : A=AD : GOSUB 90 : AD$=S$ : IF
     LEN(AD$)<4 THEN AD$=STRING$(4-LEN(AD$),"0")+AD$
1640 GOTO 290
```

DISASSEM

This disassembler, written by H. Lakser, has many nice features. One can jump or go to a subroutine with a single-letter instruction. The program keeps a stack, so one can return from a subroutine. Help can be called to explain the meaning of commands.

Here is a typical display created by the disassembler.

```
DISASSEMBLE:                              ACTION?
(LOCATION)      <ENTER>(NEXT)      S(UBROUTINE)    R(ETURN)     J(UMP)
P(RINT)         M(EMORY DUMP)      X(RESTART)      H(ELP)
...........................................................................


29DA   2A2141      LD HL,(4121H)         *!A
29DD   EB          EX DE,HL              .
29DE   CDF529      CALL 29F5H            ..)
29E1   EB          EX DE,HL              .
29E2   C0          RET NZ                .
29E3   D5          PUSH DE               .
29E4   50          LD D,B                P
29E5   59          LD E,C                Y
29E6   1B          DEC DE                .
```

The first column gives the memory location. The second column is the instruction in hex. The third column is the disassembled instruction. The fourth column prints the ASCII characters if they are printable; a period replaces an unprintable character.

Respond to the ACTION?_ query by one of the following (press ENTER after each command).

1. Type a 4-digit hex number. The instruction starting at this address will be disassembled.
2. Press ENTER. Disassembles the *next* instruction.
3. Press S, R, J, P, or X. These are explained in the HELP listing.
4. Press M for memory dump. Prints the memory location in hex.
5. Press H for HELP! This explains how the various commands work. Typing H, you are asked which of the nine commands you want explained. Type in the number of the command, and the explanation is displayed.

The help instructions do not fit into a 16K computer; they were omitted from the cassette version. For the benefit of the users of the cassette version, here are the responses to the HELP command.

```
LOCATION HELP:  ENTER THE LOCATION AS A 4 (MUST BE 4) DIGIT HEX
NUMBER AND HIT <ENTER>.  THAT MEMORY LOCATION WILL BE DUMPED/
DISASSEMBLED

NEXT HELP:  HIT <ENTER> TO DISASSEMBLE/DUMP THE NEXT MEMORY
LOCATION

SUBROUTINE HELP:  ENTER  S  AND HIT <ENTER> TO JUMP TO THE
SUBROUTINE REFERRED TO IN THE LAST INSTRUCTION IF IT IS A
'CALL' OR 'RST', OTHERWISE ERROR INDICATED

RETURN HELP:  ENTER  R  AND HIT <ENTER> TO RETURN FROM THE
SUBROUTINE.  IF THE RETURN STACK IS EMPTY AN ERROR IS
INDICATED

JUMP HELP:  ENTER  J  AND HIT <ENTER> TO JUMP TO THE
LOCATION REFERRED TO IN THE LAST INSTRUCTION IF IT IS A
JUMP OR 'DJNZ', OTHERWISE ERROR IS INDICATED

PRINT HELP:  PRINTS MEMORY LOCATIONS CONSECUTIVELY ON PRINTER.
IF 1ST LOCATION < 0002 & LAST LOCATION > FFFC THE PRINTING MUST
BE DIVIDED INTO 2 SEPARATE PASSES

MEMORY DUMP HELP:  ENTER  M  AND HIT <ENTER> TO SWITCH TO THE
'MEMORY DUMP' MENU

RESTART HELP:  ENTER  X  AND HIT <ENTER> TO GO BACK TO THE
START OF THE PROGRAM
```

To get the cassette version of the disassembler type in only lines 1 to 320.

```
1 GOTO 160
2 REM ASCII DUMP
3 IF Y>32 AND Y<128 THEN AS$=AS$+CHR$(Y) ELSE AS$=AS$+"."
4 RETURN
5 REM DISPLAY DISASSEMBLED LINE
6 H$=M$ : GOSUB 12
7 GOSUB 37
8 PRINT@ 1023," "; : PRINT L$;TAB(6)O$;TAB(16)W$;TAB(35)AS$;
9 IF PP=1 THEN LPRINT L$; TAB(6) O$;TAB(16) W$; TAB(35) AS$
10 RETURN
11 REM CONVERT 4-DIGIT HEX TO DECIMAL
12 Z=LEN(H$)-1 : X=0
13 FOR K=Z TO 0 STEP -1
14 FOR K1=1 TO 16
15 IF MID$(H$,K+1,1)=MID$(A$,K1,1) THEN K2=K1-1 : K1=16
16 NEXT K1
17 X=X+K2*K(K)
18 NEXT K
19 X=X+SHFT
20 REM GET CORRECT X
21 IF X>32767 THEN X=X-65536
22 IF X<-32768 THEN X=X+65536
23 RETURN
24 REM CONVERT DECIMAL TO 4-DIGIT HEX
25 D=D-SHFT : IF D<0 THEN D=D+65536
26 H4=INT(D/4096)
27 H3=INT((D-4096*H4)/256)
28 H2=INT((D-4096*H4-256*H3)/16)
29 H1=D-4096*H4-256*H3-16*H2
30 H$=MID$(A$,H4+1,1)+MID$(A$,H3+1,1)+MID$(A$,H2+1,1)+
   MID$(A$,H1+1,1)
31 RETURN
32 REM CONVERT DECIMAL TO 2-DIGIT HEX
```

```
33 H2=INT(D/16)
34 H1=D-16*H2
35 H$=MID$(A$,H2+1,1)+MID$(A$,H1+1,1)
36 RETURN
37 REM DISASSEMBLE MEMORY LOCATION
38 Y=PEEK(X)
39 IF Y>=64 AND Y<123 GOTO 62
40 IF Y>=128 AND Y<192 GOTO 72
41 C=INT(Y/128) : I1=VAL(A$(C,Y-192*C))
42 W$=RIGHT$(A$(C,Y-192*C),LEN(A$(C,Y-192*C))-1)
43 ON I1+1 GOSUB 46,46,46,46,133,148,110
44 RETURN
45 REM STANDARD OPCODE PROCESSING
46 IF I1<3 THEN F=0 ELSE F=1
47 IF I1=3 THEN I1=1
48 D=X : GOSUB 25
49 L$=H$ : O$="" : AS$=""
50 FOR J=0 TO I1
51 Y=PEEK(X)
52 D=Y : GOSUB 33
53 O$=O$+H$
54 GOSUB 3
55 X=X+1 : GOSUB 21
56 NEXT J
57 IF F=1 GOSUB 224 ELSE H$=MID$(O$,5,2)+MID$(O$,3,2)
58 N$=H$
59 GOSUB 217
60 RETURN
61 REM LD GROUP
62 D=X : GOSUB 25
63 L$=H$ : AS$=CHR$(Y)
64 D=Y : GOSUB 33
65 O$=H$
66 P=INT(Y/8) : P1=Y-8*P
67 W$="LD "+R$(P-3)+","+R$(P1)
68 IF Y=118 THEN W$="HALT"
69 X=X+1 : GOSUB 21
70 RETURN
71 REM REGULAR GROUP
72 D=X : GOSUB 25
73 L$=H$ : AS$="."
74 D=Y : GOSUB 33
75 O$=H$
76 P=INT(Y/8) : P1=Y-8*P
77 W$=E$(P-16)+R$(P1)
78 X=X+1 : GOSUB 21
79 RETURN
80 REM "DDCB" PROCESSING
81 AS$=AS$+"."
82 O$=O$+"CB"
83 X=X+1 : GOSUB 21
84 Y=PEEK(X)
85 D=Y : GOSUB 33
86 V$=H$ : O$=O$+V$
87 GOSUB 3
88 X=X+1 : GOSUB 21
89 Y=PEEK(X)
90 GOSUB 3
91 D=Y : GOSUB 33
92 O$=O$+H$
93 FOR I=0 TO 30
94 IF H$=LEFT$(D$(I),2) THEN W$=RIGHT$(D$(I),LEN(D$(I))-2)+
   "(I"+Z$+"+"+V$+"H)" : I=30
95 NEXT I
96 GOTO 130
97 REM "36" PROCESSING
98 O$=H$ : AS$=AS$+"6"
99 X=X+1 : GOSUB 21
100 Y=PEEK(X) : GOSUB 33
101 O$=O$+H$ : U$=H$
```

```
102 GOSUB 3
103 X=X+1 : GOSUB 21
104 Y=PEEK(X) : GOSUB 33
105 GOSUB 3
106 O$=C$+H$ : V$=H$
107 W$="LD (I?+"+U$+"H),"+V$+"H"
108 GOTO 127
109 REM PROCESS "DD-FD" CODES
110 AS$="."
111 D=Y : GOSUB 33
112 F$=H$
113 IF F$="DD" THEN Z$="X" : GOTO 115
114 IF F$="FD" THEN Z$="Y"
115 D=X : GOSUB 25
116 L$=H$ : O$=""
117 X=X+1 : GOSUB 21
118 Y=PEEK(X)
119 D=Y : GOSUB 33
120 IF H$="36" GOTO 97
121 IF H$="CB" GOTO 81
122 FOR I=0 TO 38
123 IF H$=LEFT$(C$(I),2) THEN W$=RIGHT$(C$(I),LEN(C$(I))-2) :
    I=38
124 NEXT I
125 I1=VAL(W$) : W$=RIGHT$(W$,LEN(W$)-1) : F=0
126 GOSUB 50
127 FOR I=1 TO LEN(W$)
128 IF MID$(W$,I,1)="?" THEN W$=LEFT$(W$,I-1)+Z$+
    RIGHT$(W$,LEN(W$)-I)
129 NEXT I
130 O$=F$+O$
131 RETURN
132 REM PROCESS "CB" CODES
133 D=X : GOSUB 25
134 L$=H$ : AS$=""
135 X=X+1 : GOSUB 21
136 Y=PEEK(X)
137 D=Y : GOSUB 33
138 O$="CB"+H$
139 GOSUB 3
140 P=INT(Y/8) :  P1=Y-8*P
141 IF P<8 THEN W$=R1$(P)+" "+R$(P1) : GOTO 145
142 IF P>=8 AND P<16 THEN W$="BIT"+STR$(P-8)+","+R$(P1) : GOTO145
143 IF P>=16 AND P<24 THEN W$="RES"+STR$(P-16)+","+R$(P1)  :
    GOTO 145
144 IF P>=24 AND P<32 THEN W$="SET"+STR$(P-24)+","+R$(P1)
145 X=X+1 : GOSUB 21
146 RETURN
147 REM PROCESS "ED" CODES
148 D=X : GOSUB 25
149 L$=H$ : O$="" : AS$="."
150 X=X+1 : GOSUB 21
151 Y=PEEK(X)
152 D=Y : GOSUB 33
153 FOR I=0 TO 53
154 IF H$=LEFT$(B$(I),2) THEN W$=RIGHT$(B$(I),LEN(B$(I))-2) :
    I=53
155 NEXT I
156 I1=VAL(W$) : W$=RIGHT$(W$,LEN(W$)-1) : F=0
157 GOSUB 50
158 O$="ED"+O$
159 RETURN
160 CLS
161 PRINT@ 276,"Z80 DISASSEMBLER" : PRINT : PRINT
162 PRINT TAB(20)"BY HARRY LAKSER"
163 PRINT@901,"COPYRIGHT (C) 1980 BY FORT RICHMOND SOFTWARE
    COMPANY"
164 REM MAIN PROGRAM
165 POKE 16553,255
166 CLEAR 3000 : A$="0123456789ABCDEF"
```

```
167 D2$="(LOCATION)   <ENTER>(NEXT)   S(UBROUTINE)   R(ETURN)
    J(UMP)" : REM 3 SPACES BETWEEN EACH WORD
168 D3$="P(RINT)      M(EMORY DUMP)   X(RESTART)     H(ELP)"
    : REM SPACES -- 6, 3, 5
169 M2$="(LOCATION)   <ENTER>(NEXT)   P(RINT)   I(DISASSEMBLE)"
    : REM 3 SPACES BETWEEN WORD
170 M3$="X(RESTART)   H(ELP)"  : REM 3 SPACES
171 L4$=STRING$(64,131)
172 DIM A$(1,63),B$(53),C$(38),D$(30),E$(7),R$(7),
    R1$(7),Z(10),K(3)
173 K(0)=4096 : K(1)=256 : K(2)=16 : K(3)=1 :  CT$="  (HIT ANY
    KEY)"
174 FOR I=0 TO 7 : READ R$(I) : NEXT
175 FOR I=0 TO 7 : READ R1$(I) : NEXT
176 FOR I=0 TO 63 : READ A$(0,I) : NEXT
177 FOR I=0 TO 7 : READ E$(I) : NEXT
178 FOR I=0 TO 63 : READ A$(1,I) : NEXT
179 FOR I=0 TO 53 : READ B$(I) : NEXT
180 FOR I=0 TO 38 : READ C$(I) : NEXT
181 FOR I=0 TO 30 : READ D$(I) : NEXT
182 CLS : X=0 : H$="" : INPUT"IF YOU DISASSEMBLE A PROGRAM WHICH IS
    LOCATED IN THE MEMORY
    WHERE IT IS DESIGNED TO RUN, THEN PRESS <ENTER>.
    OTHERWISE, ENTER THE OFFSET AS A FOUR DIGIT HEX NUMBER";H$
183 IF H$="" THEN SHFT=0 :  GOTO 185
184 IF LEN(H$)=4 GOSUB 12 :  SHFT=X ELSE GOTO 182
185 PRINT"MEMORY LOCATIONS SHIFTED BY ";SHFT;" IN DECIMAL" :
    PRINT : PRINT
186 S=0 : W$=""
187 PP$="" : INPUT"DO YOU WANT CONCURRENT PRINTING (Y/N)";PP$
188 IF LEFT$(PP$,1)="Y" THEN PP=1 ELSE GOTO 191
189 ST=PEEK(14312) AND 128 : IF ST<>0 THEN PRINT"TURN PRINTER  ON.
    HIT ANY KEY TO CONTINUE" ELSE 192
190 ST$=INKEY$ : IF ST$="" GOTO 190 ELSE 187
191 PP=0
192 CLS
193 REM DISASSEMBLE DISPLAY
194 PRINT @ 0,"DISASSEMBLE : "+STRING$(51," ") : PRINT D2$ :  PRINT
    D3$ : PRINT @ 192,L4$;
195 PRINT @ 32,"ACTION"; : INPUT T$ :  M$=T$ :  T$="" :  PRINT
196 IF M$="" GOSUB 7 :  GOTO 193
197 IF LEFT$(M$,1)="J" THEN IF LEFT$(W$,1)="J" OR
    LEFT$(W$,4)="DJNZ" THEN M$=N$ : GOSUB 6 :  GOTO 193 ELSE  GOSUB
    282 :  GOTO 193
198 IF LEFT$(M$,1)="S" THEN GOSUB 230 :  GOTO 193
199 IF LEFT$(M$,1)="R" THEN IF S>0 THEN S=S-1 : X=Z(S) : GOSUB 7  :
    GOTO 193 ELSE GOSUB 282 : GOTO 193
200 IF LEFT$(M$,1)="P" GOSUB 245 : GOTO 193
201 IF LEFT$(M$,1)="H" GOSUB 321 : GOTO 193
202 IF LEFT$(M$,1)="M" GOTO 206
203 IF LEFT$(M$,1)="X" GOTO 182
204 IF LEN(M$)=4 GOSUB 6 ELSE GOSUB 282
205 GOTO 193
206 REM MEMORY DUMP ROUTINE
207 PRINT @ 0,"MEMORY DUMP : "+STRING$(51," ") : PRINT M2$ :
    PRINTM3$ :   PRINT @ 192,L4$;
208 PRINT @ 32,"ACTION"; : INPUT T$ :  M$=T$ :  T$="" :  PRINT
209 IF M$="" GOSUB 237 :  GOSUB 8 :  GOTO 206
210 IF LEFT$(M$,1)="P" GOSUB 254 :  GOTO 206
211 IF LEFT$(M$,1)="I" GOTO 193
212 IF LEFT$(M$,1)="X" GOTO 182
213 IF LEFT$(M$,1)="H" GOSUB 328 :  GOTO 206
214 IF LEN(M$)=4 GOSUB 235 :  GOSUB 8 ELSE GOSUB 282
215 GOTO 206
216 REM PRINT ASSEMBLY LANGUAGE CODE
217 FOR I=1 TO LEN(W$)
218 IF MID$(W$,I,1)="-" THEN 221
219 NEXT I
220 RETURN
221 W$=LEFT$(W$,I-1)+N$+"H"+RIGHT$(W$,LEN(W$)-I)
```

```
222 RETURN
223 REM ADDRESS FOR REL JUMP
224 U=X
225 IF Y>127 THEN X=X+Y-256 ELSE X=X+Y
226 GOSUB 21
227 D=X : GOSUB 25
228 X=U
229 RETURN
230 REM S SUBROUTINE
231 IF LEFT$(W$,4)="CALL" THEN M$=N$ :  Z(S)=X :  S=S+1 :  GOTO 6
232 IF LEFT$(W$,3)="RST" THEN Z(S)=X :  S=S+1 :
    X=16*VAL(MID$(W$,5,1))+VAL(MID$(W$,6,1)) :  GOTO 7
233 GOTO 282
234 REM DUMP ROUTINE
235 H$=M$
236 GOSUB 12
237 Y=PEEK(X)
238 D=X : GOSUB 25
239 L$=H$
240 D=Y : GOSUB 33
241 O$=H$ : W$=" " : AS$=""
242 GOSUB 3
243 X=X+1 : GOSUB 21
244 RETURN
245 REM PRINTER SUBROUTINE
246 ST=PEEK(14312) AND 128 :  IF ST<>0 THEN GOSUB 279 :  RETURN
247 GOSUB 263
248 IF LEFT$(H$,1)<>"Y" THEN PRINT @ 0,STRING$(64," "); :  RETURN
249 GOSUB 37
250 LPRINT L$; TAB(6) O$; TAB(16) W$; TAB(35) AS$
251 IF X<0 THEN X1=65536+X ELSE X1=X
252 IF X1<4 AND L2>65532 RETURN
253 IF X1>L2 THEN RETURN ELSE 249
254 REM MEMORY DUMP PRINT
255 ST=PEEK(14312) AND 128 :  IF ST<>0 THEN GOSUB 279 :  RETURN
256 GOSUB 263
257 IF LEFT$(H$,1)<>"Y" THEN PRINT @ 0,STRING$(64," "); : RETURN
258 GOSUB 237
259 LPRINT L$; TAB(6) O$; TAB(11) AS$
260 IF X<0 THEN X1=65536+X ELSE X1=X
261 IF X1<4 AND L2>65532 RETURN
262 IF X1>L2 THEN RETURN ELSE 258
263 REM GENERAL PRINT ROUTINE
264 PRINT @ 0,"LINE PRINT : ";STRING$(50," ")
265 INPUT"FIRST MEMORY LOCATION IN HEX";L1$
266 IF LEN(L1$)<>4 GOTO 263
267 INPUT"LAST MEMORY LOCATION IN HEX";L2$
268 PRINT @ 192,L4$;
269 IF LEN(L2$)<>4 THEN PRINT @ 128,STRING$(60," "); :  GOTO 263
270 H$=L2$ :  GOSUB 12 :  L2=X
271 H$=L1$ :  GOSUB 12
272 D=X :  GOSUB 25 :  L1$=H$
273 D=L2 :  GOSUB 25 :  L2$=H$
274 IF L2<0 THEN L2=65536+L2
275 PRINT @ 128,STRING$(50," ");
276 PRINT @ 0,"PRINTING FROM MEMORY LOCATION ";L1$;" TO ";L2$
277 H$="" :  INPUT"IS THIS OK (Y/N)";H$
278 RETURN
279 REM LINE PRINTER CHECK
280 PRINT @ 0,"TURN PRINTER ON.  HIT ANY KEY TO
    CONTINUE";STRING$(20," ") :  PRINT
281 ST$=INKEY$ :  IF ST$="" GOTO 281 ELSE RETURN
282 REM ERROR SUBROUTINE
283 PRINT@ 0,"ERROR!!";STRING$(50," ") :  PRINT :  PRINT
284 FOR I=1 TO 1000 :  NEXT
285 RETURN
286 DATA B,C,D,E,H,L,(HL),A
287 DATA RLC,RRC,RL,RR,SLA,SRA,ERROR,SRL
288 DATA 0NOP,"2LD BC,-","0LD (BC),A",0INC BC,0INC B,0DEC B,"1LD
    B,-",0RLCA
```

```
289 DATA "0EX AF,AF'", "0ADD HL,BC","0LD A,(BC)",0DEC BC,0INC
    C,0DEC C,"1LD C,-",0RRCA
290 DATA 3DJNZ -,"2LD DE,-","0LD (DE),A",0INC DE,0INC D,0DEC
    D,"1LD D,-",0RLA
291 DATA 3JR -,"0ADD HL,DE","0LD A,(DE)",0DEC DE,0INC E,0DEC
    E,"1LD E,-",0RRA
292 DATA "3JR NZ,-","2LD HL,-","2LD (-),HL",0INC HL,0INC H,0DEC
    H,"1LD H,-",0DAA
293 DATA "3JR Z,-","0ADD HL,HL","2LD HL,(-)",0DEC HL,0INC L,0DEC
    L,"1LD L,-",0CPL
294 DATA "3JR NC,-","2LD SP,-","2LD (-),A",0INC SP,0INC (HL),0DEC
    (HL),"1LD (HL),-",0SCF
295 DATA "3JR C,-","0ADD HL,SP","2LD A,(-)",0DEC SP,0INC A,0DEC
    A,"1LD A,-",0CCF
296 DATA "ADD A,","ADC A,","SUB ","SBC A,","AND ","XOR ","OR  ","CP
    "
297 DATA 0RET NZ,0POP BC,"2JP NZ,-","2JP -","2CALL NZ,-",0PUSH
    BC,"1ADD A,-",0RST  0
298 DATA 0RET Z,0RET,"2JP Z,-",4X,"2CALL Z,-",2CALL -,"1ADC
    A,-",0RST  8
299 DATA 0RET NC,0POP DE,"2JP NC,-","1OUT (-),A","2CALL
    NC,-",0PUSH DE,1SUB -,0RST 10H
300 DATA 0RET C,0EXX,"2JP C,-","1IN A,(-)","2CALL C,-",6X,"1SUB
    A,-",0RST 18H
301 DATA 0RET PO,0POP HL,"2JP PO,-","0EX (SP),HL","2CALL
    PO,-",0PUSH HL,1AND -,0RST 20H
302 DATA 0RET PE,0JP (HL),"2JP PE,-","0EX DE,HL","2CALL
    PE,-",5X,1XOR -,0RST 28H
303 DATA 0RET P,0POP AF,"2JP P,-",0DI,"2CALL P,-",0PUSH AF,1OR
    -,0RST 30H
304 DATA 0RET M,"0LD SP,HL","2JP M,-",0EI,"2CALL M,-",6X,1CP
    -,0RST 38H
305 DATA "400IN B,(C)","4100UT (C),B","420SBC HL,BC","432LD
    (-),BC",440NEG,450RETN,460IM 0,"470LD I,A"
306 DATA "480IN C,(C)","4900UT (C),C","4AADC HL,BC","4B2LD
    BC,(-)",4D0RETI
307 DATA "500IN D,(C)","5100UT (C),D","520SBC HL,DE","532LD
    (-),DE",560IM 1,"570LD A,I"
308 DATA "580IN E,(C)","5900UT (C),E","5A0ADC HL,DE","5B2LD
    DE,(-)",5E0IM 2
309 DATA "600IN H,(C)","6100UT (C),H","620SBC  HL,HL",670RRD,"680IN
    L,(C)","6900UT (C),L","6A0ADC HL,HL",6F0RLD
310 DATA "720SBC HL,SP","732LD (-),SP","780IN A,(C)","7900UT
    (C),A","7A0ADC HL,SP","7B2LD SP,(-)"
311 DATA A00LDI,A10CPI,A20INI,A300UTI,A80LDD,A90CPD,
    AA0IND,AB0OUTD
312 DATA B00LDIR,B10CPIR,B20INIR,B300TIR,B80LDDR,B90CPDR,
    BA0INDR,BB0OTDR
313 DATA "090ADD I?,BC","190ADD I?,DE","212LD I?,-","222LD
    (-),I?",230INC I?,"290ADD I?,I?","2A2LD I?,(-)",2B0DEC I?
314 DATA 341INC (I?+-),351DEC (I?+-),36X,"390ADD I?,SP","461LD
    B,(I?+-)","4E1LD C,(I?+-)","561LD D,(I?+-)","5E1LD E,(I?+-)"
315 DATA "661LD H,(I?+-)","6E1LD L,(I?+-)","701LD(I?+-),
    B","711LD (I?+-),C","721LD (I?+-),D","731LD (I?+-),E",
    "741LD (I?+-),H"
316 DATA "751LD (I?+-),L","771LD (I?+-),A","7E1LDA,(I?+-)",
    "861ADD A,(I?+-)","8E1ADC A,(I?+-)",961SUB (I?+-),
    "9E1SBC A,(I?+-)"
317 DATA A61AND (I?+-),AE1XOR (I?+-),B610R (I?+-),
    BE1CP (I?+-),E10POP I?,"E30EX (SP),I?",E50PUSH I?,
    E90JP (I?),"F90LD SP,I?"
318 DATA 06RLC,0ERRC,16RL,1ERR,26SLA,2ESRA,3ESRL,
    "46BIT 0,","4EBIT 1,","56BIT 2,","5EBIT 3,",
    "66BIT 4,","6EBIT 5,","76BIT 6,"
319 DATA "7EBIT 7,","86RES 0,","8ERES 1,","96RES 2,",
    "9ERES 3,","A6RES 4,","AERES 5,","B6RES 6,",
    "BERES 7,","C6SET 0,"
320 DATA "CESET 1,","D6SET 2,","DESET 3,","E6SET 4,",
    "EESET 5,","F6SET 6,","FESET 7,"
321 REM HELP SUBROUTINE -- DISASSEMBLER
```

```
322 PRINT @ 0,"HELP : ";STRING$(58," ") :  PRINT"  ";D2$ :   PRINT"
    ";D3$ :  PRINT L4$;
323 PRINT @ 64,"1-"; : PRINT @ 77,"2-"; : PRINT @ 93,"3-"; :  PRINT
    @ 108,"4-"; : PRINT @ 119,"5-";
324 PRINT @ 128,"6-"; : PRINT @ 141,"7-"; : PRINT @ 157,"8-"; :
    PRINT @ 172,"9-";
325 NU$="" :  PRINT @ 32,"NUMBER"; :  INPUT NU$
326 IF NU$<"1" OR NU$>"9" GOSUB 282 :  GOTO 321 ELSE N=VAL(NU$)
327 ON N GOTO 335, 340, 344, 349, 354, 359, 364, 368, 372
328 REM HELP SUBROUTINE -- MEMORY DUMP
329 PRINT @ 0,"HELP : ";STRING$(58," ") :  PRINT"  ";M2$ :   PRINT"
    ";M3$ :  PRINT L4$;
330 PRINT @ 64,"1-"; :  PRINT @ 77,"2-"; :  PRINT @ 93,"3-"; :
    PRINT @ 103,"4-";
331 PRINT @ 128,"5-"; :  PRINT @ 141,"6-";
332 NU$="" :  PRINT @ 32,"NUMBER"; :  INPUT NU$
333 IF NU$<"1" OR NU$>"6" GOSUB 282 :  GOTO 328 ELSE N=VAL(NU$)
334 ON N GOTO 335, 340, 359, 377, 368, 372
335 REM LOCATION HELP
336 PRINT @ 0,"LOCATION HELP :   ENTER THE LOCATION AS A 4 (MUST
    BE 4) DIGIT HEX"
337 PRINT"NUMBER AND HIT <ENTER>.  THAT MEMORY LOCATION WILL BE
    DUMPED/"
338 PRINT"DISASSEMBLED"; TAB(45) CT$;
339 GOTO 380
340 REM NEXT HELP
341 PRINT @ 0,"NEXT HELP :   HIT <ENTER> TO DISASSEMBLE/DUMP THE
    NEXT MEMORY"
342 PRINT"LOCATION" :  PRINT TAB(45) CT$;
343 GOTO 380
344 REM SUBROUTINE HELP
345 PRINT @ 0,"SUBROUTINE HELP :   ENTER  S  AND HIT <ENTER> TO
    JUMP TO THE"
346 PRINT"SUBROUTINE REFERRED TO IN THE LAST INSTRUCTION IF IT IS
    A"
347 PRINT"'CALL' OR 'RST', OTHERWISE ERROR INDICATED"; TAB(45)
    CT$;
348 GOTO 380
349 REM RETURN HELP
350 PRINT @ 0,"RETURN HELP :   ENTER  R  AND HIT <ENTER> TO  RETURN
    FROM THE"
351 PRINT"SUBROUTINE.  IF THE RETURN STACK IS EMPTY AN ERROR IS"
352 PRINT"INDICATED"; TAB(45) CT$;
353 GOTO 380
354 REM JUMP HELP
355 PRINT @ 0,"JUMP HELP :   ENTER  J  AND HIT <ENTER> TO JUMP TO
    THE"
356 PRINT"LOCATION REFERRED TO IN THE LAST INSTRUCTION IF IT IS  A"
357 PRINT"JUMP OR 'DJNZ', OTHERWISE ERROR IS INDICATED";TAB(45)
    CT$;
358 GOTO 380
359 REM PRINT HELP
360 PRINT @ 0,"PRINT HELP :  PRINTS MEMORY LOCATIONS  CONSECUTIVELY
    ON PRINTER."
361 PRINT"IF 1ST LOCATION < 0002 & LAST LOCATION > FFFC THE
    PRINTING MUST"
362 PRINT"BE DIVIDED INTO 2 SEPARATE PASSES"; TAB(45) CT$;
363 GOTO 380
364 REM MEMORY DUMP HELP
365 PRINT @ 0,"MEMORY DUMP HELP : ENTER  M  AND HIT <ENTER> TO
    SWITCH TO THE"
366 PRINT"'MEMORY DUMP' MENU" : PRINT TAB(45) CT$;
367 GOTO 380
368 REM RESTART HELP
369 PRINT @ 0,"RESTART HELP : ENTER  X  AND HIT <ENTER> TO GO  BACK
    TO THE"
370 PRINT"START OF THE PROGRAM" : PRINT TAB(45) CT$;
371 GOTO 380
372 REM HELP HELP
```

```
373 PRINT @ 0,"HELP HELP : ANSWER PROMPT WITH THE APPROPRIATE
    NUMBER AND HIT"
374 PRINT"<ENTER>.  TO RETURN TO THE MENU HIT ANY KEY.  TO RETURN
    TO THE"
375 PRINT"MENU FROM  HELP  FIRST CHOOSE A NUMBER";TAB(45) CT$;
376 GOTO 380
377 REM DISASSEMBLE HELP
378 PRINT @ 0,"DISASSEMBLE HELP : ENTER  I  AND HIT <ENTER> TO
    SWITCH TO THE"
379 PRINT"'DISASSEMBLE' MENU" : PRINT TAB(45) CT$;
380 ST$=INKEY$ : IF ST$="" GOTO 380 ELSE RETURN
```

APPENDIX NINE

The Model III

In this appendix we discuss, chapter by chapter, how the differences between the Model I and the Model III TRS-80 computers affect the material covered in this book.

CHAPTER 2

The Model I character set has been considerably expanded. See Appendix C of the Model BASIC III Manual for the new special characters. Moreover, there are four characters in the Model I that are not included in the regular ASCII set, namely, the up arrow, down arrow, left arrow, and right arrow. These have been replaced in the Model III by the standard ASCII characters: [, \,], and ^.

CHAPTER 3

Memory Organization

The most important difference between the Model I and the Model III is the size of the ROM. The Model III ROM occupies the first 14K of memory. Table 9A.1 modifies Table 3.1 for the Model III.

In the Model III Disk system the top 180 bytes are used by the DO command. If DO is used, avoid this area.

Address Table

The first eight entries of Table 3.2 have all been changed in the Model III. There is no cassette select. The other seven entries are address ports. Those addresses are now in the Model III ROM. As a result those addresses cannot be used as address ports. Their functions have been taken over by ports, as shown in Table A9.2.

TABLE 9A.1. General Memory Organization for the Model III

Address	Description
	Low memory
0_H–$37FF_H$ 0_D–14335_D	ROM Model III BASIC Interpreter
3800_H–$3BFF_H$ 14336_D–15359_D	No memory Includes keyboard address ports
$3C00_H$–$3FFF_H$ 15360_D–16383_D	Video display RAM
4000_H–$43E9_H$ 16384_D–17385_D	RAM BASIC work area See Tables 3.2 and 9A.2
$43EA_H$– 17386_D– $68D9_H$– 26841_D–	RAM Model III BASIC program (in a cassette system) Model III TRS-DOS Version 1.3 BASIC program
	RAM Simple variable table (built during execution of program)
	RAM Array variable table (built during execution of program)
. . . .	RAM
	RAM BASIC stack area
	RAM String space (set aside by CLEAR)
	RAM Protected area
Top of the memory $7FFF_H = 32767_D$ $BFFF_H = 49151_D$ $FFFF_H = 65535_D$	 For 16K systems For 32K systems For 48K systems
	High memory

TABLE 9A.2. Model III Ports

Port Number		
Hex	Decimal	
F4	244	Disk drive select
F8	248	Lineprinter address port
F0	240	Disk command/status
F1	241	Disk track select
F2	242	Disk sector select
F3	243	Disk data

These ports behave the same way as the address ports discussed in Chapter 3. The disk sector select port has an additional function: Bit 7 selects the disk density (bit 7 is set for double density).

The maskable interrupts use port $E0_H$ (224_D) but the bit arrangement is completely different. The time storage area has been changed: Seconds, minutes, hours, year, day, and month are stored in 4271_H to $421C_H$ (16919_D to 16924_D). This is now available in Model III BASIC. The DOS memory size is stored at 4411_H–4412_H (17425_D–17426_D).

Status Checking

In the two-line program checking the status of the printer, replace ST = PEEK(14312) by ST = INP(248) according to Table 9A.2. Similarly, to check whether a disk is write protected, do

```
OUT 244,1 : OUT 240, 208
```

and get the result with

```
PRINT INP(240) AND 64
```

Control Blocks

The three control blocks discussed in Chapter 3 contain a number of changes as shown in Table 9A.3.

The changes reflect some of the new features of the Model III. Note that the entries of the control blocks we used in Chapter 3 remain unchanged.

Changing Drivers

A new feature of the Model III is routing input and output. This is described in detail in Section 9 of the Operation Section of the Model III Manual.

BREAK Key

Radio Shack recommends disabling the BREAK key in the Model III with

```
POKE 16396, 175 : POKE 16397, 201
```

TABLE 9A.3. Model III Control Blocks

Keyboard	Video	Printer
$4015_H = 16405_D$ Device type = 1	$401D_H = 16413_D$ Device type = 7	$4025_H = 16421_D$ Device type = 6
$4016_H = 16406_D$ LSB of driver address $= 24_H = 36_D$	$401E_H = 16414_D$ LSB of driver address $= 73_H = 115_D$	$4026_H = 16422_D$ LSB of driver address $= C2_H = 194_D$
$4017_H = 16407_D$ MSB of driver address $= 30_H = 48_D$	$401F_H = 16415_D$ MSB of driver address $= 04_H = 4_D$	$4027_H = 16423_D$ MSB of driver address $= 03_H = 3_D$
$4018_H = 16408_D$ Right SHIFT toggle	$4020_H = 16416_D$ LSB of cursor position	$4028_H = 16424_D$ Number of lines on a page + 1 = 67
$4019_H = 16409_D$ Not 00_H = capital lock 00_H = upper and lower	$4021_H = 16417_D$ MSB of cursor position	$4029_H = 16425_D$ Line counter + 1
$401A_H = 16410_D$ Cursor blink count	$4022_H = 16418_D$ 00_H = cursor on Non 00_H = character replaced by cursor	$402A_H = 16426_D$ Character counter + 1
$401B_H = 16411_D$ Cursor blink status 00_H = blinks	$4023_H = 16419_D$ Cursor character $B0_H = 176_D$	$402B_H = 16427_D$ Printed width – 2
$401C_H = 16412_D$ Cursor blink switch 00_H = blink	$4024_H = 16420_D$ 00_H = space compression Non 00_H = special chrs	$402C_H = 16428_D$ "R"

and enabling it with

```
POKE 16396, 210
```

CHAPTER 5

Ports

Since the addresses of the address ports of the Model I are taken up by the new Model III ROM, the address ports (with the exception of the video display and the keyboard arrangement) are all replaced by ports.

We have already seen some of the ports in Table 9A.2. Ports $E0_H$ (224_D) and $E4_H$ (228_D) are used by the interrupts. The RS-232-C uses $E8_H$ (232_D) to EB_H (235_D). Port EC_H (236_D) contains various controls: bit 1: cassette on (set); bit 2: 32 character/line format (set); bit 3: the Japanese Kana character set (reset).

Finally, FF_H (255_D) is the cassette port. The cassette motor is turned on and off using bit 1 of port EC_H (236_D).

Keyboard

There is one small change in the keyboard arrangement as shown in Figures 5.1 and 5.2. The SHIFT shown in the last row should be LEFT SHIFT and next to it should be a RIGHT SHIFT. Thus PEEK(14464) returns 1 if the left SHIFT key is pressed and 2 if the right SHIFT key is pressed.

Lineprinter

In all examples concerning the lineprinter (in this and other chapters), replace PEEK(14312) by INP(248) and POKE 14312, X by OUT 248, X.

Clock

The cassette routines disable the interrupt so there is no need to execute CMD "T" before a cassette operation.

PART IV

All the addresses used in this book (see Appendix 6) remain the same. In fact, with one exception the codes at these addresses remain the same. (The one exception is DELAY, which now contains JP 01FBH. At $01FB_H$, the old delay routine is repeated with an extra instruction. This is probably due to the fact that the Z-80 microprocessor runs at a slightly higher speed in the Model III and the extra instruction is supposed to compensate for this.)

The two alternatives mentioned for the label BASIC (JP 1A19H, return to BASIC), namely, $06CC_H$ and 0072_H, do not seem to help in the Model III. J. Decker in issue 1, Volume II (1981), of *The Alternate Source* recommends using

```
LD      BC,1A18H
JP      19AEH
```

instead of JP BASIC.

APPENDIX 1

There is a major change in disk input/output between the Model I and the Model III. The Model III disk file structures are much more flexible. The disk file handling code is completely new. This affects only the last two entries of Table A1.3, which should not be used in the Model III.

APPENDIX 2

The Z-80 microprocessor runs about 1.17 faster in the Model III than it does in the Model I. To get the correct execution times, multiply those given in Appendix 2 by 0.85.

APPENDIX 7

There is not much to report on software for the Model III at the time of this writing. Look for proven Model I software packages as they appear in Model III versions.

However, there is a ROM book:
MOD III ROM Commented
Soft Sector Marketing
(6250 Middlebelt Road, Garden City, Mich. 48135).

CONCLUDING COMMENTS

The examples in the text were chosen because they teach *techniques* relevant to the Model I and the Model III. Nevertheless, some of the examples themselves are of lesser importance to the Model III user. For instance, checking the status of a printer is very important for the Model I. If we try to LPRINT with no printer or a turned-off printer, the computer hangs up. The only way out is to hit the restart button. A Model III user can always get out by hitting the BREAK key, a feature missing from the Model I. Nevertheless, a careful programmer checks whether a printer is available with both models.

Some of the routing examples of Chapter 3 can be done in the Model III with the new routing feature (see Section 9 of the Operation Section of the Model III TRS-80 BASIC Manual).

The FAST BASIC string sort of Chapter 9 is less exciting for the Model III Disk BASIC users (but just as significant for the cassette-based Model III TRS-80 BASIC users) since CMD "O" sorts (single-dimensioned) string arrays without involving the string space.

Keep in mind, however, that the purpose of this book is to teach techniques. The principles of FAST BASIC, for instance, the loop structures and the string sorts, are just as relevant to the Model III user as they are to the Model I user.

Index